Miracles *of* Grace

Miracles
of
Grace

Understanding and Experiencing God's Grace

Dr. Ronald L. Thorington

XULON ELITE

Xulon Press Elite
2301 Lucien Way #415
Maitland, FL 32751
407.339.4217
www.xulonpress.com

© 2022 by Dr. Ronald Thorington

All rights reserved solely by the author. The author guarantees all contents are original and do not infringe upon the legal rights of any other person or work. No part of this book may be reproduced in any form without the permission of the author.

Due to the changing nature of the Internet, if there are any web addresses, links, or URLs included in this manuscript, these may have been altered and may no longer be accessible. The views and opinions shared in this book belong solely to the author and do not necessarily reflect those of the publisher. The publisher therefore disclaims responsibility for the views or opinions expressed within the work.

Unless otherwise indicated, all Scripture quotations taken from the New American Standard Bible (NASB). Copyright © 1960, 1962, 1963, 1968, 1971, 1972, 1973, 1975, 1977, 1995 by The Lockman Foundation. Used by permission. All rights reserved.

Paperback ISBN-13: 9781662858765
Hard Cover ISBN-13: 9781662858772
Ebook ISBN-13: 9781662858789

Acknowledgments

I greatly appreciate the assistance of my wife, Susan, in writing this book. My wife was the chief editor, and my son, Ronald L. Thorington Jr., assisted in further editing. I want to also thank those who were willing to share their testimonies of how God impacted their lives by His grace.

Preface

Do miracles really happen? A growing number of people in America do not believe in miracles, and an increasing percentage of people in American society are becoming naturalists. A naturalist is someone who does not believe in the supernatural realm; to them, everything is limited to the natural realm. Miracles cannot happen in the naturalist's worldview; they are an impossibility. When an apparent miracle occurs, the naturalist is quick to view it merely as an ordinary occurrence with a natural explanation. This worldview, with its rejection of the supernatural, is on one side of the spectrum. On the other end of the spectrum are those who think everything is a miracle. They view miracles as ordinary events that occur in everyday life. One definition of a miracle is: "an extraordinary event manifesting divine intervention in human affairs."[1] If a person does not believe in God or the supernatural, there can be no divine intervention. However, if there is a God, does He intervene in human affairs? Does God perform miracles?

Those who believe God exists should be open to the possibility of miracles. A miracle happens when God intervenes in the natural realm with His supernatural power. The Bible contains many reports of these divine interventions. Some believe the miracles recorded in the Bible are simply made-up stories intended to teach moral principles. Others believe these stories are merely tales passed on by oral tradition without any basis in reality. Most liberal theologians are naturalists who do not believe in miracles; they explain away all the miracles recorded in the Bible by attributing them to some natural cause. Some believe that miracles ceased after the apostolic age in the early church. What do you believe? Do you believe there is a God? If you believe there is a God, do you believe that He still performs miracles?

Does God involve Himself in human affairs? Does God care enough about humanity to get involved in people's lives? The God revealed in the

Bible is not the god of Deism. Deists believe in a transcendent god who is beyond the limits of all possible experience and knowledge. Miracles are not possible in their worldview because they believe that God has no interaction with humanity. However, the Bible clearly shows us that God is actively involved in His creation and is especially concerned with His relationship to humanity. God wants to be intimately involved in people's lives. He desires for people to pray to Him and trust Him to answer their prayers. Every time God answers a prayer, He works from the supernatural realm into the natural realm. Over the years, I have had several people tell me that every time someone claims God answered a prayer, it was merely a coincidence. I respond to this by saying, "Isn't it strange that the more I pray, the more coincidences I have?" I cannot remember all the prayers God has answered in my life. He has literally answered thousands of my prayers.

Yes, God is real, and He desires to perform miracles in our lives. Millions of people can testify that they have experienced God working in their lives. God typically uses natural means to answer prayers. For example, when you ask God to provide something, He will motivate someone to give you what you need. Quite often, God uses other people as a means to answer our prayers. He is not limited to work out of the supernatural realm or the natural realm; He can choose to use either one or both. Something can be considered a miracle even if natural means are involved. Just because something occurs in the natural realm does not disqualify it from being a miracle. We usually think of miracles as things that occur without a natural explanation, but this is not always the case. Miracles are extraordinary events that happen because of God's divine intervention whether there is a natural explanation or not.

This book deals with God working miracles of grace. What do I mean by a miracle of grace? Miracles of grace happen when God works by His divine power to bring extraordinary, miraculous, transformational changes in people's lives. God can transform the most wretched sinner into a saint. God can transform those who were thought to be hopeless into trophies of His grace. I have witnessed this miraculous transformation in the lives of hundreds of individuals during the course of my fifty years of pastoral ministry. *Miracles of Grace* is about lives being drastically changed by the grace of God. It has brought me great joy to see people radically changed into trophies of God's grace.

Preface

This book goes beyond sharing testimonies to thoroughly investigating the miraculous working of God's grace in transforming people's lives. How can anyone explain the miraculous? How does God transform the lives of people? *Miracles of Grace* is not written as a casual read, but rather as an in-depth, scriptural study of the topics relating to God's transforming grace as it relates to salvation, sanctification, and service. This book will endeavor to explain the miraculous work of God's grace from the beginning of God's work in a person, before his salvation, to the day the believer experiences the glories of heaven. It will examine the various scriptural terms used to describe the multifaceted aspects of salvation. Throughout this book there will be word studies to determine the exact meaning of key words. I believe these word studies are necessary in order to have a deeper understanding of each topic. I will explain the various aspects of the Holy Spirit's work of grace during the transformational process in a person's life. I will also explore how the Holy Spirit works through grace to enable believers to serve God in ministry. My desire in providing this in-depth study is to assist you in developing a much deeper understanding of the extraordinary work of God's grace.

Interspersed throughout this book, you will find true stories of a few people in my life whose lives were either radically changed or enabled by God's marvelous grace. As you read their testimonies, I hope you are inspired by God's transformational work in their lives. You may identify with some of the things shared by these people. I hope their testimonies will increase your faith to believe that God's grace can also radically change and empower your life. I have given these people the title "Trophies of God's Grace." By calling someone a trophy of God's grace, I am not implying that they have arrived at perfection; they are still a work in progress.

It is my aspiration to help you experience the transforming power of God's grace in your life. It is my hope and prayer that you will become a miracle of God's love and grace. God desires all of us to become trophies of His grace. In order to assist you in your development, I have included personal application sections throughout the book. As you learn about the wonderful working of God's grace, hopefully you will want to fully and personally experience all the blessings of this grace. If you sincerely complete the questions in the personal application sections and apply them accordingly in your life, you will experience an abundance of God's grace. I recommend using a selected notebook to write out your answers to the questions in the application sections. My purpose for including personal application in this book is that you will be able to transition from acquiring more information to experiencing transformation. The intent of this book is to go far beyond being merely informational and to truly be, most importantly, transformational.

Grace, God's Indescribable Gift

Who can measure the vastness of the universe? Who can probe the depths of God's love? Who can describe the beauty of God's holiness? Who can calculate the strength of an omnipotent God? Who can fully comprehend the omniscience of God? Who can behold the splendor of God's glorious majesty and live? Who can count the riches of God's grace? Numerous books and songs have been written to describe the vast array of God's attributes. No volume of words can come close to fully explaining the greatness of God. Not even the vastness of the universe, with its millions of galaxies, can come close to displaying the vastness of God's greatness. Mark Altogge's song, "You are Beautiful Beyond Description," expresses the inability of man to comprehend and describe God's majesty:

You are beautiful beyond description

> Too marvelous for words,
> Too wonderful for comprehension,
> Like nothing ever seen or heard.
> Who can grasp Your infinite wisdom?
> Who can fathom the depths of Your love?
> You are beautiful beyond description,
> Majesty, enthroned above.
>
> And I stand, I stand in awe of You,
> I stand, I stand in awe of You,
> Holy God to whom all praise is due,
> I stand in awe of You.

As humans, our finite minds are limited in comprehending the seemingly immeasurable expanse of space, let alone grasp the magnificence of God. The Bible states, "The natural mind does not understand the things of God" (1 Cor. 2:14). It is only with the aid of the Holy Spirit that one can even begin to know God. This is especially true concerning our understanding of all the riches of God's grace. The apostle Paul, in his second letter to the Corinthian church, speaks of God's grace as an indescribable gift (2 Cor. 9:15).

It is definitely a challenging task to explain the grace of God in a way that can be easily understood. Understanding what grace is and how it works is essential to understanding how God transforms a person's life. Without the grace of God, there will be no true transformation of a person's character. I desire to explain God's grace accurately but not in a complicated manner. I will explain God's grace as simply and as thoroughly as I can so that every reader will have the maximum impact of God's grace on his life. Prayerfully ask God to open the eyes of your understanding to comprehend the deep things of God.

Trophy of Grace: Isidro Oyola

My name is Isidro Oyola. I was born in 1943, the seventh of ten siblings in the beautiful town of Humacao, Puerto Rico. I praise God that at the age of seventy-eight, I can share my personal story of redemption. In His mercy, my Lord, Savior, and Redeemer delivered me from the slavery of drug addiction. God drew me from a deep pit where I was imprisoned and set me free. By the grace of God, He has made my deliverance secure. Today, God is my anchor of hope. I am eternally grateful to God for His work of grace in my life. I have been asked by Pastor Ronald Thorington to share a brief summary of how God's grace is transforming my life.

My upbringing was pretty sound; I grew up in a Christian family. Both of my parents had accepted the Lord before I was brought into this world. From an early age, I was taught the gospel of Jesus Christ. However, right about the age of twelve or thirteen, I started drifting away from what I had learned from my parents and church. As soon as I became a young adult, my life took another course. I became more and more unrestrained and eventually lost control of my life. I eventually became a renegade. I attribute it to my own foolishness. It all started not long after I arrived at New York City from Puerto Rico in the summer of 1956.

I was thirteen when I arrived in New York City. I experienced quite a cultural shock and had great difficulty in adapting to what was going on in New York City. I left behind closely bonded friends, and now I found myself in a big, metropolitan city without friends. When I arrived in New York City, school was closed for the summer. I remember how I longed for school to start, hoping to meet new friends. I remember friends of the family warning me of the dangers of becoming a gang member and telling me that once I crossed that line, there would be no turning back. Their warnings had an adverse effect on me; instead of causing me to stay away from gangs, they caused me to be all the more attracted to them.

It was the same way with the drug awareness education workshops that I attended at school. I remember the first time I viewed a film about the effects of smoking marijuana. My attitude after watching the film was, "Yeah, right. I wish that would happen to me." From that point on, I planned to experience that aura. I started smoking marijuana at the age of thirteen. As you can imagine, I already had a dash of rebellion in me.

When it was time to go to school, I attended School 57 in the neighborhood of Bedford-Stuyvesant in Brooklyn, New York. Although school started well and my teachers liked me, I did not see the potential of becoming an outstanding student they said that I possessed. Instead, I chose to hang out with my Puerto Rican friends from school and became close comrades. These new friends were taking drugs and were already members of a street gang. We all lived in the same neighborhood, so it was almost impossible not to become members of the local gang. Eventually, I joined their gang, known as "The Jesters."

Unaware of whom I was hurting, I became a very problematic, cold-blooded juvenile delinquent. The police were always doing stop and searches on me. The police frequently took me in for questioning at the police station. They hated my "Al Capone" attitude, and they did not want to see me hanging around the neighborhood. By the time I was fifteen, I started experimenting with recreational drugs like cocaine and hashish. Most of my acquaintances were already into using drugs and, to me, they seemed to be no different from other people. So, as curious as I was, I decided to experiment also.

It was a disastrous mistake! These recreational drugs were definitely a gateway for me to taking heroin, cocaine, and speed-ball which is a combination of both heroin and cocaine. These drugs created a physical and psychological dependency that led me to take harsher substances. My addiction to drugs all started in the fall of 1958.

For twenty years, I roamed the streets of New York City, chasing after my addiction to heroin and cocaine. I had become a hardcore junkie. For more than twenty years, my life literally became a garbage can. I should have died many times and would be rotting in hell except for the grace of God.

Jesus was watching over me and eventually He would, with His outstretched hand like a drag hook, pull me from the garbage dump

Miracles of Grace

and rescue me. In 1963, for three months, I lay in a jail hospital ward at Riker's Island, infected with hepatitis B caused by the use of dirty needles to shoot heroin. In drug culture, it is very common for multiple people to use the same needle to save money. Again, by the grace of God, I did not die of it. I served close to eight years in prison for drug-related charges and for violation of the Sullivan Law (possession of a firearm without a permit). I was incarcerated in 1959 and was released on parole for a brief time in 1962.

While on parole, I was arrested for another crime and was sentenced to five years and was released in 1967. I did not stay out of jail for long because I was sent back the same year due to a parole violation. I was accused of consorting with known felons. I remember, as clearly as if it were today, the words of the parole officer before he sent me back. He said I was incorrigible and that I was going to be a junky all of my life and that there was no hope for me. I spent eight years in jail, feeling isolated and lonely.

It was awful being alone especially around Christmastime, although, I must confess, that being in jail for Christmas was not as bad as being strung out on heroin on the streets of New York City. Even when you are stoned out of your mind, surrounded by thousands of people on the streets, you are never more lonesome than when you are in jail. One could be a prisoner of his own mind when he allows himself to be captivated by the uncontrollable passion for the gratification of the next high from drugs. I finally finished serving my time in November 1968.

Since I was no longer under parole supervision, I felt free to immerse myself into the use of heroin immediately after I was let out of prison. Do you see how pervasive addiction to heroin can be? As a heroin user, I had no resistance against the lure of this addictive drug. I am not saying that other addictions cannot be just as harmful; I am only speaking as an ex-heroin user. It was later that I discovered that only the supernatural power of God could set me free. Lost and without hope, the words of my parole officer that there was no hope for me still rang in my ears. My heart became more hardened, and I even began to think that perhaps there was no God.

I said to myself, "Life has no meaning, so why not continue in your present state of stupor?" I was deluded into believing that the human race's objective should be to experience pleasant emotions and that the embodiment of happiness was the pleasant tranquility of the mind.

Under that premise, I made it my mission to seek after my opiates. Heroin became my god. I was always looking to satisfy my own desires, as if life was all about me.

My search for joy, peace, and purpose began as a journey that led me from the Christianity of my early youth into skepticism. As a result, I became sort of a libertine and lived mostly for myself. Indulgence became my motto: "Eat, drink, and be merry today because tomorrow you will die." That is how despondent I had become. Some addicts use drugs to live; other addicts live to use drugs. I found myself in the latter category. That is all I did for a very long time. I went through many counseling and treatment programs but none of them worked for me.

After I got out of jail, I stayed in a five-story apartment building located near 110th Street between Madison and Lexington in Manhattan, New York. The area was known as "El Barrio," a.k.a. Spanish Harlem. To my knowledge, everyone who lived in the building either was on drugs or was selling them. I usually got my drugs from a dealer in the building. Whenever he would leave the apartments, he would carry a duffel bag with a sawed-off shotgun inside. One morning in 1978, after I awoke, I could not think of anything else but getting my next fix. I had some money but not enough to buy drugs so I waited on the outside steps to partner with someone to buy more drugs.

As I was waiting on the steps, the drug dealer came down the stairs. I tried to do a trade for drugs, but he was in a hurry to go across the street to a housing project. He was carrying the duffel bag with his shotgun. It was only a few minutes later that I heard some gunshots coming from the housing project. After an ambulance came, I rushed over to see what had happened. I saw the dealer's body fully covered by a sheet. The dealer from our apartments was killed by gunshots to his head.

Eventually, that day, I got the drugs I wanted and went up to my apartment to "get off." I injected a needle into a vein and "boosted" (drawing your blood back and forth) several times. I don't know what happened to me, but as I was standing there next to my table, I experienced what I would describe as a visual ecstasy. I had a vision of the police coming to arrest me. The police took me and threw me into an elevator full of men, including the dead dealer. The elevator descended down into a dark cave. There were hundreds of people in that cave. Many whom I recognized were people that I hated. I recognized the dealer who had just been killed so I went over to him to talk with him.

I said to him, "I don't think that we will ever get out of here." He agreed that we would never leave this dark place. As I was there, I became extremely thirsty, so I began to dig in the dirt for water. I soon awoke from my vision to find myself still standing at my table with the needle still stuck in my arm. A few months after that traumatic experience, I was advised by my family to leave New York City and go live with my brother in Springfield, Missouri. My brother and his beautiful wife were very gracious to me and very supportive in their efforts to help me.

My brother and his wife were professors at Evangel University and were held with high esteem both by the students and faculty. Even though they had a position of being highly respected, they chose not to look on me with distain as a drug addict but instead treated me with much regard. My brother and his wife were instrumental in eventually leading me back to Christ. Their love and compassion for me were not in vain. It was their loving treatment that made a lasting impact on my heart. Even though my heart was touched, my change of heart did not come quickly because God still had a lot of work to do in my obstinate and hardened heart.

In fall of 1979, I left Springfield, Missouri, without a trace. No one in my family knew my whereabouts. Not even my brother, with whom I was very close, knew where I was. I said goodbye to no one. I just took off. I went to Chicago and settled on the south side. I was not there but a month or two before I got connected to a Mexican drug ring. I won the confidence of a leading member of a Mexican drug ring and eventually became sort of a go-between distributer with my connections to the Puerto Rican gangs of north Chicago.

It was around 1982 that I began to feel apprehensive that something bad was about to happen to me. I was getting deeper into gang leadership, and I believe I was being considered to be a hit man. There is a lot of double crossing and throat cutting in the drug culture. You need to be witty and cunning to survive. It is either kill or be killed. I do not know if it was the cocaine that I was using that was making me paranoid, but I smelled a rat. I really believed someone was setting me up for a trap to have me killed. I have now come to believe that it was the divine providence of God warning me.

With this apprehension that I was feeling, I had no peace and nothing could satisfy me anymore, not even heroin, my drug of choice.

At this time in my life, I sort of wore two hats. One was the hat of a tough guy on the streets and the other a hat of a sad and remorseful person when I was alone in the privacy of my apartment. A sadness came over me, and I cried out in solitude. This misery drove me to use heroin more and more, thinking that perhaps it would satisfy me. I know now that only God can satisfy men's souls. Nothing but the living God could satisfy my soul. Man's shattered heart is a black hole that only Christ can fill.

God was dealing with me in His grace during this very distressing time. God was demonstrating to me what hell was really like. I have no doubt it must have been because of my mother and a host of Pentecostal churches interceding for me in prayer that my heart became overwhelmed. I desperately called on God and humbled myself before Him. I asked Him to forgive me for my transgressions. I prayed that if He would help me get out of the mess, I would forever be grateful to Him. Because of the danger I felt, I knew I could not stay in Chicago. I believed the best decision for me was to leave Chicago and to go live with my sister in Buffalo, New York.

As soon as I got to Buffalo, I committed myself to a six-month, Christian-based rehabilitation program called Teen Challenge. The first days were very difficult for me as I was going through withdrawal from drugs. I could not sleep for days and was very uncooperative with the program. Every day, we were required to attend chapel services, but I refused to attend. I came very close to being kicked out, but something happened that changed my attitude. Because my bedroom was close to the chapel, I would listen to the men joyfully singing and praising God in the services. I realized that these men had a joy that I did not have. I asked God to give me this joy, but if He didn't, it would be His fault that I never knew Him. I prayed that I would not leave this place without experiencing this joy.

One night, I had a dream in which I saw Christ. I was walking on a beautiful Puerto Rican beach when I saw Christ walking up to me. Christ was very tall in my dream, and as I came up to Him, He embraced me. After my dream, I decided to commit my life to Christ. I humbled myself before God and asked for His forgiveness and help to overcome my drug addiction. From that point on, things really began to change in me. The leaders at Teen Challenge commented that they could see a real change in me. Initially, I refused to attend the chapel services but now I could not get enough chapel service time, prayer, and Bible study. I was so hungry to learn all I could about God. I did not just learn about God; I came to know Christ personally as my Lord and Savior.

The factor that makes Teen Challenge different from most other drug rehabilitation programs is the "Jesus factor." What is missing in so many drug rehabilitation programs is the spiritual aspect of treating this disease. The "Jesus factor" is what makes Teen Challenge so successful in fully delivering a person from drug and alcohol addictions. When people come to know Christ personally, they have God's power to overcome their addictions. There is hope for addicts in Christ Jesus. Through the power of God, I was able to successfully complete the program and, by the grace of God, I have been set free from substance abuse since 1983. Praise the Lord!

Moreover, my sins are forgiven. This is an example of the manifold grace of God. All I know is that once I was blind, but now I see. So, if the Son sets you free, you will be free indeed. I must confess that Jesus Christ is the Son of the living God and that He is my Redeemer. The Bible says in Psalm 107:20, "He sent forth His word and healed them; He rescued them from the grave." I am one of those whose life was rescued from the grave.

My life's story does not end with my deliverance. By the grace of God, He has blessed me in so many ways since my deliverance. After I finished the Teen Challenge program, I went back to live with my sister. I got a job working in a factory for minimum wage. The work was difficult for me because it was a dirty job, and I was not used to working. Many times, I felt like quitting because I was not making much, and it was not providing the lifestyle that I was used to when selling drugs. Every day that I went to work I would ride the Metro Bus.

While riding the bus, I became friends with a woman. One day, she mentioned that she attended a Bible study, so I asked if I could attend. She welcomed me to come, so I began attending. After three of years of courtship, I married my wife, Nelly. My wife is such a blessing to me. She is a very dedicated believer in Christ and a wonderful wife to me. God has truly blessed me in a multitude of ways.

God was gracious to me in providing better jobs. An opportunity opened up for me to work at an HIV testing and rehabilitation center. I worked at testing for HIV for several years at the rehab center. Then

I was offered a job doing the same type of work at Columbus Hospital in Buffalo. I also became a counselor working with those with drug addictions. This was the perfect job for me. I was able to turn all the bad experiences I had with drug addiction into being able to help those with addictions. I knew what they were going through; so, with God's help, I was able to help many come to know Christ and experience freedom from their addictions.

Over the thirty-eight years since my deliverance from drugs, the Lord has opened many doors of ministry opportunities for me. I have faithfully attended church for the last thirty-five years. By the grace of God, He has allowed to serve in many ways. One of my passions has been to disciple men and help them grow in Christ. By the grace of God, He has allowed me to serve as an elder for over thirty years, and I am now a council member at Victory International Assembly of God. God's grace has radically transformed my life from being a hopeless drug addict to being a servant of God. It is my hope and prayer that my testimony will give you hope to trust in the grace of God. So, if you find yourself in the same predicament I once was in, bound by the chains of addiction, do not let anyone tell you that there is no hope for you like I was once told. Jesus can set you free. So, by all means, do not lose hope. There is hope for you if you can believe and humble yourself to receive God's grace.

Contents

Acknowledgments v
Preface vii
Trophy of Grace: Isidro Oyola xii

PART ONE: THE SOURCE OF GRACE 1
    Chapter 1: Our Perception of God 3
    Chapter 2: The Moral Nature of God 14
    Chapter 3: The Ultimate Expression of God's Love 30
    Trophy of Grace: Pedro Arroyo 45

PART TWO: GOD'S SAVING GRACE 49
    Chapter 4: Removing the Penalty of Sin 51
    Chapter 5: Being Made Righteous 59
    Chapter 6: Starting a New Life 65
    Chapter 7: Having a New Relationship with God 70
    Trophy of Grace: Doug 86

PART THREE: GOD'S ENABLING GRACE 91
    Chapter 8: The Grace of God That Strengthens 93
    Chapter 9: The Grace of God That Sustains 109
    Chapter 10: The Grace of God That Sanctifies 125
    Chapter 11: The Grace of God that Serves 131
    Chapter 12: The Grace of God That Secures 140
    Trophy of Grace: Marsha Thomas 144

PART FOUR: THE AGENT OF GRACE 147
    Chapter 13: The Agent of Salvation 149

Chapter 14: The Agent of Sanctification.....................168
Chapter 15: The Agent of Service 208
Trophy of Grace: Ann Winfield 217

PART FIVE: THE MEANS OF GRACE 223
Chapter 16: Regular Bible Study 225
Chapter 17: Daily Prayer................................243
Chapter 18: Regular Christian Fellowship 256
Chapter 19: Heart-felt Worship..........................256

PART SIX: HORIZONAL GRACE 223
Chapter 20: Speaking Words of Grace 256
Chapter 21: Showing Acts of Grace........................256
Chapter 22: Showing Grace in Our Attitudes 256
Trophy of Grace: Pastor Kenneth H. Wilson 330

Conclusion 345
End Notes 363
About the Author 361

PART ONE

THE SOURCE OF GRACE

CHAPTER 1

Our Perception of God

In order to understand God's grace, we first need to look at the source of God's grace. The source of God's grace is the moral nature of God. What one believes about the moral nature of God has a powerful impact on how one perceives and relates to God. An unbiblical perception about the nature of God will hinder one's understanding of the grace of God. How does someone come to his personal opinion concerning the nature of God? Everyone seems to have his own conception of God's nature. Who determines whether one's view of God is correct? Are all views about the nature of God of equal value? Is there a correct view of the nature of God?

We must not fall prey to the relativism of our day by allowing it to influence our comprehension of God's nature. Postmodernism, which has become the prominent worldview during the last four decades, declares that each culture can determine its own truth. Therefore, each culture's values and beliefs are of equal value to any other cultural truth. Postmodernists do not believe that there is a truth or worldview that supersedes all others. They believe that whatever a culture considers as truth is equal to that of any other culture. Postmodernists say all worldviews are equal, but in reality, they look with distain on Western culture because of its Christian heritage.

Western culture has its roots in Christian values and Greek culture; however, during the last three hundred years, Western culture has been heavily influenced by Modernism. Modernism is skeptical of both the supernatural and the authority of Scripture. Modernism replaces belief in God with belief in rationalism and science. Over the last fifty years,

Modernism is being replaced by Postmodernism. Postmodernists reject Christian and Modernist beliefs.

I want to make it clear from the start that this book rejects all non-biblical worldview concepts of God's nature and relies solely on the revelation of God's Word, the Bible. Yes, there is a correct view of God's nature, and it is found in Scripture. The Bible and Christ incarnate are God's special revelation of Himself to mankind. By studying God's Word, and by coming to know Christ as one's Lord and Savior, one can come to know the true character of God.

How does a person come to perceive the nature of God? There are many factors that influence a person's perception of God, some of which can lead a person to a faulty perception. Five major influences that impact the development of a faulty view of God's nature are: (1) difficult life experiences; (2) unanswered prayers; (3) unanswered philosophical questions; (4) unbalanced interpretation of certain biblical passages; and (5) nonbiblical worldviews.

How do difficult life experiences impact one's concept of God's nature? I believe that one of the most powerful life experiences that can influence the development of a faulty perception of God is one's relationship with his earthly father. Why would I say that? We tend to subconsciously or consciously equate God with our earthly father. If we had a less-than-ideal father (which almost everyone had), we will struggle with improper perceptions of God as our heavenly Father.

If we had an absentee father, we may struggle with believing that God will be available. If we had a weak, passive father, we may believe that God is unreliable. If we had a very strict and non-affirming father who was impossible to please, we may struggle with trying to please God. With a non-affirming father, we may feel that we have to earn God's affirmation and love. If we had an angry father who was harsh in his punishment, we may have an unhealthy fear of God, a fear that drives us away from God. If we have an unhealthy fear of God, we may feel that God is unapproachable and that it is best for us to stay as far away from Him as possible.

I know from experience that one's view of God the Father can be deeply impacted by the experience we have with our earthly fathers. My father was a good father in many ways, but he struggled with anger and would frequently explode with rage. Even though my father was a Christian for most of my life, he struggled with anger, stemming from the abuse he experienced when he was a young boy. My father was very strict, non-affirming, and never verbally expressed his love for his three children until we were adults. My father would only say he loved me after I had told him that I loved him first. I do not remember my father ever initiating any verbal expression of his love for me. My mother would often tell my siblings and me that our father loved us but he just had difficulty in expressing it. I certainly struggled with the feeling that my father did not love me. As I look back at my childhood, I now realize that he did express his love for me, just not verbally; he showed his love by doing things for me.

Even though I was a dedicated Christian from about ten years old, I struggled with believing that I could ever please God. Although I knew I was saved by God's grace, I still struggled with the sense of a dark cloud of condemnation hanging over my head that badgered me and made me feel that God was not pleased with me, no matter how hard I tried to please Him. For many years, I grappled with trying to gain God's love through my performance. It took a considerable amount of intervention by God's Spirit to finally convince me that I was already accepted by God's love and grace. Time after time, I felt God was telling me He was not like my father; He loved and accepted me. I now realize that God accepted me, not because of my performance, but solely by His grace.

Believe me, it was very liberating to know God was pleased with me even if I did not deserve it. Because of God's grace, He gives those who believe in Christ His love and acceptance even though they do not deserve it. No one can earn God's love and acceptance; these are received as a gift from God as a result of faith in Christ. Do you feel you must earn God's love and acceptance? If you can identify with perceiving God as similar to your earthly father, then it is important that you develop a deeper and biblically accurate understanding of the nature of God. He is not like our earthly fathers; He is holy and, therefore, does not possess any of the character flaws we may have seen in our fathers who were imperfect humans. God is a perfect being. The Bible states numerous times that God is a compassionate, loving, and merciful God. Early in His relationship with the people of Israel, God described Himself as: "compassionate and gracious, slow to anger, and abounding in lovingkindness and truth" (Exod. 34:6).

Have you experienced traumatic events in your life? Do you have difficulty believing that God is a good God? How could a good God allow something so terrible to happen in your life? How could a good God allow your child to die? How could a good God take away your spouse? How could God allow your child to be born with birth defects? How could God allow you to be abused as a child? How could God allow you to get cancer? The list goes on and on. Has this been your experience? Do you find it difficult to believe God is a good God because of what you have experienced? If you question God's goodness because of some experience you have had, I encourage you to keep reading this book and pray for God to open the eyes of your understanding to know Him as He truly is.

Unanswered prayers can also adversely affect our perception of God. Many believe God has failed them because He did not answer certain prayers. Some have the rationale that if God were a good God, He would have answered their prayers. If God did not answer their prayers, they reason He must not be a good God. When prayers go unanswered, people conclude that either God must not care enough to give them what they needed or that there is no God at all. This reaction to unanswered prayer demonstrates a lack of understanding about the ways and nature of God. Frequently, God works in ways we do not understand. People think God should do things the way they would. As we grow in our understanding of God, we will learn to trust His goodness even if what is happening to us does not make any sense.

My wife, Susan, underwent difficult teenage years. Her greatest difficulty came when her mother, Esther, began dying of cancer. Her mother was a godly woman, a dedicated Christian, and a firm believer in prayer. Esther prayed countless hours for God to heal her. Esther had the whole church and many of her friends praying for her healing for several years. She even traveled to attend services of a famous healing evangelist to pray for her. After years of praying, Esther eventually died of her cancer at the age of forty-three.

Susan was only sixteen years old when her mother died, and that was a devastating experience for her. Even though she remained a dedicated Christian, she struggled with trusting God for her own health. How could God allow such a tragic thing to happen? Why did God not answer all those prayers? These unanswered prayers can cause some to question God's nature and to struggle with trusting God.

Unanswered philosophical questions are another cause of a faulty perception of the nature of God. What are some of the common questions regarding the goodness of God? Probably the most common question that people will ask is, "How could God be a good God if He allows so much evil and suffering in the world?" Other common questions are: "How could a good God allow so many children to starve to death?" "How could a good God allow so many tragedies to occur?" "How could a good God send people to hell?" Trite answers to these deep questions are not enough to help a person overcome his doubts about God's character. Those who seriously ponder these questions can distrust God or even give up believing that there is a God at all.

A fourth thing that can cause a person to develop a faulty perception of God is having an imbalanced interpretation of Scripture. If one only focuses on certain passages of Scripture, one can develop an imbalanced understanding of God. If we only look at part of a picture and do not look at the rest of the picture, we will most likely not understand fully what we are perceiving. Similarly, Scripture must be understood in context. In order to get a full understanding of the nature of God, one must look at all of what Scripture says about God. Atheists love to selectively choose passages from the Old Testament that show God as angry and judgmental. Atheists assert that God authorized genocide in the annihilation of whole nations, including women and children. They try to instill disbelief in the God of Jews and Christians. Those who are not familiar with all of what the Bible says about God may be deceived and discouraged from seeking a God who truly loves them.

Unfortunately, it is not only atheists who misrepresent God. Well-meaning Christian leaders and teachers can have an imbalanced interpretation of scripture. Within Christianity, there are many groups that go to extremes in their portrayal of God's nature. At one end of the spectrum are those who only emphasize God's holiness and His judgment of sin. These groups focus on Scriptures that speak about God's judgment of sin. God is portrayed as one who must be feared and obeyed. In order to please God, a person must live by a certain code of conduct. This code of conduct is based not only on the commands of Scripture, but on countless rules that are added by these present-day Pharisees. Those who follow these Christian Pharisees are under a tremendous weight of condemnation because they know that they will never fulfill all the requirements of being holy. Legalists are not more holy; they are just better at hiding their sins. Legalists often focus on outward sins while overlooking the greater sins of the heart. Instead of viewing God as merciful and gracious, legalists tend to view Him as eager to punish sinners by casting them into hell.

Those who overemphasize the love of God are at the other end of the spectrum of Christian teaching. They focus exclusively on verses relating to God's love, mercy, and grace. Scriptures that speak about repentance and the need for obedience are ignored. There is seldom, if ever, any mention of hell. People are given the impression that God is so loving that He is not concerned about sin. Some people believe that God must overlook sin in order to be loving. People who think this way have the misconception that God is fine with sinners living however they please. They view God as both loving and approving of sin. This misconception of God's nature is very popular in American churches today. Even though this is a popular view today, it is not biblically balanced.

One must consider the totality of biblical teaching in order to have a balanced view of the nature of God. We must be careful to view God as both holy and loving. If we emphasize one of these truths at the expense of the other, we run the risk of becoming imbalanced. There is a common aphorism that states, "God loves the sinner, but hates the sin." This short statement is packed with truth; it shows how God can be both merciful in His dealing with sinners and just in His dealing with sin.

The fifth thing that can cause a person to develop a faulty perception of God is his worldview. It is critically important to possess a correct worldview. Many people have developed a faulty conception of God's nature and essence because of their nonbiblical worldview. A large percentage of Americans is adversely affected by nonbiblical worldviews regarding the existence and nature of God. It is not just non-Christians who have been influenced by nonbiblical worldviews, however. A large percentage of those who call themselves Christian are also highly influenced by secular and pantheistic (New Age) worldviews.

All worldviews either contain religious beliefs concerning God and His nature or deny God's existence through ignoring the topic all together. There are two essential questions that every worldview must answer: "Is there a God?" and "If there is a God, what is He like?" The religious aspect of nonbiblical worldviews has probably done more damage to the perception of God's good nature than anything else. There are many contrasting views of the nature and essence of God among the different religious worldviews. Religious worldviews fall into four major categories: Monotheism, Pantheism, Polytheism, and Atheism.

Monotheism is the theological belief in the existence of only one supernatural deity who created all things and is distinct from creation. The three major monotheistic religions are Christianity, Judaism, and Islam. Christianity and Judaism share belief in the same God. A different understanding of the being of God is the primary distinction between Christianity and Judaism. Christians believe the one God exists as three persons. This doctrine is known as Trinitarianism in which one being of God is shared by three divine persons: the Father, the Son, and the Holy Spirit. There are other distinctions between these monotheistic religions. Judaism stresses the holiness of God and the necessity to please Him through keeping the Old Testament Law. It also rejects the Christian belief that Jesus Christ is the Son of God who died on the cross for the forgiveness of sins. Furthermore, it views God as loving toward those who keep the Jewish law. Finally, Judaism does not embrace the Christian concept of salvation by grace through faith in Christ. Islam, the third major monotheistic religion, is distinct from Christianity and Judaism in its doctrine of the nature of God. The god of Islam does not possess the same moral attributes as the God of the Bible. Despite these clear differences, many today blur the lines between these religions. The following quote makes an important point:

> In an effort to seek peace, Western political leaders will commonly say things like "Christians, Jews, and Muslims worship the same God." This is misleading. Even if it were true that all three theistic religions worshipped the same God, and this is a matter of much controversy, Islam defines the nature and character of God very differently than Christianity or Judaism.[2]

There are significant differences between Islam and Christianity that cannot be ignored. One important difference is in the ability to have a personal relationship with God. Christians are encouraged to seek a personal relationship with God. Muslims, on the other hand, do not seek this relationship because of a dissimilar view of how their god interacts with humanity. "Muslims traditionally view God as utterly transcendent. He relates to people only through the prophets and authoritative teachings."[3] Two other key differences between Christianity and Islam are: Islam rejects the Christian doctrine of the divinity of Christ, viewing Him merely as one of the great prophets, but not as the Son of God or as divine; Islam rejects the Christian doctrine of substitutionary atonement (that Jesus died in mankind's place to pay for man's sins).

Now that we have considered the three great monotheistic religions, let us take a look at other major belief systems. One major belief system is Pantheism that holds the theological belief that god is everything and everything is god. A Pantheist is someone who believes that god is impersonal; this god is an essence that indwells everything. There are three major pantheistic religious worldviews: Zen Buddhism, Hinduism, and New Age. New Agers do not believe in a personal god. Their concept of god is an impersonal cosmic force that resides in everything. They believe that everyone can, with proper guidance, discover his cosmic consciousness and become god.

Another major belief system is Polytheism. Polytheism is the theological belief that there are many gods. Hinduism's beliefs concerning god are both pantheistic and polytheistic. Most ancient cultures held to the belief in many gods. For example, the ancient Egyptians believed in many gods, and their pharaohs were considered gods. The Greeks believed in mythological gods who were both human and god. These Greek gods took on many of the worst characteristics of human nature. The Greek gods were often portrayed as jealous, vengeful, angry, sexual, and competitive with other gods. The Romans adopted some of the Greek gods and added some of their own gods, including many of the Roman emperors.

One more belief system is Atheism. Atheism is the theological belief that there is no god. Secular Humanists, Marxists, and Naturalists are all atheistic in their beliefs concerning the existence of God. Even though most Postmodernists do not openly claim to be atheistic, it is safe to assume they are. Postmodernism is actually a worldview that does not acknowledge the existence of worldviews. Postmodernism is an outgrowth of Secular Humanism and Marxism, both of which are atheistic.

With all these different views of God's existence and character, it is no wonder that there is so much confusion concerning the essence and nature of God. In order to truly understand God's grace, one must have a biblical worldview concerning the essence and nature of God. God's grace flows from His nature. What is it about God's nature that moves Him to demonstrate such grace?

Understanding God's essence is foundational for comprehending who God is. In His essence, God is a personal, spiritual being who is immaterial (John 4:24). As a spiritual being, He is alive. He is called the "living God" (Matt. 16:16). God has life in Himself (John 5:26), and is the source of all life (Ps. 36:9). God is self-existent, which means He is not dependent on anything to exist (Exod. 3:14). He is eternal, meaning He has no beginning or end of existence (Gen. 21:33). This one true God is omnipresent (everywhere; Ps. 139:7–12), omniscient (all knowing; Ps. 147:5), omnipotent (almighty; Gen. 17:1), and immutable (never changing; Mal. 3:6).

In order to help you better understand the essence and moral nature of God, I designed diagrams to illustrate the various aspects of God's nature. I used a triangle to represent the triune nature of God, and inside the triangles that represent God, I sequentially displayed the different aspects of God's essence and moral nature. At the base of the triangle, I placed the essence of God as the foundational characteristic of God.

The Essence and Nature of God

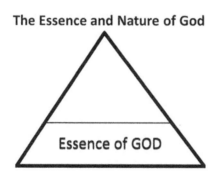

The Essence of God

Application

1. Has your perception of God been influenced by your life experiences? If so, how?

2. What are your feelings about your father?

3. Are there any similarities between how you view your father and how you view God? If so, in what ways?

4. Do you struggle having faith in God because of unanswered prayers?

5. Do you have any unanswered philosophical questions about God? If so, what are they?

6. Do you see God as being judgmental and condemning? Or, do you see God as so loving that He condones sin?

7. Do you believe that your view of God has been influenced by nonbiblical worldviews? If so, how?

8. Do you believe that God is everything, and everything is God?

9. Do you believe that God is the creator of everything and is separate from His creation?

10. Do you believe in many gods or just one God?

11. Do you believe that everyone's view of God is equally valid?

12. Have you decided to believe what the Bible says about the nature of God's essence?

CHAPTER 2

The Moral Nature of God

The moral nature of God flows from His essence. As a divine being, God possesses moral attributes, such as holiness, righteousness, justice, truthfulness, and love. It is imperative for one to have a basic knowledge of the moral attributes of God. Through understanding His moral nature, one can better understand God's plan of salvation and how God's moral nature is the source of His grace.

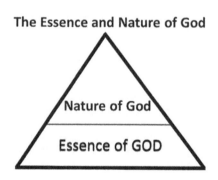

The Nature of God

God's Holy Moral Nature

Holiness is the primary attribute of God's nature and the foundation for His moral character. His glorious perfection is demonstrated by this holiness. God is holy in all of His actions and attributes; this shows the centrality of holiness to His nature. "The holiness of God is his glory, as his grace is his riches: holiness is his crown, and his mercy is his treasure. This is the blessedness and nobleness of his nature; it renders him glorious in himself, and glorious to his creatures, that understands anything of this lovely perfection."[4] The Scriptures declare the holiness of God: "Who is like You among the gods, O Lord? Who is like You, majestic in holiness, Awesome in praises, working wonders?" (Exod. 15:11); "Exalt the Lord our God and worship at His holy hill, for holy is the Lord our God" (Ps. 99:9). There are two places in the Bible, one in the Old Testament and one in the New Testament, where God is seated on His throne with angels surrounding Him crying, "Holy, Holy, Holy." In so doing, the angels continuously identify holiness as the primary attribute of God's nature (Isa. 6:3; Rev. 4:8). Because God is holy, "He is absolutely separated from, and exulted above all His creatures and He is equally separated from moral evil and sin."[5]

According to the Bible, at the beginning of human history, Adam and Eve possessed a pure, unspoiled relationship with God. This perfect relationship was forfeited when they sinned and, as a result, were separated from God. This separation from God occurred because God's holiness requires that no sin or evil can enter His presence. As a consequence of their sin, a great gulf was created between God and sinful humanity. How could sinful man ever have hope of approaching a holy God?

By itself, humanity is incapable of restoring its relationship with God. Apart from the intervention of God, all of man's efforts toward restoration have proven futile. Humanity cannot approach God on the basis of its own righteousness or merit. Humanity's relationship with God can only be restored by a gracious act of God. God devised a plan to restore this relationship with humanity because He knew that everyone would sin and be separated from Him. This plan of salvation created a way for mankind to be reconciled with God and restore the relationship that was broken when Adam and Eve sinned.

God revealed this plan of salvation through His dealing with His chosen people, the nation of Israel. When God progressively revealed Himself to the nation of Israel, He first revealed to them that He is a holy God. The strict instructions He gave to Israel concerning the appropriate way to approach Him show the importance of recognizing His holiness. God did provide a way for the Israelites to approach Him in a way that would not violate His holiness. They were required to build a tabernacle according to specific instructions and to only approach God in the way that He prescribed. People cannot approach God in any means other than on His terms.

God's terms for approaching Him are demonstrated in the design of the tabernacle. As we study the design of the tabernacle, we will discover what it reveals about the nature of God. When we examine the layout of the grounds of the tabernacle, we learn that the structure was surrounded by heavy curtains. This created only one entrance. Once inside the curtains, the first object that came into view was the altar of sacrifice. Only priests were allowed past the altar of sacrifice and only after they had offered sacrifices for their sins. Inside the partitioned grounds stood a tent that was considered the tabernacle where only approved priests could enter. The inside of the tabernacle was divided into two sections: the Holy Place and the Holy of Holies. There was a heavy veil that separated the Holy Place from the Holy of Holies. Inside the Holy of Holies was the ark of the covenant where God's holy presence was manifested. Once a year, on the day of Atonement, the selected high priest was permitted to enter the Holy of Holies. Years later, when the Israelites built the temple, it was constructed according to the same pattern as the tabernacle. The construction demonstrated many spiritual principles. A person can learn from the layout of the tabernacle grounds that God is a holy God who cannot be approached without the issue of sin being dealt with through sacrifices to atone for sin.

How could the sacrifice of an animal atone for sin? The bringing of a sacrifice demonstrated a person's recognition of God's holiness and his own sinfulness. Additionally, the sacrifice showed one's desire to obtain God's forgiveness. The Israelites learned from this ritual sacrifice that God required a penalty to be paid for sin. Even though the offering of an animal would never fully pay the price for sin, it was still an act of faith that looked forward to the great sacrifice of Christ. It was the sacrifice of Jesus Christ, the Lamb of God, that would fully pay the penalty for the sin of the whole world (John 1:29). As the Jewish people looked forward in faith to the sacrifice of the Lamb of God, so all those after Christ's sacrificial death can look back, in faith, to that sacrifice as an atonement for their sins. There is no need for additional sacrifices for sin because Christ's death completely paid the punishment for all sins. "For Christ also died for sins once for all, the just for the unjust, in order that He might bring us to God, having been put to death in the flesh, but made alive in the spirit" (1 Pet. 3:18). We can only approach a holy God through faith in Christ.

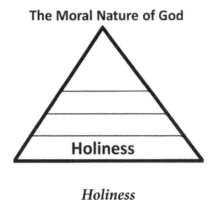

Holiness

Application

1. Do you believe that God is holy?

2. How does your level of holiness compare to God's level of holiness?

3. Does sin in your life separate you from God?

The Righteousness and Justice of God's Moral Nature

Building on the foundational attribute of holiness, we will now consider God's righteousness and justice. Because God is holy, He is righteous and just in all His dealings with creation. Remember that God's holiness regulates all that He is and does. God's righteousness is His holiness displayed in all His actions. The Greek word use for the noun *righteousness* is transliterated *dikaiosunë* (1343), (*Note—whenever I show a number after a Greek or Hebrew word, that number is the number one can use to find the exact word in the *Zondervan's NASB Exhaustive Concordance*). *Vine's Complete Expository Dictionary of Old and New Testament Words* defines righteousness as:

> The character or quality of being right and just"; it was formerly spelled "rightwiseness," which clearly expresses the meaning. It is used to denote an attribute of God, e.g., Rom. 3:5, the context of which shows that "the righteousness of God" means essentially the same as His faithfulness and truthfulness, that which is consistent with His own nature and promises; Rom. 3:25, 26 speaks of His "righteousness" as exhibited in the death of Christ, which is sufficient to show men that God is not indifferent to sin nor regards it lightly.[6]

Righteousness and justice are the foundation of God's throne. Psalm 89:14 declares, "Righteousness and justice are the foundation of Your throne; Lovingkindness and truth go before You." God's throne represents His exclusive position of authority above all other authorities. God's righteousness and justice are the foundation of His authority. The Greek word for "righteous" transliterated as *dikaios* (1342) signifies 'just' without prejudice or partiality."[7] The judgments of God are righteous and just as stated in Revelation 16:7, "And I heard the altar saying, 'Yes, O Lord God, the Almighty, true and righteous are Your judgments.'" Because God is a righteous and just God, He will always be a righteous judge (2 Tim. 4:8). All His ways are righteous, "The Lord is righteous in all His ways and kind in all His deeds" (Ps. 145:17).

The Law Was Given

God's righteousness required that He establish a standard for His chosen people that distinguished between what is holy and unholy, good or evil, and right and wrong. This standard reflected the moral nature of God. He gave the Israelites the Ten Commandments (Exod. 20) at the beginning of His dealings with them in order to establish that He is a holy God. His people must live in accordance with His moral nature as revealed in the law because He is holy and righteous. Any violation of God's moral nature would be considered sinful. The Israelites were to be a witness to the Gentiles about the nature of the one true God. In order to encourage His people to be a good witness for Him, God promised blessings for obedience to His laws and punishment for disobedience (Deut. 11:26–28). Unfortunately, the Israelites miserably failed to represent God by their disobedience to His laws. Because God is just, He cannot overlook or condone sin. Because God's justice demands a consequence for sin, to condone sin would be a violation of His righteousness and justice. The punishment for sin must be executed, or God would not be just. God cannot be partial or prejudiced in His dealing with sin; He must be equitable in His punishment of sin.

Righteousness

Application

1. Do you believe God should just overlook your sins?

2. Do you believe you can live up to God's holy standard by keeping the law, the Ten Commandments, or any set of rules?

3. How would you rate yourself in goodness on a scale of 1–10?

4. Are you evaluating your goodness as you compare to others or how you compare to God's standard? On a scale of 1–10, how would you rate yourself according to God's standard of holiness?

The Truthfulness of God's Moral Nature

Just as God's righteousness determines what is right or wrong, holy and unholy, good or evil, God's truthfulness determines what is true or false, what is genuine or fake. Truthfulness is an essential part of God's moral nature. All of God's actions and words are true and just. Psalm 111:7 declares, "The works of His hands are truth and justice; All His precepts are sure." The Scriptures declare that God is the only true God (John 17:3; 1 Thess. 1:9). God's truthfulness is our standard of truth. What His Word says is truth. What God has revealed about Himself is true.

There is much confusion today about what is truth. In America's postmodern society, it is not acceptable for anyone to say he has the truth or that the god he believes in is the only true God. Postmodernism proclaims that there can only be truth for an individual or a cultural group; there is no overall truth that applies to everyone. What is true for one person is not necessarily true for anyone else. When it comes to religion, Postmodernists reason that no religion has all the truth. They believe that each religion only has part of the truth. Christians who say they have the truth are considered to be narrow-minded and bigoted. This postmodern way of thinking is totally incompatible with a biblical worldview. In contrast to Postmodernism, the biblical worldview holds that the revelation of God through His Word is the truth. This truth is a universal truth that applies to everyone. God is the true God for everyone to believe in, to love, and to serve.

It is important to understand the meaning of "truth" as it is used in the Scripture. According to the *International Standard Bible Encyclopedia*, the word most frequently used for "truth" in the Old Testament is the Hebrew word *met*. This word, "*met*, occurs about 126 times in the Old Testament. It basically denotes a reality that is firm, stable, valid and binding."[8] When this Hebrew word *met* is used:

> In a legal sense "met" denotes the actual truth of a cause, the authentic facts (cf. Dt. 22:20) or an authentic guarantee (Josh. 2:12). More generally it describes the reality or authenticity, e.g. of the revelation in Dnl. 10:1;, from this developed the broad sense of the genuine as opposed to the false."[9]

When this Hebrew word for "truth" is used in reference to God's character, it speaks of God's truthfulness and faithfulness; "in the theological sense *met* is used for the truthfulness of God and has a close approximation to "faithfulness."[10] "A further implication is that God is the true God as distinct from false gods."[11]

In the New Testament, the concept of "true" is very similar to the Old Testament word *met*. One Greek word used for "true" is an adjective *alēthinos* (228), which "denotes "true" in the sense of real, ideal, genuine."[12] This Greek word for "true" is used concerning God as the only true God in John 17:3, "And this is eternal life, that they may know Thee, the only true God, and Jesus Christ whom Thou hast known." This Greek word is used again in 1 Thessalonians 1:9 comparing God to idols, "For they themselves report about us what kind of a reception we had with you, and how you turned to God from idols to serve a living and true God." First John 5:20 states that God is the true God, "And we know that the Son of God has come, and has given us understanding so that we may know Him who is true; and we are in Him who is true, in His Son Jesus Christ. This is the true God and eternal life."

The Greek word for "truth" as a noun is *alētheia* (225). "'Truth,' when used objectively, signifies 'the reality lying at the basis of an appearance, the manifested, veritable essence of a matter (Cremer).'"[13] This Greek word for truth has an "absolute force in John 14:6; 17:17; 18:37, 38; Eph. 4:21."[14] In John 14:6, Jesus Christ refers to Himself as the "truth," "And Jesus said to him, I am the way, the truth, and the life; no one comes to the Father, but through Me." Ephesians 4:21 states that the truth is in Jesus, "If indeed you have heard Him and have been taught in Him, just as truth is in Jesus." In these verses, the use of the Greek word for "truth" takes on a deeper meaning. "The meaning is not merely ethical 'truth,' but 'truth' in all its fullness and scope, as embodied in Him; He is the perfect expression of the truth."[15] In summary, to be "true" means to be genuine, real, and authentic. When applied to God's nature, it speaks of His truthfulness, faithfulness, and reliability. When applied to God's existence, He is the only true God. God is genuine and real, not something made up or just a figment of our imagination. Jesus not only spoke the truth but He is the embodiment of truth.

What God reveals about Himself is true. His Word is true: "The sum of Your word is truth, and every one of Your righteous ordinances is everlasting" (Ps. 119:160); "Sanctify them in truth; Thy word is truth" (John 17:17). Since God's moral nature is to be truthful, it is impossible for Him to lie or deceive. Hebrews 6:18 declares that God cannot lie, "so that by two unchangeable things in which it is impossible for God to lie, we who have taken refuge would have strong encouragement to take hold of the hope set before us." God is faithful to keep His promises because He is truthful. Believing that God is faithful in keeping His promises is essential to having faith concerning the promise of salvation, forgiveness of sin, being accepted by grace into His family, and receiving the gift of eternal life.

Truthfulness

Application

1. Do you believe there is only one true God or that there are many gods?

2. Do you believe what is true for one person is true for him but not necessarily for anyone else?

3. Do you believe that there is truth that applies to everyone?

The Love of God as Part of His Moral Nature

Since there is such a strong emphasis on God's holiness in the Old Testament, many wrongly conclude that the God revealed in the Old Testament is not loving and compassionate. On the contrary, God's love is seen throughout the Old Testament. The misconception that the God of the Old Testament is unloving stems partly from a lack of understanding of a certain Hebrew word that is not translated as "love" in English but as "lovingkindness." The Hebrew word for God's lovingkindness is *hesed* (2617), meaning "loving-kindness; steadfast, love, grace, mercy, faithfulness, goodness, and devotion."[16] God's *hesed* includes three qualities: strength, steadfastness, and love. "This word is used 240 times in the Old Testament, and is especially frequent in the Psalter."[17] The covenant love of God means that He is personally involved in, and committed to, His relationship with His chosen people. God describes Himself in Exodus 34:6–7 as: "compassionate and gracious, slow to anger, and abounding in lovingkindness and truth; who keeps lovingkindness for thousands, who forgives iniquity, transgression and sin." In the Psalms, God is characterized numerous times as compassionate, gracious, and abounding in lovingkindness (Ps. 103:8, 11). God's lovingkindness is described as everlasting (Ps. 103:17–18; 118:1–4; 136:1–26). He possesses a devoted love.

The recipients of God's lovingkindness in the Old Testament were His covenant people, the nation of Israel. Jeremiah described God's love for Israel as everlasting, saying that God has drawn them with His lovingkindness (Jer. 31:3). Since the death of Christ, God's covenant people are those who become the children of God through faith in Jesus Christ, both Jews and Gentiles. God will show His lovingkindness to His chosen people throughout eternity.

The New Testament word used to describe God's love is the Greek word "*agape*" (26). The noun form is used 116 times, while the verb form, *agapaō*, is used 137 times.[18] "*Agape* and *agapaō* are used in the NT (a) to describe the attitude of God toward His Son, (John 17:26); and the human race, generally, (John 3:16; Romans 5:8); and to those who believe on the Lord Jesus Christ, particularly (John 14:21)."[19] These two words, *agapao,* and *agape* are rich in meaning. "*Agapao* properly denotes a love founded on admiration, veneration, and esteem. It means to have a preference for, wish well to, regard for, the welfare of (Matt. 5:43f). It is to be full of good will both in thought and deed. (Luke 7:42ff.) The noun form (*agape*), is defined as "affection, good will, love, benevolence," as seen in numerous references (John 15:13; Rom. 13:10; 1 John 4:18)."[20] The emphasis of "*agape*" love is not how one *feels* toward another person, but rather how one thinks of and acts toward others. "Love can be known only for the actions it prompts. God's love is seen in the gift of His Son, 1 John 4:9–10."[21]

When one considers the love of God, one should not deem it as an emotional response by God but rather as an act of His good will in both His thoughts and actions. God's love for humanity means that He favors us; He desires to treat us well and has regard for our welfare. God shows His compassionate will toward humanity through His goodness, benevolent care, mercy, and grace. There are many Scriptures in the New Testament that speak of God's love. John 3:16 is probably the most well-known passage in the Bible proclaiming, "For God so loved the world, that He gave His only begotten Son, that whoever believes in Him shall not perish, but have eternal life."

In order to come to a greater understanding of God's love, there are a number of truths to consider. First, it is essential for one to understand that God's love is a predominate attribute of His moral nature. God does not just show love; He is love. The apostle John declared, "Beloved, let us love one another, for love is from God; and everyone who loves is born of God and knows God. The one who does not love does not know God, for God is love" (1 John 4:7–8). Just as God is holy, righteous, just, and true, He is also love.

The second truth of God's love is that, because love is part of God's moral nature, His love is eternal (Jer. 31:3). God's love never dies nor vanishes. God's love cannot be depleted; it will never run out. The existence of God's love is not dependent on the actions of mankind.

The third truth of God's love is that it is unchanging. Because God's love is part of His moral nature, His love will never change. The God portrayed in the Old Testament is the same God of love seen in the New Testament, and His love is the same in both the Old and New Testaments. In contrast to the kind of love that man possesses, God's love is not fickle or dependent on emotion. God's love was demonstrated when we were still sinners according to Romans 5:8, "But God demonstrates His own love toward us, in that while we were yet sinners, Christ died for us."

The fourth truth is that God is free to demonstrate His love whenever, to whomever, and in whatever manner He desires. God cannot be commanded or obligated to love against His sovereign will. How God chooses to exercise His love is up to Him. God told Moses that He will have mercy on whom He will have mercy, and compassion on whom He will have compassion (Rom. 9:15). Love must freely flow from a choice to love; love that is forced is not love. The fifth and final truth is that God's love can be demonstrated in multiple respects, including His goodness, benevolent care, mercy, and grace. God can choose to demonstrate His love in just one or through combinations of these ways.

Love

Application

1. Do you view God as loving and compassionate?

2. If you do not view God as loving, how then do you view Him?

3. What has influenced your view of God?

CHAPTER 3

The Ultimate Expression of God's Love

There is an abundance of Scripture that portrays God as loving in addition to being holy, righteous, just, and truthful. Love is a significant aspect of God's moral nature. Like sunlight refracting through a prism, showing various colors of light, so God's love is manifested in its various dimensions. Out of God's love flow His goodness, benevolent care, mercy, and grace. Just like a beautiful rainbow that appears after a rainstorm, so God's love is manifested in much greater beauty for humanity to experience.

God's Goodness as an Expression of His Love

In order to have a more complete understanding of God's grace, we need to understand how God's grace fits in with His other expressions of love. First, let's consider how God's love is shown through His goodness. The most basic expression of God's love is His goodness. When a person thinks of the goodness of God, he should understand that there are several aspects of God's goodness. One aspect is that God is good in His nature. God is good because His nature is infinitely perfect. Only God is absolutely perfect, and nothing is absolutely good except God (Matt. 19:17).

Flowing out of God's goodness is His good will and intention toward His creation. God's inclination to deal favorably and bountifully with His creation is an expression of his goodness. God has good intentions for all of his creatures, especially for humanity. From God's good intentions flows the last aspect of His goodness, His good works. God's good works of creation and providential care demonstrate His goodness. God demonstrated goodness toward mankind from the very beginning of creation.

God demonstrates His goodness to all of mankind in a general sense. When God created the earth and brought life to it, He concluded that His creation was very good (Gen. 1:31). God causes the sun to rise on the evil and the good, and sends rain on the righteous and the unrighteous, thus blessing all of mankind (Matt. 5:45). In a more specific way, God demonstrates His goodness especially toward His chosen people. In the Old Testament, God's chosen people were the Israelites. After the sacrificial death of Christ, God's chosen people are all those who choose to believe in and follow Christ.

God's goodness is pleasant to experience, "O taste and see that the Lord is good; How blessed is the man who takes refuge in Him!" (Ps. 34:8). God's goodness bestows great blessings on those He chooses. God's goodness protects those who take refuge in Him, "The Lord is good, A stronghold in the day of trouble, And He knows those who take refuge in Him" (Nahum 1:7). God has good plans for His people, "For thus says the Lord, 'When seventy years have been completed for Babylon, I will visit you and fulfill My good word to you, to bring you back to this place. 'For I know the plans that I have for you,' declares the Lord, 'plans for welfare and not for calamity to give you a future and a hope'" (Jer. 29:10–11). God's intentions are good for His chosen people and for their children as in Jeremiah 32:38–41:

> They shall be My people, and I will be their God; and I will give them one heart and one way, that they may fear Me always, for their own good and for *the good of* their children after them. "I will make an everlasting covenant with them that I will not turn away from them, to do them good; and I will put the fear of Me in their hearts so that they will not turn away from Me. "I will rejoice over them to do them good and will faithfully plant them in this land with all My heart and with all My soul.

God has a vast amount of goodness in store for those who fear Him, "How great is Your goodness, Which You have stored up for those who fear You, Which You have wrought for those who take refuge in You, Before the sons of men" (Ps. 31:19). Those who take refuge in the Lord can have confidence that God will bless them with an abundance of His good works.

Goodness

God's Benevolent Care as an Expression of His Love

Second, God's love is demonstrated through His benevolent care. God has loving care for all of His creation; however, He shows special care for humanity. God shows a special care for humans because they are made in His image and are the pinnacle of His creation. He manifests His benevolence for the benefit of mankind. In Matthew 6:25–33, Christ enlightens us to the nature of the Father's loving care for all of His creation and especially His providential care for all those who seek Him. God's benevolent care is shown in His constant concern for us (Ps. 115:12). God cares about us because we are of great value to Him, "Are not five sparrows sold for two cents? Yet not one of them is forgotten before God. Indeed, the very hairs of your head are all numbered. Do not fear; you are more valuable than many sparrows" (Luke 12:6–7).

Since God cares so much about us, He does not want us to be anxious about anything. Instead, He calls us to bring our needs before Him in prayer, "Casting all your anxiety on Him, because He cares for you" (1 Pet. 5:7). God knows all of our needs and desires to provide for them, "Do not worry then, saying, 'What will we eat?' or 'What will we drink?'

or 'What will we wear for clothing?' 'For the Gentiles eagerly seek all these things; for your heavenly Father knows that you need all these things'" (Matt. 6:31–32).

Care

God's Mercy as an Expression of His Love

A third way God demonstrates His love is in how He shows mercy. God's mercy is demonstrated by how He shows compassion toward those who are in misery and distress. The Hebrew word used for mercy in the Old Testament is the word *rāham* (7355). This term refers to the seat of compassion. "It was used for the deep, tender feeling of compassion that was awakened by the trouble, weakness, suffering, or vulnerability of another in need of help."[22] The Old Testament affirms that mercy is an element of God's moral nature, "The Lord passed before him and proclaimed, "The Lord, the Lord, a God merciful and gracious, slow to anger, and abounding in steadfast love and faithfulness" (Exod. 34:6, ESV); "Gracious is the Lord, and righteous; our God is merciful" (Ps. 116:5, ESV). God shows His mercy in great abundance, "Nevertheless, in your great mercies you did not make an end of them or forsake them, for you are a gracious and merciful God" (Neh. 9:3, ESV). The psalmist appeals to God's abundant mercy, "Answer me, O Lord, for your steadfast love is good; according to your abundant mercy, turn to me" (Ps. 69:16, ESV).

How do you perceive God? Do you see Him as mostly an angry, harsh, unforgiving God? Or, do you see Him as He really is, a loving and merciful God? Since mercy is a part of God's moral nature, it will never fail, "Remember your mercy, O Lord, and your steadfast love, for they have been from of old" (Ps. 25:6, ESV); "As for you, O Lord, you will not restrain your mercy from me; your steadfast love and your faithfulness will ever preserve me!" (Ps. 40:11, ESV).

In the New Testament, the Greek word most commonly used for "mercy" is *Eleos* (1656). This term refers to "the outward manifestation of pity, it assumes need on the part of him who receives it, and the resources adequate to meet the need on the part of him who shows it."[23] Ephesians 2:4 proclaims that God is rich in mercy, "But God, being rich in mercy, because of His great love with which He loved us." God's mercy is an outward expression of His compassion. God's loving compassion is what motivates Him to show mercy. Compassion is something a person feels, while mercy is an action someone takes because of compassion. For example, God shows mercy by giving deliverance from trouble, rescuing from danger, healing from sickness, supplying a desperate need, relieving suffering, and forgiving sin. In general, God's mercy assists those in great need of help who call upon Him and who fear Him, "Have mercy on me, O God, according to your steadfast love; according to your abundant mercy blot out my transgressions" (Ps. 51:1, ESV); "And his mercy is for those who fear him from generation to generation" (Luke 1:50, ESV).

God showed great mercy when He devised a plan of salvation to deliver all of humanity from their hopeless, sinful condition. The human race is helpless; it cannot rescue itself from its sinful nature. Mankind cannot fully pay for its own sins. It is only because God showed mercy that man can be saved from his sinful condition. God showed mercy by sending His only begotten Son to become a sacrifice for the sins of all mankind. God's love and compassion compelled Him to show mercy to humanity in their greatest need.

> ***Humanity's greatest need is for God's forgiveness and the restoration of a right relationship with Him.***

"He saved us, not because of works done by us in righteousness, but according to his own mercy, by the washing of regeneration and renewal of the Holy Spirit" (Titus 3:5, ESV); "Blessed be the God and Father of our Lord Jesus Christ! According to his great mercy, he has caused us to be born again to a living hope through the resurrection of Jesus Christ from the dead" (1 Pet. 1:3, ESV).

Mercy

God's Grace as an Expression of His Love

Grace is the culmination of all the other ways God expresses His love. He shows His graciousness through His goodness, benevolent care, and mercy. Grace is the highest expression of God's love, exceeding all others. God's grace is built on these other demonstrations of love but is distinct from all of them. God's goodness, care, and mercy are what God does for humanity and especially His chosen people. Grace is what God bestows out of His love, especially to those who have faith in Christ.

> *Grace is something that God gives freely without obligation or regard to merit.*

It can never be demanded of God nor earned by merit. God's grace is so important that man cannot be saved without it. Without grace no one would have the power to live a godly life. God's grace is an essential aspect in a believer's life. We are all helpless and hopeless without God's grace. But with it, all things are possible even the miraculous transformation of the most wretched sinner!

Understanding the Grace of God

Understanding God's grace is essential to fully understanding salvation, experiencing spiritual growth, and maintaining spiritual stability. The apostle Paul conveys the importance of understanding the grace of God when receiving the gospel, "which has come to you, just as in all the world also it is constantly bearing fruit and increasing, even as it has been doing in you also since the day you heard of it and understood the grace of God in truth" (Col. 1:6). The gospel is both the word of truth and the grace of God in truth. The truth concerning God's grace is central to the gospel message. In order to better understand God's grace, it should be viewed from two perspectives: the perspective of the giver (God) and the perspective of the recipient (those who have faith in Christ).

From God's perspective as the giver, grace is the fullest expression of His love. Grace involves all the expressions of God's love (goodness, care, and mercy) that are given freely without regard to the merit of the recipient. God's blessing and favor in our lives are manifestations of His grace. The most common definition of God's grace is the unmerited favor of God. This grace is His favorable disposition toward those who are in Christ. From this favorable disposition, God lavishes out His blessings and power. One can observe that the apostle Paul commonly greeted the various churches in his letters with the phrase, "Grace to you and peace from God the Father and the Lord Jesus Christ (Rom. 1:7; 1 Cor. 1:3; 2 Cor. 1:2; Gal. 1:3; Eph. 1:2; Phil. 1:2). Paul used the term "grace to you" as a statement of God's blessing and favor on those he greeted.

The gifts that God gives us are blessings from Him. Many Scriptures speak of grace as a gift (Rom. 3:24; 5:15, 17; 12:3; 15:15; 1 Col. 3:10; Eph. 1:6; 2:8; 3:7, 8; 4:7; James 4:6; 1 Pet. 4:10). Because God delights in showing His grace, His gifts are infinite. God's grace is measureless because it is part of His moral nature. Who can measure the riches of God's grace? The Scriptures proclaim the abundant riches of God's grace, "so that in the ages to come He might show the surpassing riches of His grace in kindness toward us in Christ Jesus" (Eph. 2:7). God's grace abounds to many (Acts 4:33), and God's "abundant grace was upon them all" (Acts 4:33).

The Bible describes some as being full of grace. Jesus Christ is said to be full of grace and truth (John 1:14), and Stephen was "full of grace and power" (Acts 6:8). The apostle Paul described God's grace as abounding and all sufficient, "And God is able to make all grace abound to you, so that always having all sufficiency in everything, you may have an abundance for every good deed" (2 Cor. 9:8). Paul proclaimed God's abundant grace as "surpassing grace" (2 Cor. 9:14). In his letter to Timothy, Paul described God's grace as more than abundant, "and the grace of our Lord was more than abundant, with the faith and love which are found in Christ Jesus" (1 Tim. 1:14). The Greek word used in 1 Tim. 1:14 for "more than abundant" is *huperpleonazö* (5250). I love how *Vine's Complete Expository Dictionary of Old and New Testament Words* defines the word as, "to abound exceedingly."[24] God's grace "abounds exceedingly." God's supply of grace is like an ocean compared to man's small bucket of need. God's grace will always be more than what we need.

Grace and God's Plan of Salvation

In order to fully understand God's grace from His perspective, we need to understand God's plan of salvation. Out of God's infinite knowledge and wisdom, He foreknew before creation that humanity would need a way to be restored from their fallen sinful state. Humanity's disobedience and rebellion were not a surprise to God, and He did not have to come up with a "Plan B" when Adam and Eve sinned. God already had His "Plan A" that anticipated man's fall. In love, God devised a perfect plan of salvation to pardon and restore man to a right relationship with Him. This plan would fully provide forgiveness and restoration to man and, most importantly, it would not in any way violate God's moral nature.

All of humanity need salvation because all have sinned and fall short of the glory of God (Rom. 3:23) and all are under the sentence of death (Rom. 6:23). The "glory of God" in Romans 3:23 refers to His holiness. So, when the Bible states that all fall short of the glory of God, it is saying that no one comes anywhere close to reaching God's standard of holiness. When we compare ourselves with others, we might conclude that we are less sinful than others and, therefore, worthy of God's acceptance. However, the standard that we will be judged by is not the standard of man, but rather, by God's standard. There are certainly those who are worse sinners than others, but that is not consequential because we will all be judged by the standard of God's holiness.

I played on a basketball team when I was a junior in high school. Even though I was six feet tall, I was not able to dunk the basketball. The best I could do was to grab the ten-foot-high rim. In order to dunk the ball, I would need to be able to jump at least another six to eight inches higher. Even after training myself to jump higher, I was never able to jump high enough to dunk the ball. My inability to dunk a basketball by a few inches is similar to how some people think about achieving God's standard. People believe that if they just put more effort into it, they can achieve God's standard of holiness. This belief is incorrect and far from spiritual reality. Everyone must realize that there is no one who is even close to reaching God's standard of holiness. No one is just a few inches away from reaching God's standard of holiness; everyone is miles away from reaching it.

Can a person jump hundreds of feet high just on the strength of their legs? No one would believe that is possible. Similarly, is it impossible for anyone to measure up to God's holy standard. It doesn't matter how a person compares to others; it only matters how he or she compares to God's requirement. There is no way for us to save ourselves. We cannot save ourselves through keeping the Law, "because by the works of the Law no flesh will be justified in His sight; for through the Law comes the knowledge of sin" (Rom. 3:20). The purpose of the Law was not to save us but to show us our sinfulness. It is only until a person realizes that he is a sinner and has no hope of saving himself that he can appreciate God's offer of grace and mercy.

Compassion and mercy drove God to rescue humanity from its sinful condition. His plan of salvation truly satisfies the standard of His love for all of humanity. He desires to show love to all of humanity through His goodness, benevolent care, mercy, and grace. Because of God's love, He does not want anyone to be punished for his sins, "The Lord is not slow about His promise, as some count slowness, but is patient toward you, not wishing for any to perish but for all to come to repentance" (2 Pet. 3:9). God demonstrated His love through the sacrifice of His Son to make salvation available to all. "But God demonstrates His own love toward us, in that while we were yet sinners, Christ died for us" (Rom. 5:8). This plan of salvation allows God to freely express His love for all who respond in faith.

God's demonstration of grace is central to salvation. Grace is the greatest expression of God's love, the apex of His love. Grace is what God freely gives to those who have faith in Jesus Christ, regardless of merit. Grace is always undeserved; He gives it as a free gift and not as a reward for anything we have done to earn it. Through grace, God freely offers pardon for sins, imputes righteousness, and brings reconciliation. The Scriptures are very clear about the importance of grace in one's receiving of salvation, "For by grace you have been saved through faith; and that not of yourselves, it is the gift of God" (Eph. 2:8). Second Timothy 1:9 states, "who has saved us and called us with a holy calling, not according to our works, but according to His own purpose and grace which was granted us in Christ Jesus from all eternity." Romans 3:24 says that we are "being justified as a gift by His grace through the redemption which is in Christ Jesus."

God's plan of salvation not only satisfies His love, but it also satisfies His justice. God cannot just overlook or condone sin; sin cannot go unpunished (Rom. 6:23). God's love can never violate God's righteousness or justice. When we ask a person to forgive us for an offense against him, that offended person might make light of it by saying, "Oh, it was nothing." We need to understand that God can never make light of sin. To make light of sin would then make light of God's holiness and justice. The penalty for sin must be paid in order for God's justice to be satisfied.

In God's plan, the debt of sin for all of humanity could only be fully paid by God Himself. God would pay the debt of sin Himself through Jesus Christ taking upon Himself the punishment for sin, "and He Himself bore our sins in His body on the cross, so that we might die to sin and live to righteousness; for by His wounds, you were healed" (1 Pet. 2:24). Through faith in Christ's vicarious death, God's grace will pay off every penny of the debt of sin. Everyone owes God such a debt of punishment for his sin that it could never be paid. It is like we all owe over a billion dollars each, but only have a few pennies to our name. By God's grace paying the debt of punishment for our sins, we will escape God's wrath of justice, "For God has not destined us for wrath, but for obtaining salvation through our Lord Jesus Christ" (1 Thess. 5:9).

God's plan of salvation satisfies His love, His justice, and also His holiness. A holy God cannot allow any sin or unrighteousness to enter His presence; only righteousness can enter. Even if the full penalty for our sins were paid, we still could not enter God's presence because we would not possess any holiness of our own. Pardon for sin in itself does not make us righteous; it just clears our spiritual account from any debt of punishment. There is more to righteousness than the removal of the penalty of sin. Everyone needs the spiritual capital of God's righteousness added into his account to make him righteous. This is what God's grace does for those who have faith in Christ; it pays off all the debt of punishment for sin and, very importantly, it provides God's righteousness. Because God loves us and wants to have a close relationship with us, He has deposited His own righteousness into the believer's spiritual account. Through grace, God ascribes His righteousness to those who believe in Christ, "He made Him who knew no sin to be sin on our behalf, so that we might become the righteousness of God in Him" (2 Cor. 5:21). The marvelous grace of God credits into the believer's spiritual account what amounts to billions of dollars of "spiritual credit." Just as Abraham was made righteous through his faith, so are believers in Christ are made righteous:

> [22] This is why "it was credited to him as righteousness." [23] The words "it was credited to him" were written not for him alone, [24] but also for us, to whom God will credit righteousness—for us who believe in him who raised Jesus our Lord from the dead (Rom. 4:22–24, NIV).

This spiritual credit of righteousness gives believers a distinctive spiritual status. In some cultures, there is still a caste system, recognizing diverse social levels. If a person is not of a certain income level or heritage, he is not allowed to associate with those of higher social status. There are exclusive clubs where only those of a certain status are allowed. For example, there are millionaire clubs where only millionaires are accepted. What God's grace has done is to give those who have faith in Christ the status of righteousness and thus are welcomed into His holy presence. God grace has given believers a spiritual billionaire status! God's grace gives believers the most favored status without having earned it in any way. Believers have a restored relationship with

God because they are made righteous through the imputed righteousness of Christ.

This reminds me of something that happened to my wife, Susan, and me on a trip to Africa. We were in London for over a week, attending services and speaking at some services. We stayed in London an additional four days after the conference to do some sightseeing around London and Portsmouth. When it was time to depart for Africa, we went through the whole process of finding the right terminal for our fight. When we handed in our tickets, the clerk looked at our tickets and then at his computer screen. He had a puzzled look on his face when he informed us that there must have been some confusion about our tickets because those seats were given to someone else. Our hearts sank. What were we going to do? The clerk tried to reassure us by telling us that he would find a solution.

After a few minutes, the clerk asked us if we would mind riding in first class at no extra cost? Are you kidding? Of course, we would not mind riding in first class! My wife and I had never ridden in first class before. Whenever we flew, we could only afford the economy seats at the back of the plane. We flew all the way from London to Africa in first-class seats! Riding first class was so much better than what we had experienced before. We enjoyed first-class seating, first-class menus, and first-class service. We could lie all the way back in a horizontal position and sleep through the night on our way to Africa. What a blessing from God! This is similar to the way the grace of God works in our lives. God's grace offers believers first-class, favored, spiritual status with Him paying the whole bill!

Unfortunately, many Christians think they only deserve to ride in the spiritual economy class because they are spiritually unworthy to ride first class. God's grace freely offers believers in Christ first class spiritual status. Ephesians 2:5–7 describes this first-class spiritual status as being seated with Christ in heavenly places, "even when we were dead in our transgressions, made us alive together with Christ (by grace you have been saved), and raised us up with Him, and seated us with Him in the heavenly places in Christ Jesus, so that in the ages to come He might show the surpassing riches of His grace in kindness toward us in Christ Jesus" (Eph. 2:5–7). First-class spiritual status is not something that happens to believers when they get to heaven; this is speaking about the believer's present spiritual status given to him because of the surpassing riches of God's grace.

A significant part of this new spiritual status given to those who have received God's grace is the ability to freely approach God in prayer. Some people falsely believe that they will not be allowed into God's presence in prayer because they have sin in their lives and are thus disqualified from receiving God's attention. We must never forget that we are allowed into God's presence solely because of God's grace and never based on our own merit. If we confess our sins and apply the blood of Christ by faith to cleanse us from all our sins, we can boldly enter God's presence. "Since therefore, brethren we have confidence to enter the holy place by the blood of Jesus…let us draw near with a sincere heart in full assurance of faith, having our hearts sprinkled clean from an evil conscience and our bodies washed with pure water" (Heb. 10:19, 22).

An additional benefit of this new spiritual standing through God's grace is having an assurance of one's salvation. Our assurance of salvation does not come from a confidence in good works to qualify us but from a trust in God's faithfulness to keep His promises. As stated earlier, an important aspect of God's moral nature is His truthfulness. His truthfulness speaks of God being faithful and reliable. What God has revealed about Himself is reliable; it can be trusted. God's promises will most assuredly be fulfilled. When God promises salvation by grace through faith in Christ, we must believe the promise is true. Having faith to believe God for salvation is not based on human reasoning or feelings; rather, it is based solely on the truthfulness of God. We must take God at His Word.

The spiritual status given to believers should never lead to pride. Since the righteousness that has been received is by grace through faith, there is no place for pride. Those who have been given this new status are not to consider themselves as an exclusive group. The spiritual status given to believers comes with many benefits, but it also comes with a responsibility to share God's plan of salvation with others. God's plan of salvation through grace is the one and only, true plan. All other ways that proport to be the way of salvation are lies and deceptive scams. Jesus declared the truth concerning the one way of salvation, "I am the Way, and the Truth, and the Life, no one comes to the Father, but through Me" (John 14:6).

Since God's plan of salvation is the only way to be saved, this gospel of grace must be made known to everyone. God desires everyone to have an opportunity to at least hear the good news about His offer of salvation through grace. God has given the responsibility of presenting this gospel of good news to the whole world to those who have received His grace by faith (Mark 13:10). The task of presenting the gospel is every believer's responsibility. If some never hear the gospel message, it will not be God's failure but of those believers who disobeyed His command to preach the gospel to all nations. Once a person hears the gospel, he then will be held responsible for how he responds to the message. God will not violate the will of any person. God gives each individual a choice in the matter of his salvation. A person is given the freedom to choose to reject the message or to receive the message of God's grace by faith. Those who respond in faith to the gospel message will be recipients of the marvelous riches of God's grace.

Grace

Application

1. Do you believe that God is a God of love and that He loves you?

2. Do you believe that God is a good God and that He wants to do good things for you?

3. Do you believe that God is a benevolent God who cares for you?

4. Do you see God as an angry, harsh, unforgiving God or as a loving and merciful God?

5. Have you cried out to God for mercy?

Trophy of Grace: Pedro Arroyo

This testimony was written from several interviews that I had with Pedro Arroyo. Pedro and his family faithfully attended Victory International for over two years but have since moved to another city and are faithfully attending church there. I believe that what was shared with me about his life is true. Isidro Oyola, who was the first Trophy of Grace in this book, has known Pedro for many years and is a witness to truth of his statements. Pedro was one of the persons that Isidro Oyola helped while he worked for the Columbus Hospital as a drug rehabilitation counselor. Pedro is an example of many that Isidro helped to escape drugs.

Pedro's story begins on June 14, 1959, when he was born in a small town called Puerto Chico, Puerto Rico. His father divorced his mother when he was only six months old. He grew up not having any relationship with his father. At the age of six, his mother moved to the United States and left him behind with his grandparents. At the age of nine, he moved to Buffalo, New York, to stay with his mother.

Once Pedro moved to Buffalo, he quickly learned the English language. He attended schools until he graduated from high school. After graduation, he got caught up in drugs as a user and a dealer. At the age of nineteen, Pedro became a heroin dealer. At the age of twenty, he stabbed a customer who refused to pay what was owed on some drugs. It was a whole year after the stabbing that the person called the police. Pedro was arrested and brought to court.

During his stay in prison, he promised God that he would serve Him the rest of his life if he would get out of jail. He believed that his promise was sincere. He stayed in jail for only a couple more weeks until he was brought to court concerning the stabbing. The person who was stabbed never showed up for the court case so the charges were dismissed. After his release, Pedro did not keep his promise to God but went right back to using and selling drugs.

At the age of twenty-one, Pedro got married and eventually had three children. The years from nineteen to twenty-eight of Pedro's life could be characterized as on and off with drugs. He would attend church with his family and be clean from drugs for a while; then he would fall right back into drugs. During the time of being on and off with drugs, Pedro confessed that he never really made a full commitment to God. At that time in his life, he confessed that he did not know how to apply God's Word nor did he understand how the grace of God operated.

At the age of thirty, Pedro said, "Everything went crazy; things went from bad to worse." He stopped doing heroin in his twenties but got right back on heroin in his thirties. During this time, his wife divorced him because of the drugs. Getting divorced only made things worse for him. From his thirties to fifty-seven years of age, his life continued to go downward into a deadly spiral. He was constantly in and out of jail and the hospital. Pedro was taken to the hospital an unbelievable twenty-two times for drug overdoses. When he was not in jail or the hospital, he lived as a homeless person on the streets of Buffalo. Pedro slept in abandoned houses and stayed short times at the Buffalo City Mission and the Harbor House (a place from the homeless to stay overnight during cold weather). There were no beds at the Harbor House, only chairs for people to sit in during the night. Pedro described his stays at the Harbor House as "hell."

Because getting drugs was the most important thing for Pedro, he resorted to picking food out of garbage bins to save money for drugs. He was drawn into a life of crime and stealing to feed his drug habit. He and a partner in crime would rob people on the streets. The last time they robbed a person on the street, they beat him up to rob his money. They fled from the scene, leaving him lying on the street not knowing if he were dead or alive. From that time on they decided to rob houses. Pedro's life continued downward into a "dark world."

"It was only God who could rescue me from the darkness," Pedro declared. Pedro described his life as being "numb." In the five years before Pedro finally got off of drugs, he stated, "Drugs were the most important to me, more than my mother, my kids, more important than God, more important than anything." Pedro tried rehab centers for short stays, but they did not work because he would go right back to drugs after he got out. Pedro had made many promises to God to quit, but for most of forty years, all he lived for was to get the next fix.

Pedro confessed that, "Drugs destroyed everything in my life." All his attempts to get off of drugs always failed. If there ever were a hopeless case, Pedro was a prime candidate. Pedro came to the conclusion that he could never quit drugs on his own.

Pedro came to the place of humbling himself before God and confessing his total need for God to rescue him from a lifelong addiction. He had come to the realization that only God could make a difference in his life and submitted himself to a three-year-long rehab program at Erie County Medical Center. During that long stay in the hospital, God began to work in his life. He began to pray and read the Bible a lot more. The more he read the Bible, the more he understood about God's love and grace. At a certain point in his growing relationship with the Lord, he experienced the presence of God in his life. Pedro explained that the Holy Spirit came into his life and took up residence there. Pedro had what many describe as a "born-again" experience.

With the Holy Spirit now in his life, God began to make genuine changes in Pedro's life. His desires completely changed, and he now possessed a new desire and hunger for the righteousness of God. God had changed his heart so much that he did not want to have anything to do with the sinful things of the world. Pedro stated, "I know that I know that it was God who changed my life. God went inside of me and pulled the desire for drugs out of me and the desire to live that way any longer. No words can express what God has done for me. It is not about me and what I can do; it is about God and what He can do."

Pedro discovered first hand that there is no such a thing as a hopeless case with God. Pedro has been drug-free for six years as of 2022. He is now back with his second wife and family and working construction jobs to provide for his family. Before Pedro moved to another city, he was involved briefly with the homeless ministry of Victory International to provide warm clothing and food for the homeless in downtown Buffalo during the cold winter months. Where once he suffered the misery of homelessness, Pedro has been used to minister to the homeless at Harbor House. This is the miracle of God's grace; God can take a homeless person, destitute and hopelessly addicted to drugs, and set him free. Now Pedro is able to minister to those who are in his previous condition. Pedro Arroyo is another one of the millions of people that have experienced the miracle of the power of God's grace.

PART TWO

GOD'S SAVING GRACE

CHAPTER 4

Removing the Penalty of Sin

How does a person receive the benefits of God's grace? In order to receive all the benefits of God's grace, a person must first be saved. How does a person experience salvation by grace? This salvation is a gift given by God (Rom. 3:24). Salvation cannot be earned or merited in any way (Eph. 2:8–9). Salvation cannot be earned through keeping the law or any set of rules (Gal. 2:16).

When a person hears and understands God's offer of forgiveness of sins, he must respond in faith to the message in order to receive salvation. Ephesians 2:8 clearly states that a person is saved by grace through faith, which is believing the Gospel message to be true and then acting on God's offer to receive His gift of salvation. Faith believes that God will keep His promise of forgiveness to those who believe in Christ. Faith reaches out to take hold of God's gift. It is through faith that we obtain our introduction into God's grace, "through whom also we have obtained our introduction by faith into this grace in which we stand; and we exult in hope of the glory of God" (Rom. 5:2).

In Romans 10:9–10, the apostle Paul explained how a person is to believe, "that if you confess with your mouth Jesus *as* Lord, and believe in your heart that God raised Him from the dead, you will be saved; for with the heart a person believes, resulting in righteousness, and with the mouth he confesses, resulting in salvation." Having faith to receive salvation includes several things: faith to confess Jesus as Lord, faith to believe in one's heart that God has raised Christ from the dead (Rom.10:10), and faith to receive Christ into one's life (John 1:12). Exactly what happens to someone when he is saved by grace through faith? After a thorough study of the words used in Scripture concerning salvation, I concluded that there are four major factors that take place at salvation. I divided these into four categories. First, is the removal of the penalty of sin; second, is the imputation of God's righteousness; third, is the creation of new spiritual life, and finally a new relationship with God is established.

There are certain scriptural terms that apply to each particular aspect of salvation. The first element of salvation is the removal of the penalty of sin. This removal of the penalty of sin must happen before any of the other aspects of salvation can occur. I am not suggesting that there is a sequence of time between each aspect of salvation, but only that an order of importance exists. For example, a person cannot be born again without first being forgiven of his sins. Similarly, a person could not be reconciled to God without first having his sins forgiven. When someone repents and asks God's forgiveness through faith in Christ, all the elements of salvation should occur simultaneously.

There are a number of terms used in Scripture to describe the removal of the penalty of sin. Terms that describe how the penalty of sin can be removed are: forgiveness of sin, pardon for sin, redemption/ransom, propitiation, atonement, and justification.

Terms Describing the Removal of the Penalty of Sin

Forgiveness of Sins

To forgive sins means to grant relief from payment of a debt for the punishment of sins. When God forgives our sins, He cancels the debt of punishment that is due for our sins. Forgiveness from God is more than just canceling a debt; it is also the cessation of resentment against the offender. We need to understand that sin does not just incur debt for punishment; it also deeply offends God. When God forgives, He removes the penalty for sin; additionally, He removes any disfavor towards the offender. When God forgives us, He is no longer at odds with us but is at peace with us (Rom. 5:1).

When we have offended someone and go to ask his forgiveness, he may forgive us, but he may still hold on to resentment toward us. You may have heard someone say to the one they supposedly forgave, "I forgive you, but I will never forget." To thoroughly forgive as God forgives means to completely forget the offense ever happened. When God forgives us, He will act toward us like we never offended Him by our sins. When we forgive a person of an offense against us, we still may not have any desire to renew a friendship. When God forgives us, He desires for us to be reconciled to Him. Through reconciliation with God, we can now begin a lifelong discovery of God's great love for us.

There are several verses in the Old Testament that metaphorically describe the completeness of God's forgiveness. One of those verses is Psalm 103:12, "As far as the east is from the west, so far has He removed our transgressions from us." This verse describes the boundlessness of how God removes transgressions from a person He forgives. If a person would circle the earth going west or east, he would never come to a place where he could not go farther in either direction. Thus, this verse assures believers that when God forgives their sins, He completely removes them so far that they can never return.

Another verse in the Old Testament describes God's forgiveness as putting people's sins behind His back, "Lo, for *my own* welfare I had great bitterness; It is You who has kept my soul from the pit of nothingness, For You have cast all my sins behind Your back" (Isa. 38:17). What does "behind God's back" mean? This is an anthropomorphic or symbolic statement of God having "a back." In human terms, when a person puts something behind his back and keeps looking forward, he will not see it. This means that when God forgives, He puts sins behind His back and, therefore, is choosing not to focus on a person's sins.

Another verse describes God's forgiveness as crushing our sins under His feet and casting all our sins into the depths of the sea, "He will again have compassion on us; He will tread our iniquities under foot. Yes, you will cast all their sins into the depths of the sea" (Mic. 7:19). Again, understand this is another anthropomorphic description of God having feet. This expression is symbolic of God's forgiveness destroying the memory of our confessed sins. When God forgives our sins, He cast our sins into the depths of the sea. Our sins, which are heavy, will sink to the bottom of the sea where they will never be seen again.

> *God covers our sins with an ocean of mercy and grace.*

Another insightful verse concerning God's forgiveness is Isaiah 43:25, "I, even I, am the one who wipes out your transgressions for My own sake, And I will not remember your sins." In this verse, God is saying that when He forgives, He wipes out transgressions for His own sake. "Wipes out" means that when God forgives sins, He erases the memory of those sins. He promises not to remember those sins. It is like God hitting delete and then emptying the recycle bin on His spiritual computer. Obviously, God cannot forget anything because He is omniscient. He cannot forget anything in a strict literal sense, but God will never recall or bring up again any sins that He has forgiven.

Proclaiming the opportunity for forgiveness of sin is the central emphasis of the gospel, "Therefore let it be known to you, brethren, that through Him forgiveness of sins is proclaimed to you" (Acts 13:38). Because of Christ's death on the cross and through faith in Him, our sins can be forgiven. "Of Him all the prophets bear witness that through His name everyone who believes in Him receives forgiveness of sins" (Acts 10:43). Through Christ we have redemption and the forgiveness of sins, "In Him we have redemption through His blood, the forgiveness of our trespasses, according to the riches of His grace" (Eph. 1:7). The heavy burden of the guilt from sin is lifted when we realize, as believers in Christ, our sins are forgiven.

It is important to understand that God's forgiveness is part of the daily life of believers. After salvation, everyone needs to practice daily confession of sin and believe that God will forgive every sin. Somehow, many Christians act like God's grace only covers sins before salvation but not afterward. The same grace of God that forgives the sinner when he comes to believe in Christ is the same grace that will continue to forgive the penitent believer.

The apostle John addressed the topic of sin in a believer's life in 1 John 1:7–9. When a believer sins, he needs to confess his sins and fully believe that his sins are indeed forgiven. A believer in Christ can enjoy assurance of forgiveness through faith in God's promise to forgive. In addition to God's promise of forgiveness, every believer has the assurance that his appeal for forgiveness will be presented to God the Father by his extremely successful defense attorney. Jesus is the believer's Advocate (defense attorney) who has never lost an appeal for forgiveness for His children, "My little children, I am writing these things to you so that you may not sin. And if anyone sins, we have an Advocate with the Father, Jesus Christ the righteous" (1 John 2:1).

Pardon for Sin

Another term that is primarily used in Old Testament to describe the removal of punishment for sin is the word *pardon*. Webster's Dictionary defines the word as: "to absolve from the consequences of a crime."[25] This word takes on legal usage when a government official, such as a governor, chooses to absolve a person who is charged with a crime. A pardon usually comes after a person has served some time in prison for a crime that was committed. Once a person is pardoned, he is immediately set free from incarceration or payment of penalties. We are all sinners who have committed crimes against God's holy standard and, as a consequence, have the sentence of death hanging over us (Rom. 6:23). We are all on sin's "death row." Everyone is a sinner imprisoned by his sins with no hope of escape or release.

People who are on death row can appeal to a governor for a pardon or a stay of execution. God, in His great mercy and love, has offered pardon for those who call on Him, asking for His forgiveness. Psalm 103:2–3 speaks about God pardoning all our iniquities, "Bless the Lord, O my soul, And forget none of His benefits; Who pardons all your iniquities, Who heals all your diseases." Isaiah 55:7 speaks about how God will abundantly pardon those who turn to Him in repentance, "Let the wicked forsake his way, And the unrighteous man his thoughts; And let him return to the Lord, And He will have compassion on him, And to our God, For He will abundantly pardon." Other Scriptures that mention God remitting sin are Jeremiah 33:8 and Micah 7:18.

Redemption

The words *redeem*, *redeemed*, and *redemption* are rich in meaning concerning absolution of sin. Webster's Dictionary defines redeem as, "To free from the consequences of sin"[26] and redemption as, "the act, process, or an instance of redeeming."[27] In the Old Testament, these words take on the general meaning of deliverance. When redemption is used for dealings between people, "Its basic use had to do with deliverance of persons or property that had been sold for debt, as in

Leviticus 25:25."[28] The legal practice of the Israelites for settling debts was to sell property or, if an Israelite was too poor, he could sell himself to a fellow Israelite (Lev. 25:39) or to an alien living in Israel (Lev. 25:47). "The responsibility to redeem belonged to the nearest relative—brother, uncle, uncle's son, or a blood relative from the family (Lev. 25:25, 48–49)."[29] The redeemer could buy back property such as land or pay back the debt to set free the person who sold himself to pay for the debt. Once the ransom was paid, the property or persons enslaved would be either returned or set free. The book of Ruth is a beautiful account of a kinsman-redeemer named Boaz who redeemed a woman named Naomi and her daughter-in-law, Ruth. When used of God in the Old Testament, redemption is used most often concerning His deliverance of His chosen people Israel, such as their deliverance from Egypt (Isa. 51:10; 63:9) and from the Babylonian captivity (Isa. 48:20; 52:3).

The Greek words used in the New Testament for *redeem, redeemed,* and *redemption* take on a similar meaning to the Old Testament meaning of deliverance. One of the Greek verbs for redeem is transliterated *exagorazō* (1805), which "denotes "to buy out" especially of purchasing a slave with a view to his freedom."[30] This Greek word for redeem is used metaphorically of Christ, "Christ redeemed us from the curse of the Law, having become a curse for us—for it is written, "Cursed is everyone who hangs on a tree" (Gal. 3:13); "so that He might redeem those who were under the Law, that we might receive adoption as sons" (Gal. 4:5). Christ's death was the ransom paid for humanity's deliverance. Ransom means to free from captivity or punishment by paying a price. Christ declared that His major purpose for coming to earth was to give His life as a ransom for many, "just as the Son of Man did not come to be served, but to serve, and to give His life a ransom for many" (Matt. 20:28).

Another Greek word for redeem is *lutroō* (3084), which means "to release on receipt of ransom."[31] Though both "*exagorazō* and *lutroō* are translated "to redeem," *exagorazō* does not signify the actual redemption, but the price paid in view of it, *lutroō* signifies the actual "deliverance," the setting at liberty."[32] Christ has redeemed believers from every lawless deed and purified them, "who gave Himself for us to redeem us from every lawless deed, and to purify for Himself a people for His own possession, zealous for good deeds" (Titus 2:14). Christ purchased humanity's redemption through the shedding of His blood, "knowing that you were not redeemed with perishable things like silver or gold from your futile way of life inherited from your forefathers, but with precious blood, as of a lamb unblemished and spotless, *the blood* of Christ" (1 Pet. 1:18–19).

The Greek word for "redemption" is *lutrōsis* (3085); it "is used in a general sense for the deliverance of the nation of Israel."[33] It is through the redemptive work of Christ's death that people are delivered from the guilt and power of sin, "and not through the blood of goats and calves, but through His own blood, He entered the holy place once for all, having obtained eternal redemption" (Heb. 9:12).

To summarize, the meaning of "redeem" or "redemption" is to be set free from the bondage of debt for sins. We are all sold into the bondage of sin and its punishment without the ability to redeem ourselves. We all need a deliverer (redeemer) to pay our debt of punishment for sin. Jesus Christ is the Redeemer who came to pay the ransom for our sins through the shedding of His blood on the cross, "In Him we have redemption through His blood, the forgiveness of our trespasses, according to the riches of His grace" (Eph. 1:7).

Propitiation for Sin

Most people are not familiar with the word *propitiation*. With that in mind, let us explore what the word means and how it applies to the removal of the penalty of sin. Webster's Dictionary defines the verb *propitiate* as: "to gain or regain the favor or goodwill of: appease, conciliate."[34] Because God is a righteous and just God, He will judge all sin, "For the wrath of God is revealed from heaven against all ungodliness and unrighteousness of men who suppress the truth in unrighteousness" (Rom. 1:18). God sent His Son to be the propitiation for sin because of His great love for mankind. The penalty for sin had to be paid in full. "In this is love, not that we loved God, but that He loved us and sent His Son *to be* the propitiation for our sins" (1 John 4:10). The price for sin would be paid in full through the sacrificial death of Christ. Christ's substitutionary death propitiated God's wrath toward sin, "Much more then, having now been justified by His blood, we shall be saved from the wrath *of God* through Him" (Rom. 5:9). Christ's vicarious death is the propitiation for the sins of the whole world, "and He Himself is the propitiation for our sins; and not for ours only, but also for *those of* the whole world" (1 John 2:2).

The Greek word used in the New Testament for "to propitiate" is *hilaskomai* (2433). Christ's "expiatory work on the Cross is therefore the means whereby the barrier which sin interposes between God and man is broken down. By the giving up of His sinless life sacrificially, Christ annuls the power of sin to separate God and the believer."[35] Through Christ's propitiation, God's wrath toward a believer's sin is appeased and, as a result, those who have faith in Christ gain a favored status.

Atonement for Sin

The terms *propitiation* and *atonement* have a similar meaning. The noun *atonement* or the verb *atone* were primarily used in the Old Testament, especially in connection with sacrifices. The word *atonement* is used only once in the New Testament in the King James Version (Rom. 5:11) and is translated *reconciliation* in the New American Standard Bible. In the Old Testament, atonement was made through offering animal sacrifices. Sacrificing of animals to atone for sin was done both for individuals (Lev. 4:13–20) and for the whole nation of Israel on the day of Atonement (Lev. 16).

The Hebrew term for "atone" is *kāpar* (3722). As a verb *kāpar* means, "'to cover over, atone, propitiate, pacify.' This root is found in the Hebrew language at all periods of its history, and perhaps best known for the term Yom Kippur, "day of Atonement." Its verbal forms occur approximately 100 times in the Hebrew Bible." [36] "Most uses of the word, however, involve the theological meaning of *"covering over,"* often with the blood of a sacrifice, in order to atone for some sin. It is not clear whether this means that the *"covering over"* hides the sin from God's sight or implies that the sin is wiped away in the process."[37]

Webster defines the verb *atone* as "to become reconciled, to supply satisfaction for: expiate: to make amends."[38] The noun *atonement* is defined as: "reconciliation, the reconciliation of God and man through the sacrificial death of Jesus Christ, reparation for an offense or injury."[39] In order to grasp the full meaning of atonement, we need to combine two concepts: *"to cover"* and reconciliation. The concept of atonement includes both the covering of sin through the blood of Christ and, as a result of that covering of sin, full reconciliation with God.

CHAPTER 5

Being Made Righteous

Terms Describing God Crediting Righteousness to Man

Righteousness as a Gift from God

When people think about salvation, they usually consider it merely the forgiveness of sin. Having one's sins forgiven is a wonderful act of God's grace, but there is still more God wants to grant believers by His grace. The removal of the penalty for sin is the initial part of salvation. However, there is so much more to salvation than just the removal of this penalty. Salvation also includes the imputation of Christ's righteousness. God not only graciously forgives the believer's sins; He also gives them the perfect righteousness of Christ. "For if by the transgression of the one, death reigned through the one, much more those who receive the abundance of grace and of the gift of righteousness will reign in life through the One, Jesus Christ" (Rom. 5:17).

Because of Christ's substitutionary death on the cross, believers can *become* the righteousness of God, "He made Him who knew no sin *to be* sin on our behalf, so that we might become the righteousness of God in Him" (2 Cor. 5:21). This righteousness is not a righteousness that can be earned through keeping the law. The apostle Paul explained the righteousness that is received through faith in Christ, "and may be found in Him, not having a righteousness of my own derived from *the* Law, but that which is through faith in Christ, the righteousness which *comes* from God on the basis of faith" (Phil. 3:9).

Imputed Righteousness

The Bible describes this gift of righteousness as an imputation of righteousness. What is meant by imputation of righteousness? Let us look first at the meaning of "impute" or "imputation." Webster defines *impute* as "to credit to a person or a cause."[40] The Greek word used in the New Testament for "impute" is *logizomai* (3049) which means "to reckon, to consider, to count, to credit, to regard, to take into account."[41]

In his letter to the Galatians, Paul revealed how Abraham was made righteous because of his faith. "Even so Abraham believed God, and it was reckoned to him as righteousness" (Gal. 3:6). When God "imputes" righteousness or "reckons" a person as righteous, He takes into account the person's faith in Christ and equates it to righteousness. God never considers a person righteous in himself without faith in Christ. Why is it so important to be "reckoned" as righteous before God? Is not the forgiveness of sins sufficient enough to allow believers to have fellowship with God? The answer is, "No, having one's sins forgiven is not enough to qualify one to enter God's presence." God demands that only righteousness can be in His presence. Being righteous is more than just being pardoned for sin; it is possessing God's righteousness. No one can approach God in his own righteousness. It is only when God gives His righteousness to a believer that he is qualified to enter God's holy presence. When God clothes the believer in the righteousness of Christ, he can freely enter into God's presence.

Justification

Justification is the act of God declaring a person righteous through faith in Christ. Webster defines *justify* as, "to prove or show to be just, right, or reasonable, to judge, regard, or treat as righteous and worthy of salvation."[42] There are two Greek words for "justification" used in Scripture. The first is *dikaiōsis* (1347), which "denotes "the act of pronouncing righteous, justification, acquittal."[43] The second is *dikaioma* (1345), which is defined as, "a sentence of acquittal by which God acquits men of their guilt, on the condition of His grace in Christ, through His expiatory sacrifice, the acceptance of Christ by faith (Rom. 5:16)."[44] Justification is a forensic or legal act of God as Supreme Judge where He pronounces a person acquitted of all guilt and, furthermore, pronounces the sinner who has faith in Christ as righteous. Justification is a declarative act on God's part. As Supreme Judge, God declares those who have faith in Christ as righteous in His sight. Justification deals with our standing or status before God; whereas, sanctification deals with our actual growth in personal righteousness. Our favored status with God is based solely on Christ's perfect righteousness, obtained through faith in Him.

Even though the development of a believer's personal righteousness is a matter that is very important to God, it is not the basis of a believer's standing before God. If one's status with God were established on one's personal holiness, then salvation would not be based on God's grace. Instead, it would be based on man's righteousness. This type of thinking was an issue in the churches of Galatia. The apostle Paul had to correct the erroneous belief that a believer was initially saved by God's grace but then had to maintain his salvation through works, "Are you so foolish? Having begun by the Spirit, are you now being perfected in the flesh?" (Gal. 3:3). It is by grace we are saved, and it is by grace that we continue to be saved.

Picture God sitting on His holy throne. He is the holy, righteous, and just God who will judge all sins and cannot be approached by sin. But, because of a person's faith in Christ, God declares a full acquittal of his sins and then declares him righteous in his standing before God.

> *Where once God's throne was a throne of judgment, it is now, for those who have faith in Christ, a throne of grace.*

"Therefore let us draw near with confidence to the throne of grace, so that we may receive mercy and find grace to help in time of need" (Heb. 4:16). As believers in Christ, we have assurance that we can approach God's holy throne because of His lavish grace, "Since therefore, brethren we have confidence to enter the holy place by the blood of Jesus" (Heb. 10:19).

Justification consists of two parts: (1) forgiveness of sins, remission of penalty; and (2) imputation of righteousness. Forgiveness is the negative side of salvation which is the removal of debt; whereas, justification is the positive side of salvation or the deposit of righteousness. A good analogy here is to compare financial accounting with spiritual accounting. According to God, everyone has a spiritual bank account. Because of sin, our spiritual account is bankrupt. We all owe a huge debt that we can never repay. It is like everyone having a billion dollars of debt.

Then, because of one's saving faith in Christ, God's grace cancels the debt. The debt is paid in full; not even a penny is owed. The believer's spiritual account is at zero. Then, after canceling our debt of sin, God does something so wonderful it is difficult for us to comprehend. He deposits a billion dollars of spiritual righteousness into our spiritual account. God's grace credits our spiritual account with His righteousness. We can never deplete the gift of righteousness that God gives us by His grace; God's grace will be more than sufficient for all eternity.

To better understand justification, it is helpful to look at its opposite. "The opposite of justify is not "be a sinner" but is "accuse" or "condemn" (Rom. 8:33), and the opposite of justification is *condemnation* (Rom. 5:18).[45] From this contrast, we understand that justification is not dealing with personal holiness but with a believer's standing before God. The question of one's status with God comes down to whether one stands justified or condemned. Romans 5:18 demonstrates this contrast, "So then as through one transgression there resulted condemnation to all men, even so through one act of righteousness there resulted justification of life to all men."

How can a person be justified? Everyone must first understand that it could never be by works of the Law. No flesh is justified in His sight, "nevertheless knowing that a man is not justified by the works of the Law but through faith in Christ Jesus, even we have believed in Christ Jesus, so that we may be justified by faith in Christ and not by the works of the Law; since by the works of the Law no flesh will be justified" (Gal. 2:16). The purpose of the law was never to justify man but only to reveal man's sin, "because by the works of the Law no flesh will be justified in His sight; for through the Law *comes* the knowledge of sin" (Rom. 3:20). The revelation of our sinfulness should drive us to seek God for His help. Realizing our sinfulness ought to lead us to Christ, "Therefore the Law has become our tutor *to lead us* to Christ, so that we may be justified by faith" (Gal. 3:24).

It is only by God's grace that anyone is justified. Justification is a gift given through the grace of God, "being justified as a gift by His grace through the redemption which is in Christ Jesus" (Rom. 3:24). Titus 3:7 confirms that justification is only through God's grace, "that being justified by His grace we might be made heirs according to *the* hope of eternal life." Justification takes place at the moment an individual confesses his faith in Christ. Justification is based on the shedding of Christ's blood at His crucifixion, "Much more then, having now been justified by His blood, we shall be saved from the wrath *of God* through Him" (Rom. 5:9). God can freely justify those who have faith in Christ because Christ fully paid for all sin. God can freely show His grace because His justice was satisfied by Christ's death. "Because Jesus Christ has borne the punishment of our sins in His own body, God is able to remit the penalty and to restore us to His favor."[46]

> But He was pierced through for our transgressions, He was crushed for our iniquities; The chastening for our well-being *fell* upon Him, And by His scourging we are healed. All of us like sheep have gone astray, Each of us has turned to his own way; But the Lord has caused the iniquity of us all To fall on Him. (Isa. 53:5–6)

> And He Himself bore our sins in His body on the cross, so that we might die to sin and live to righteousness; for by His wounds you were healed. (1 Pet. 2:24)

Sanctification (positional)

There are two types of sanctification. The first type of sanctification is what happens instantaneously when a person is saved. The second is the type of sanctification that happens gradually during the entire life of a believer. Justification is a declarative act by which God confirms a believer's forgiveness of sins and his righteous standing through faith in Christ. When a new believer is declared righteous by God, he is then sanctified or set apart unto Christ. With this "setting apart" to be "in Christ," God imputes His righteousness to the new believer. First Corinthians 1:30 states, "But by His doing you are in Christ Jesus, who became to us wisdom from God, and righteousness and sanctification, and redemption."

At the beginning of 1 Corinthians, Paul addresses believers as those who have been sanctified in Christ, "to the church of God which is at Corinth, to those who have been sanctified in Christ Jesus, saints by calling, with all who in every place call on the name of our Lord Jesus Christ, their *Lord* and ours" (1 Cor. 1:2). This righteousness is obtained by grace through faith in Christ, "to open their eyes so that they may turn from darkness to light and from the dominion of Satan to God, that they may receive forgiveness of sins and an inheritance among those who have been sanctified by faith in Me" (Acts 26:18). This initial act of sanctification happens immediately at salvation when a person is set apart unto God by the Holy Spirit through his faith in Christ. The believer is sanctified through the blood of Christ, "Therefore Jesus also, that He might sanctify the people through His own blood, suffered outside the gate" (Heb. 13:12).

The sanctified believer is reckoned holy by God who looks upon those who are in Christ as covered by the righteousness of Christ (Rom. 4:24). This type of sanctification is described by some as positional sanctification. A believer's standing before God is holy when he is "in Christ." This is evident in the naming of all born-again believers as saints (Rom. 1:7; I Cor. 1:2; Eph. 1:1; Phil. 1:1; Col. 1:1). It is important that all believers know that through God's grace, they are considered as saints before God. Being considered a "saint" by God does not mean that believers are perfected and that their transformation into Christlikeness is complete. Being a saint is the believer's standing before God because of God's grace. The believer's personal growth in holiness comes under the second type of sanctification which is a progression of development into the likeness of Christ.

CHAPTER 6

Starting a New Life

Terms Used to Describe the New Spiritual Life that Occurs at Salvation

From Spiritual Death to Spiritual Life

All of humanity is separated from God and spiritually dead because of the fall of Adam. Without God, all of humanity is dead in trespasses and sins (Eph. 2:1). Sin prevents humanity from having the spiritual life that comes from God, "being darkened in their understanding, excluded from the life of God because of the ignorance that is in them, because of the hardness of their heart" (Eph. 4:18). The only way for humanity to regain this spiritual life is to be reunited with God who is the source of life (John 5:26; 1 John 1:2). The Bible declares that Jesus Christ came to give abundant spiritual life (John 10:10). It is solely through Christ that a person can receive this new spiritual life. "Jesus said to them: "I am the bread of life; he who comes to Me will not hunger, and he who believes in Me will never thirst" (John 6:35). Jesus claimed that He was the source of life, "Jesus said to him, I am the way, and the truth, and the life; no one comes to the Father but through Me" (John 14:6).

Even though Adam and Eve's sinful failure brought spiritual death to everyone, there is hope for humanity; we can be made spiritually alive through faith in Jesus Christ! "For as in Adam all die, so also in Christ all will be made alive" (1 Cor. 15:22). Through faith in Christ, we can experience this spiritual life, "He who believes in the Son has eternal life; but he who does not obey the Son will not see life, but the wrath of God abides on him" (John 3:36). Through believing that Jesus is the Christ, we will have life through His name, "but these have been written so that you may believe that Jesus is the Christ, the Son of God; and that believing you may have life in His name" (John 20:31). When a person comes to believe in Christ, he will experience a wonderful salvation which includes the forgiveness of his sins, the imputation of Christ's righteousness through justification, and the receiving of new spiritual life. Salvation brings us from spiritual death to spiritual life. "When you were dead in your transgressions and the uncircumcision of your flesh, He made you alive together with Him, having forgiven us all our transgressions" (Col. 2:13). First John 3:14 declares, "We know that we have passed out of death into life, because we love the brethren. He who does not love abides in death."

This new spiritual life is often termed "eternal life." Eternal life is the spiritual life that indwells the believer at his salvation. Eternal life is a new type of life that a believer possesses because of his relationship with Christ, "so that whoever believes will in Him have eternal life" (John 3:15). Eternal life is both a new quality of life here on earth and the kind of life believers will enjoy throughout eternity, "He who loves his life loses it, and he who hates his life in this world will keep it to life eternal" (John 12:25). Eternal life is the "abundant life" (John 10:10) that believers can experience during this life and for all eternity.

Born Again or Born of the Spirit

Scripture describes this abundant life in a variety of ways. One description that Christ used was "being born again." The term *born again* describes the creation of a new spiritual life in the believer at salvation. In His conversation with a Pharisee, a very devout Jewish leader named Nicodemus, Jesus explained that Nicodemus must be born again. Even though he was very knowledgeable in Jewish laws and customs, Nicodemus lacked understanding of spiritual matters. He was confused by what Jesus said to him concerning being born again. He thought Jesus was saying that he had to be born again physically from his mother's womb. Jesus clarified by explaining that He was referring to being born again a second time in the spirit, "That which is born of the flesh is flesh, and that which is born of the Spirit is spirit" (John 3:6). Jesus made it clear that what Nicodemus needed was to be born of the Spirit. Nicodemus was a very religious man but did not possess any spiritual life. Jesus explained that being born again spiritually was necessary for him to see the kingdom of God, "Jesus answered and said to him, 'Truly, truly, I say to you, unless one is born again, he cannot see the kingdom of God'" (John 3:3). Jesus continued by explaining that this new spiritual birth could be received through believing in Him (John 3:14–17).

Being born of the Spirit means that the Holy Spirit comes into us and dwells within us. At the moment of salvation, the Holy Spirit comes into us and creates a new spiritual nature in us. If a person does not have the Holy Spirit in him, he is not saved. "However, you are not in the flesh but in the Spirit, if indeed the Spirit of God dwells in you. But if anyone does not have the Spirit of Christ, he does not belong to Him" (Rom. 8:9). Without the indwelling of the Spirit of God, there is no spiritual birth or life.

I can bear witness in my own life to what the Scriptures say regarding the experience of new spiritual life through faith in Christ. I grew up in a Christian home and regularly attended church with my parents. In my preteen years, I went forward to the church altar two times to pray to accept Christ as my savior. After going forward to the altar, I never felt much of a difference in my life. As far as I could discern, there was no new spiritual life occurring in my life. I attribute this lack of change in my life to my lack of understanding of what I was doing when I went forward for salvation. A few years later, when I was thirteen years old, a pastor explained to me personally how I could be saved, or born again. I prayed again asking God's forgiveness and invited Christ to come into my heart. This time I had a much better understanding of salvation. Since I prayed that prayer, my life has never been the same. From that point on, God became so real to me. I felt I had a true, personal relationship with God.

I had a new spiritual hunger for God that I never had before. I loved spending time with my Lord in prayer and Bible study. The Bible came alive to me. It seemed that God was speaking directly to me as I read the Scriptures. I felt convicted about some of the sins that I had recently committed, so I went to as many people as I could and asked their forgiveness for whatever I had done against them. Some of those people questioned what prompted me to ask their forgiveness. My response was that I had become a Christian. I realize now that I was previously a Christian by religion only, but I had not become a born-again Christian. I truly experienced, and continue to experience to this day, this new spiritual life. Jesus said that He came to give "abundant life" (John 10:10). I truly have enjoyed that "abundant life" now for fifty-eight years and, by my faith in Christ, I am assured that I will enjoy it for eternity.

New Creation, Newness of Life

There are other terms used to describe the new quality of spiritual life that begins at salvation. One phrase that is found in Scripture is "new creation" or "new creature," as in "Therefore if anyone is in Christ, *he is* a new creature; the old things passed away; behold, new things have come" (2 Cor. 5:17). This verse describes the drastic change that happens in a person when he is saved. We have seen how salvation includes pardon for sin, imputation of righteousness, and impartation of new spiritual life to the believer. Imputation of righteousness has to do with the believer's status before God as justified. This impartation of new spiritual life is different from the imputation of righteousness. Impartation of new spiritual life is God giving the believer a new nature. Whereas, justification deals with the believer's status before God; the impartation of a new nature results in an actual change in the believer's character.

The believer's nature is radically changed when God gives him spiritual life. Through the indwelling of the Holy Spirit, God makes drastic changes in a believer's life. The Holy Spirit will remove aspects of the old sinful nature and replace them with a godly nature, "and put on the new self, which in *the likeness of* God has been created in righteousness and holiness of the truth" (Eph. 4:24). This new spiritual birth or new creation is an essential part of salvation. Without the creation of a new nature, there will be no radical change in that person's life. The apostle Paul explained to the church at Galatia that experiencing the new creation was much more important than whether they were circumcised or not: "For neither is circumcision anything, nor uncircumcision, but a new creation" (Gal. 6:15).

Another phrase that describes this spiritual birth is "newness of life." "Therefore, we have been buried with Him through baptism into death, so that as Christ was raised from the dead through the glory of the Father, so we too might walk in newness of life" (Rom. 6:4). This verse speaks about walking in the newness of life that was received at salvation. It is through the indwelling of the Spirit of God that the believer receives a new nature. However, this does not mean the believer is completely and immediately transformed into his new nature. It is a process of transformation that will require cooperation between the believer and the Holy Spirit to accomplish real change in character. Without the indwelling of the Spirit and the creation of a new nature, there will be no real change in character. With the Spirit of God indwelling the believer and with his new nature, the believer is now capable of overcoming his fallen, sinful nature. Learning to walk in newness of life means a believer is progressing from being controlled by his fleshly, carnal nature to being controlled by the Holy Spirit in his new nature.

CHAPTER 7

Having a New Relationship with God

At the time of salvation there are many wonderful things that happen to the new believer. First, through a person's faith in Christ, he is forgiven of all his sins. Second, through justification, the new believer is declared righteous in God's sight. Third, the new believer is "born-again." This means that at salvation the Holy Spirit comes into the believer, and he becomes alive spiritually.

The Holy Spirit births a new, holy nature within the believer. The removal of the debt of sin, the imputation of righteousness to make the believer righteous in his standing with God, and the holy nature causes the wall of separation between man and God to be removed. Man's relationship with God can be restored to what it was before the fall. There are several terms used in scripture to describe this new relationship made possible through God's grace. The word *reconciliation* describes the act of restoring a person's relationship with God. The word *adoption* is used to describe the type of close relationship believers have with God. The phrases "in Christ" or "united with Christ" are descriptive of the type of union believers have with Christ.

The Terms Describing a New Believer's Relationship with God

Reconciliation

Humanity is alienated from God because of sin. Through the hardness of people's hearts, humanity has become hostile toward God. Romans 8:7 tells us that the fallen, human mind is set on the flesh and is therefore hostile toward God, "because the mind set on the flesh is hostile toward God; for it does not subject itself to the law of God, for it is not even able *to do so.*" There is an impenetrable barrier between God, and man because of man's transgressions and rebellion. There is enmity between God and humanity because God is opposed to sin and humanity is opposed to being judged for its sins. Humanity is in a state of perpetual rebellion. People want to do whatever they please without any accountability to God. Colossians 1:21 describes humanity's condition of separation from God as being alienated and hostile in mind because of their participation in evil behavior: "And although you were formerly alienated and hostile in mind, *engaged* in evil deeds." Romans 5:10 describes humanity's relationship with God as being enemies: "For if while we were enemies we were reconciled to God through the death of His Son, much more, having been reconciled, we shall be saved by His life."

The enormity of humanity's separation from God is like a great abyss that can never be crossed. Not only is humanity not able to cross over this abyss, it does not even want to cross over it. In John 3:19–20, Jesus explains sinful humanity's aversion to God, "And this is the judgment that the light is come into the world, and men loved the darkness rather than the light; for their deeds were evil. For everyone who does evil hates the light, and does not come to the light, lest his deeds should be exposed." It is God who desires to have a relationship with mankind. It is God who loves humanity and made a way, through His grace, for people to have close fellowship with Him.

This restoration of fellowship with God is described as being "reconciled" with God. The words *reconcile* and *reconciliation* are used primarily by the apostle Paul in Romans 5 and 2 Corinthians 5:18–21. In Romans 5, Paul describes reconciliation as a result of being justified by God's grace through faith. Webster defines the verb *reconcile* as, "to restore to friendship or harmony, settle or resolve."[47] The Greek definition: for the word used in these passages for reconcile is *katallassō* (2644). This word "properly denotes "to change, exchange" (especially of money); hence of persons "to change from enmity to friendship, to reconcile."[48] "Primarily "reconciliation" is what God accomplishes, exercising His grace toward sinful man on the grounds of the death of Christ in propitiatory sacrifice under the judgment of sin (2 Cor. 5:19)."[49]

God is the reconciler. He is the one who took the initiative to restore His relationship with humanity. "He reconciled the world to Himself, namely, that God was in Christ reconciling the world to Himself, not counting their trespasses against them, and He has committed to us the word of reconciliation" (2 Cor. 5:19). God does not need to be reconciled to the world. He is not the offender. God has done nothing wrong toward humanity. It is not God who needs to make any changes to be reconciled to the world. He is righteous in all His dealings with humanity. He can do no wrong.

God is a holy and just God who cannot tolerate sin. He cannot just overlook sin; sin must be punished. But, because of His love, He made a way for man to be reconciled to Him. "But God demonstrates His own love toward us, in that while we were yet sinners, Christ died for us" (Rom. 5:8). Christ's death propitiated (appeased) God's wrath and, as result, He reconciled believers to Himself, "Much more then, having now been justified by His blood, we shall be saved from the wrath *of God* through Him" (Rom. 5:9).

As a result of a person being justified by faith, he has peace with God (Rom. 5:1). That means the great abyss that separated man from God has been bridged through the death of Christ. So, those who put their faith in Christ as their savior are forgiven and considered righteous before God and, therefore, have full access to God. There is something else that happens at salvation that is essential for this reconciliation. It is the change of the nature of the person who is saved. Man's sinful nature caused him to have an attitude of hostility toward God but, with salvation, a person experiences a complete change in attitude toward God. A new believer receives a new nature that now loves God and desires fellowship with Him. Not only has God made the way clear for us to come to Him, He also has created a longing in our hearts for close fellowship with Him.

The Believer's Union with Christ or Being "In Christ"

God's Word assures everyone that He is not a God who is far off. Psalm 145:18 states just how near the Lord is, "The Lord is near to all who call upon Him, to all who call upon Him in truth." The Lord declares Himself to be a God who is near, "Am I a God who is near," declares the Lord, "And not a God far off?" (Jer. 23:23). In Acts 17, Paul described the nature of the only true God to the Greeks assembled at the Areopagus on Mars Hill. This true God is the creator of the world and all that is in it. God is the Lord of heaven and earth and does not dwell in temples made with hands. Instead, He is a God who is near "that they would seek God, if perhaps they might grope for Him and find Him, though He is not far from each one of us" (Acts 17:27).

Believers are close to God because of His grace. This closeness is much more than God being near to a person; it is God indwelling him with the Spirit of Christ. Christ tells His followers, "you will know that I am in My Father, and you in Me, and I in you" (John 14:20). Jesus continues His words concerning a believer's relationship with the Father and Him in John 14:23, "Jesus answered and said to him, "If anyone loves Me, he will keep My word; and My Father will love him, and We will come to him and make Our abode with him."

Paul described his personal relationship with Christ as having died to himself and Christ living within him. "I have been crucified with Christ; and it is no longer I who live, but Christ lives in me; and the *life* which I now live in the flesh I live by faith in the Son of God, who loved me and gave Himself up for me" (Gal. 2:20). Paul frequently used the phrase "in Christ" when writing to the churches. In Paul's letter to the church in Rome, he used the phrase two times (Rom. 6:11; 8:1). In Paul's letters to the Corinthian church, he described the results of being "in Christ": "Therefore if anyone is in Christ, *he is* a new creature; the old things passed away; behold, new things have come" (2 Cor. 5:17). Paul's letter to the Ephesian church explained how their relationship changed through being "in Christ": "But now in Christ Jesus you who formerly were far off have been brought near by the blood of Christ" (Ephesians 2:13). Paul prayed for the believers in Ephesus that "Christ may dwell in your hearts through faith" (Eph. 3:17). Paul told the church of Colossae that Christ being in them was their hope of glory (Col. 1:27). Being "in Christ" is descriptive of being so close to Christ that the believer is now one with Christ. Being "one with Christ" means a believer cannot be separated from Christ.

Let's look at a practical example of believers being adorned by the goodness of God's grace. Have you ever used a product called "Great Stuff"? Last week, I was doing some work on the church nursery, which is in the church basement. I was trying to seal off leaks around the window. I used Great Stuff which comes in a spray can about the size of spray paint. It does an impressive job of filling in holes. You spray just a little into a crack, and in a few minutes, it will expand to fill in the hole. However, there is one real problem you might encounter. Do not ever get it on your skin! If you read the instructions, you will read a warning about having proper covering of your skin. You are instructed to wear gloves and to avoid getting it on your skin.

Being true to form, I never read the instructions the first few times I used it. I discovered that you cannot not get it off your skin, no matter what you try to use to remove it. I used soap and water, which did nothing. I used paint thinner; that did nothing. Great Stuff will literally bond with your skin and will only come off days later when your skin sheds. God's grace is like Great Stuff in that it fills in the gaps of our imperfections and weaknesses. How it bonds with our skin is like God's grace bonding us to God. God's grace really is great stuff!

Scripture uses various analogies to represent the union of believers with Christ. Ephesians 2:20-22 compares the church to a spiritual building with the apostles and prophets being the foundation and Christ being the corner stone, "having been built on the foundation of the apostles and prophets, Christ Jesus Himself being the corner *stone*, in whom the whole building, being fitted together, is growing into a holy temple in the Lord, in whom you also are being built together into a dwelling of God in the Spirit." Just as a physical building is connected together to form a structure, so believers are connected with each other and to Christ. As believers are attached to Christ, they also are to be attached to other believers. This analogy speaks of the strength of commitment in relationships between believers and with Christ. Bricks that are mortared to a wall of a building are much more secure than a pile of loose bricks. There is a strong, lasting bond between Christ and believers. God's love is the mortar that binds believers to Christ and each other.

An interesting analogy used in Scripture is Christ being united with the church (all believers) in the same way a husband and wife are united in marriage. "For this reason a man shall leave his father and mother and shall be joined to his wife, and the two shall become one flesh. This mystery is great; but I am speaking with reference to Christ and the church" (Eph. 5:31-32). Another analogy is Christ as the head of the church: "And He put all things in subjection under His feet, and gave

Him as head over all things to the church, which is His body, the fullness of Him who fills all in all" (Eph. 1:22–23).

In an agricultural sense, Christ compares His relationship to believers as a vine to its branches. Christ is the vine, and believers are joined as the branches (John 15:1–10). As Christ is the vine and believers are the branches, they are to "abide" in Christ and He in them. "Abide in Me, and I in you. As the branch cannot bear fruit of itself unless it abides in the vine, so neither can you unless you abide in Me" (John 15:4).

After studying many verses dealing with the unity between Christ and believers, we can rightly conclude that there is a powerful unity between Christ and His people that can never be broken. Paul assures all believers that nothing can separate them from the love of God. "For I am convinced that neither death, nor life, nor angels, nor principalities, nor things present, nor things to come, nor powers, nor height, nor depth, nor any other created thing, will be able to separate us from the love of God, which is in Christ Jesus our Lord" (Rom. 8:38–39).

Adoption

One of the most personal terms used to describe the new relationship that believers have with God is *adoption*. Through experiencing salvation, a person is reconciled in his relationship with God. As a result of this reconciliation, a unity between God and the believer is created. This new relationship with God is the most wonderful relationship that one can experience. A significant benefit of God's grace is that born-again believers become participants in a favored relationship with God. Being a member of God's family immerses believers into God's loving care and grace. Becoming a child of God ushers the believer into the ultimate relationship that mankind can experience.

What does it mean to be a child of God? Biblical terms such as "children of God" and "sons of God" are descriptive of the familial relationship that believers have with God as their Father. This is a unique family relationship. Before experiencing salvation, people are not children of God. In contrast, according to Scripture, they are children of wrath (Eph. 2:3), or sons of disobedience (Eph. 5:6; Col. 3:6), and children of the devil (1 John 3:10).

In a serious conversation with Jews who were not receptive to His message, Jesus clarified that they were not children of God but were children of the devil. These Jews claimed to be children of God because they were descendants of Abraham. Jesus responded to their claim, "If God were your Father, you would love Me, for I proceeded forth and have come from God, for I have not even come on My own initiative, but He sent Me" (John 8:42). Jesus proceeded to tell them that not only were they not children of God but they were children of the devil, "You are of *your* father the devil, and you want to do the desires of your father. He was a murderer from the beginning, and does not stand in the truth because there is no truth in him. Whenever he speaks a lie, he speaks from his own *nature,* for he is a liar and the father of lies" (John 8:44).

An individual becomes a child of God at salvation. "But as many as received Him, to them He gave the right to become children of God, *even* to those who believe in His name, who were born, not of blood nor of the will of the flesh nor of the will of man, but of God" (John 1:12–13). The preceding verse mentions the "right to become children of God" which strongly implies that not everyone will become a child of God. One can only become a child of God on the basis of one's faith in Christ. Becoming a member of God's family does not happen because of heritage; it happens solely on the basis of faith, "For you are all sons of God through faith in Christ Jesus" (Gal. 3:26). Many mistakenly believe that everyone is a child of God; that belief is scripturally inaccurate. Everyone is a creature made by God, but not everyone is a child of God. In order to become a child of God, a person must be born of the Spirit.

When a person is saved, he is adopted into God's family. It is important to understand that a believer is adopted into God's family only on the basis of his faith and not because of family lineage. The Jews believed that they were children of God because they were children of their father Abraham. Many assume that because their parents are Christians, they are automatically children of God. If one's relatives are saved, one might falsely conclude that he belongs to their spiritual family. You may have heard the saying, "God has no grandchildren." The influence of Christian parents certainly increases the likelihood of a child becoming a follower of Christ, but there is no guarantee that it will happen. Becoming a believer in Christ is a personal decision of faith. No one else can make that decision on a person's behalf.

It is important to grasp why believers are considered adopted rather than being considered sons of God through likeness of nature. Jesus Christ often referred to God as "My Father." Jesus Christ, as the Son of God, has a unique and exclusive relationship with God the Father. When Jesus is referred to as the Son of God, it is a reference to Jesus's deity. Jesus Christ is of the same likeness and nature as God the Father. Jesus Christ is a member of the Trinity: God the Father, Jesus Christ the Son, and the Holy Spirit. Jesus often proclaimed that He and the Father were one (John 10:30, 38; 14:10; 17:11). The difference between believers being considered sons of God and Jesus Christ being the "Son of God" is that Jesus Christ is God's Son by right of His divine nature. We, as believers, are sons of God by God's grace and His work of regeneration. Jesus is the Son of God by nature; believers in Christ become sons of God by faith, "For you are all sons of God through faith in Christ Jesus" (Gal. 3:26).

This adoption by God shifts believers in Christ from the status of being children of the devil to being children of God. The concept of adoption is used exclusively in Scripture by the apostle Paul. Paul, being a Roman citizen, understood the Roman custom of adoption and used it as an analogy to compare what happens in a believer's relationship with God at salvation. "Under this figure, he teaches, that God, by the manifestation of His grace in Christ, brings men into the relationship of sons to Himself, and communicates to the experience of sonship."[50] The Roman custom of adoption gave the adopted person new privileges and position. An adopted person, who may have previously been a slave or servant, is no longer considered a servant; he is now a full member of the family, assuming all the rights of children naturally born into the family.

Paul made it clear that the newly adopted believer is delivered from the bondage of the Law, "so that He might redeem those who were under the Law, that we might receive the adoption as sons. Because you are sons, God has sent forth the Spirit of His Son into our hearts, crying, "Abba! Father!" Therefore, you are no longer a slave, but a son; and if a son, then an heir through God" (Gal. 4:5–7). Not only are God's adopted children no longer servants to the law, through the power of the indwelling Spirit, they are no longer slaves to fleshly desires (Rom. 8:13–15).

In addition to a new status as adopted children of God, believers are given privileges that come with being members of God's royal family. Becoming a member of God's family means that God truly becomes your heavenly Father. The fatherhood of God is nothing like the fatherhood people experience with their human fathers. Everyone has had an imperfect earthly father in contrast to God, the perfect Father. As our heavenly Father, God is the most loving, kind, benevolent, and caring Father that anyone will ever have. Even God's discipline of His children is done for their spiritual benefit (Heb. 12:4–11). When God disciplines His children, He does it not to punish sin but to correct and assist in His child's growth in holiness.

God is not a father who acts out of a selfish desire to serve himself. Instead, He does what is best for us. "He predestined us to adoption as sons through Jesus Christ to Himself, according to the kind intention of His will" (Eph. 1:5). Even fathers who are dominated by the sinful nature know how to give good gifts to their children, so much more does our Heavenly Father. "If you then, being evil, know how to give good gifts to your children, how much more will your Father who is in heaven give what is good to those who ask Him!" (Matt. 7:11).

Jesus assured His followers that they did not have to worry about their provision because their heavenly Father would take care of those needs.

> Look at the birds of the air, that they do not sow, nor reap nor gather into barns, and *yet* your heavenly Father feeds them. Are you not worth much more than they? Do not worry then, saying, 'What will we eat?' or 'What will we drink?' or 'What will we wear for clothing?' "For the Gentiles eagerly seek all these things; for your heavenly Father knows that you need all these things. (Matt. 6:26, 31–32)

As a child of God, you can enjoy freedom from worry because you know that your heavenly Father watches over you. The same love that moved God the Father to give His Son to die for your sins will continue providing all that you need. "What then shall we say to these things? If God *is* for us, who *is* against us? He who did not spare His own Son, but delivered Him over for us all, how will He not also with Him freely give us all things?" (Rom. 8:31–32). Children of God need to learn to trust Him and to break free from comparing God to their earthly father. The more we see God as our loving heavenly Father, the more we will trust Him.

Adoption into the family of God brings an individual near enough to God to refer to Him as "Abba Father" (Rom. 8:15). The title "Abba Father" is an expression of endearment. Abba is an Aramaic expression used by children and is equivalent to the English "daddy." The title Abba is always joined with Father in the New Testament. "*Abba* is the word framed by the lips of infants and betokens unreasoning trust; father" expresses an intelligent apprehension of the relationship. The two together express the love and intelligent confidence of the child."[51] Jesus used this expression of endearment to God, His Father (Mark 14:36). Believers can also experience this very close relationship of trust and dependence on God.

Those who have been adopted into God's family by the grace of God have become heirs of the unfathomable riches of Christ (Eph. 3:8). It is difficult for the human, finite mind to grasp the unfathomable. The apostle Paul prayed for believers to be able to comprehend what are the riches of the glory of His inheritance for the saints, "*I pray that* the eyes of your heart may be enlightened, so that you will know what is the hope of His calling, what are the riches of the glory of His inheritance in the saints" (Eph. 1:18). A person becomes qualified to share in the inheritance of the saints through the grace of the Father, "giving thanks to the Father, who has qualified us to share in the inheritance of the saints in Light" (Col. 1:12).

Adopted into the King's Family

There is a beautiful Bible story that demonstrates the wonders of God's grace. This is the story of a boy whose life was drastically changed in one day when he was just five years old. On that fateful day, the boy's father and grandfather were both killed, and he broke both of his feet in an accidental fall. This injury left him crippled for life. From that day on, the boy hid in exile, fearing for his life. This boy certainly was a victim of bad circumstances. Maybe you are reading this book today, and you have experienced some devastating setbacks in your life. You may feel like you are the victim of bad circumstances. If you have lost hope, this story is for you.

This account, found in 2 Samuel 9:3–11, is of a boy named Mephibosheth and a king named David. Who was Mephibosheth? He was the grandson of King Saul and the son of Jonathan who was one of the sons of King Saul. At the age of five, it appeared that Mephibosheth had a great future. He could possibly become the king of Israel following his father, Jonathan, as king. What looked like an optimistic future quickly turned into a dismal prospect in just one day. What happened on that fateful day was that Mephibosheth's grandfather, King Saul, and father, Jonathan, were both killed in battle. When news of his grandfather's and father's death came, a nurse who was caring for Mephibosheth fled with him to spare his life. Unfortunately, in her haste to protect the child, the nurse dropped him and injured both of his feet, crippling him for the rest of his life (2 Sam. 4:4). The reason he was taken into exile for his safety was due to the common practice of a new king killing any remaining male descendants of the previous king. This practice of exterminating male family members was done to eliminate future threats to the new king's reign.

Maybe you can identify with this young boy. You may have experienced some tragic events in your life that radically changed you for the worse. Have you experienced the death of one or both of your parents? Have you experienced something that was very detrimental to your health, your emotions, or self-esteem due to someone else's carelessness? Have you been physically or sexually abused? Perhaps life has not been good to you and you have been a victim of injurious circumstances. Have you been crippled by life circumstances? Take courage; there is hope.

It was a number of years after the death of King Saul before David became king over all of Israel. A few years after the death of King Saul, the tribe of Judah was the first to recognize David as king. King David reigned for seven years in Hebron over the tribe of Judah (2 Sam. 5:1–5). It was only after the death of Ishbosheth, the last remaining son of Saul, that David became king of all Israel (2 Sam. 5:3). Scripture does not tell us how many years after David became king that he inquired into the existence of any remaining family members of King Saul (2 Sam. 9:3). David sent people to search the kingdom for anyone related to Jonathan's family.

Ziba, a head servant who cared for the house of King Saul, was located and brought before King David. Ziba informed King David that there was only one remaining male family member of the household of Jonathan. There was a crippled young man named Mephibosheth who was Jonathan's son. Most likely, Ziba thought that King David was planning to kill any remaining male descendants in Saul's family. Ziba was fearful for his own life and for the life of Mephibosheth. As sinners, all of us were like Mephibosheth, living in exile fearing the judgment of God. Mephibosheth was hiding from King David; we were fleeing from the King of kings. We fear that God is looking to judge and destroy us. We do not believe that God has good intentions for us. We are in exile hiding from God.

When King David heard about Mephibosheth, he sought to see him right away. How would Mephibosheth respond to David's request? Would he escape in fear or would he comply with the request and come? God is sending forth His Spirit and is calling mankind to come to Him. Will we respond to His call or run away in fear? What was King David's motive for having Mephibosheth come to him? Was David seeking to execute him or to get revenge for how he was treated by King Saul? What will you do with people who have hurt you in the past? Will you seek revenge? If you had the chance to get even with someone, would you do it?

Mephibosheth decided to accept King David's welcome. Second Samuel 9:6 describes the manner in which he presented himself to the king, "Mephibosheth, the son of Jonathan the son of Saul, came to David and fell on his face and prostrated himself. And David said, "Mephibosheth." And he said, "Here is your servant!"" It is interesting to see how Mephibosheth came before King David. Mephibosheth came in meekness by falling on his face and prostrating himself before King David. This posture was a demonstration of complete humility and surrender. His words showed submission by referring to himself as "your servant." When we approach God, we must come before Him in complete humility. Remember that God humbles the prideful but exalts the humble (Luke 14:11). When a person comes before God, he cannot come in pride with his religious merit or self-righteousness. Every person must come before God trusting fully in God's mercy and grace.

Undoubtedly, Mephibosheth feared for his life as he lay prostrate before King David. Would King David show mercy or would he seek revenge? Would King David act to preserve his throne and execute this potential rival? What will God do with you when you are brought before Him? Will God judge you for your sins, or will He show mercy? King David expressed his good intentions to alleviate Mephibosheth's fears: "David said to him, "Do not fear, for I will surely show kindness to you for the sake of your father Jonathan, and will restore to you all the land of your grandfather Saul; and you shall eat at my table regularly" (2 Sam. 9:7).

David's intention was to keep a promise he had made to his close friend Jonathan. Somehow, Jonathan foreknew that David would be king, so he pressed David to make a promise to treat his family with lovingkindness. David, being a man of principle, was committed to fulfilling his promises. Are you faithful in keeping your promises? God is always faithful to keep His promises. He will be faithful by showing His lovingkindness to all who have faith in Jesus Christ. God has good intentions for us. He desires to pour out blessings on us.

David fulfilled the promise he made to Jonathan by returning all the land and possessions of King Saul to Saul's grandson, Mephibosheth. King David commissioned Ziba and his family to cultivate the land now owned by Mephibosheth to ensure Mephibosheth's prosperity. David did something else that is extraordinary and beyond anyone's expectations. While David could have just assured Mephibosheth that his life was not in danger, he surpassed showing mercy to showing grace. David demonstrated grace by going beyond what was required. Grace always goes beyond what is required; it bestows much more than the minimum. Grace lavishes by giving abundantly far above what we deserve.

What did David do that was so astonishing? David welcomed Mephibosheth to regularly eat with him at his table. This was more than just providing food for Mephibosheth; it was offering him fellowship and exclusive sonship. David treated Mephibosheth like one of his sons, "Then Ziba said to the king, "According to all that my lord the king commands his servant so your servant will do." So, Mephibosheth ate at David's table as one of the king's sons" (2 Sam. 9:11).

God offers more than mercy by forgiving us; He offers fellowship with Him in order that we may be part of His family. God will adopt us into His family and treat us as favored family members, "He predestined us to adoption as sons through Jesus Christ to Himself, according to the kind intention of His will" (Eph. 1:5). Where are you in your relationship with God? Are you hiding from Him? Are you fearful of God's judgment? Know that God has kind intentions for you if you come to Him in humility and put your faith in Christ for salvation. God has promised those who humble themselves that they will be exalted and receive an abundance of His grace. God, the heavenly Father, invites you to come to Him and be part of His royal family.

Application

1. Have you asked God's forgiveness for your sins?

    If you are not sure if God has forgiven you of your sin, you can pray this prayer with sincerity:

    Dear God, I believe that you sent Your Son to die on a cross for my sins. Believing that Christ paid for my sins, I ask you to forgive me of all my sins. I invite Christ to come into my life to be my Lord and Savior. Thank you, Lord, for forgiving me and including me in your family as a child of God.

2. Do you believe that God has forgiven your sins?

3. Why do you believe that God has forgiven you?

4. What did God do with your sins when He forgave them?

5. Has your spiritual debt of sin been paid in full?

6. Do you believe God has made you righteous in your standing with Him?

7. What is your standing with God?

8. What do you have in your spiritual account?

9. Are you spiritually alive?

10. Have you been born again?

11. How would you describe your relationship with God?

12. Have you been adopted into God's family?

13. Are you experiencing the benefits of being a child of God?

    If so, what are some of those benefits?

Trophy of Grace: Doug

The earliest recollection I have about heaven is my mom telling me that the gates of heaven were closed until Jesus went up there to open them up. I just assumed that all good people went there. We went to church every Sunday, and I went to religious instruction for ten years. That should have taught me all I needed to know about heaven, right?

I learned about the Ten Commandments, doing good things, going to church every Sunday, giving money to the church, baptism, first communion, confirmation, confession, penance, and not eating meat on Friday during Lent. Well, if I do my best to follow all these religious rules, I can get to heaven, right? It gets more complicated now. There's this thing about venial sin, mortal sin, indulgences, and purgatory. Even if you do all that, you might not make it in the Roman Catholic Church's eyes. You'd make a good church member, but the Roman Catholic Church wasn't going to make any promises of heaven. They like that element of fear from their subjects. You know what I said as a rebellious young teenager, "Keep it, forget it, I give up!"

But, you know what? Something used to bother me. I used to lie in bed at night, and I used to be so scared of dying and of not knowing what, if anything, was going to happen after I died. Directly or indirectly because of that fear, I found comfort and a cushion from life's problems in three things: sex, alcohol, and drugs. The first letters from these words (sad) pretty much tell the end result. In a blur of Budweiser, pot smoking, and girlfriends, all of a sudden, twenty years went by. All I was doing was passing time. By now I had fathered two daughters, married, and divorced, and I was working, drinking, partying and being a drunk on weekends. I got a DWI in 1992 and then finally bottomed out and reached the bottom of the barrel. I went through financial failure, also.

It's tough to think you can't get to heaven, and you can't make in this world, too! Then came hope, and God sent it in the love of my brother

Donald. He started me in a work at home business to make some extra money. Dealing with people face-to-face required me to sober up. But after a week of not drinking and smoking pot, being straight, thinking about my life again, I woke up on the morning of February 22, 1998, scared again. I mean freaking out, waking-up-screaming scared. The same fear I had hidden twenty years before about dying and not knowing what was going to happen was back in my face.

God knew the timing was right. My brother Donald called early that morning and talked to me a bit to try and calm me down. Then he asked me if I would go to church with him. It was too late to go to his church, but instead, we went to Raymond Community Church. It always seemed to be a beacon, this little church on the hill, calling out to me the first four years I lived out here. And the sign with its messages out front used to grab my attention and somehow touch my heart when I was driving by. From the moment my kids and I came in, I felt at home. Across the aisles, people greeted us, and I felt they were genuinely glad we were there, ponytailed biker Doug with his two daughters. There was an elderly woman named Ann Prafke in the pew behind us who helped us out by showing us the hymns and the Bible verses. After the service, I was invited to a dinner in the church. I really knew I was in the right place when my favorite meal was served—lasagna!

During the service, Pastor Quenton Blueye gave the message and closed with the gospel. My mom has always told me it's not the speaker that's important but the words that they are speaking. Now, Pastor Blueye is one of the best speakers I have heard, but the words that he spoke made a difference in my life. They were God's words about salvation and getting to heaven and that there was nothing I could do to get there. That's because what was needed to be done Jesus Christ had done for me. It was God's grace that I did not deserve, but it was a gift if I would just accept it.

By putting my faith and trust in Jesus's death and resurrection instead of anything I can do, I have come to know and experience eternal life through Jesus Christ our Lord. Romans 6:23 says, "For the wages of sin is death, but the free gift of God is eternal life in Christ Jesus our Lord. First John 5:13 says, "These things have I written unto you that believe on the name of the Son of God; that ye may know that ye have eternal life, and that ye may believe on the name of the Son of God." This was not just a teaching of the church, but it was God's

Word from the Bible. The new church I was attending showed me the Scriptures, and I was actually encouraged to read the Bible for myself.

Can you imagine the difference hearing the clear and simple gospel would have made in my life twenty years earlier? I realize now that we serve a living God. He knew my fears, heard my brother's prayer for me, and led me to a church to hear the words I needed to hear my whole life. And, all this time it was a free gift; it is free to all who have faith to accept it. I decided that Sunday that, as a sinner, to trust Jesus Christ and His sacrifice for me was the only way that God would accept me into heaven. Jesus said in John 8:32, "and ye shall know the truth, and the truth shall make you free." The proof of that has been that the heavy weight or burden of the guilt and shame from my sins has been lifted off of me. My anxiety and fear of dying was replaced with the security and confidence in God's Word that I will go to heaven when I pass from this life. I have this confidence not because of anything I have done to deserve it but solely based on God's grace.

Out of a relationship with God, not religion, I can know my Creator, Sustainer, and Savior, Jesus Christ. Out of gratitude, not obligation, I seek to know God more through the Bible and prayer. Out of gratitude, I will seek to serve in any way that He leads me. I know the way is not easy, but with God's Holy Spirit in me as a believer, He will give me the strength I need to get through the trials of this life. I know I cannot do it on my own, but as it says in Matthew 19:26, "with men this is impossible, but with God all things are possible."

For the seven years, I remained clean and sober, doing nothing more than trusting the Lord, having a relationship with Him and trying to faithfully serve Him. I tried a relationship with someone, not in God's way though, and I ended up drifting in my relationship with God. Then came one of those life-changing events; I was diagnosed with a serious, possibly incurable disease. For my treatment I had to give myself a shot once a week, take eight of these pills which together left me nauseous, weak and in pain in my whole body for forty-eight weeks. At the same time, I had to keep working. Then mentally, depression set in as I lay on a cot in my living room whenever I could for eleven months. I became resentful. How come with all the drugs I did, then trusting in Lord, serving, having a relationship with someone who was clean and sober, and going to church, after all this, why did I get sick? Why God?

Through the stress of the pain of my treatment, my relationship with my girlfriend ended, and my relationship the Lord was at a standstill. I stopped reading God's Word and praying—the simple things that used to keep me strong, clean and sober. As a result, after a year or so of relying on myself and my own thinking, I started drinking first and then using drugs again. For nine months, I used alcohol and drugs. I was right back where I left off before I came to have faith in Christ as my Savior. Getting high, working and then coming home to drink was extent of my life.

One of my lifelong friends called one day, needing a place to stay. He was a few months into recovery from drugs, and things were not working out so well, so I let my friend Mike move in. We had started thirty years before in our drug habit, so I knew the old person. But this man was different now. He had God in his life, and he was going to those meetings. He invited me and took me to his first Narcotics Anonymous meeting. I lied that first meeting and said I was there for his support. That's where the NA literature and conviction by the Lord opened my eyes to see that I am an addict. I was powerless over my use of alcohol and drugs, and my life was definitely unmanageable.

Although I had turned my back on God for a while, He brought people into my life to bring me to a place where I could stop the use of alcohol and drugs. When the time was right, He put someone else in my path who brought me to Celebrate Recovery, a Christ-based, twelve step program. My heart and mind were now ready to let God guide me, not in just abstaining from drugs and alcohol, but recover and grow into the person that God wants me to be.

Then one day, when I was not looking or even expecting it, God blessed me by bringing the woman who is now my wife into my life. She loves the Lord with her whole heart and gives me such joy. We have six grown kids and seven grandchildren between us, which does make for some challenges. But, with God at our core, there is plenty of love to go around and never a dull moment. I feel I am living the "abundant" life that God intended. The broken road the Lord carried me through was just part of the journey to bring me here. Out of gratitude and love for the Lord, we serve our local church wherever there is a need. There are usually many needs, but after what God has done for us, nothing is too much.

I am still a work in progress but I look forward to what He has in store for me every day. I have to endure His chastisement, as well as His blessings, but I can rest assured He knows what is best for me. As we stay in a close relationship with the Lord, it is truly amazing what He will do. By God's grace, we can have joy in this life, as well as the security of eternal life with Him through Jesus Christ our Lord. Amen.

PART THREE

GOD'S ENABLING GRACE

CHAPTER 8

The Grace of God That Strengthens

It is vital for those who have been saved by God's grace to come to a full understanding of the boundless blessings of His grace. Not having a proper understanding of what God's grace does after salvation can greatly hinder a believer's spiritual wellbeing. If a Christian believes that salvation is maintained by good works, he will continually struggle with assurance of salvation. Trying to serve God in one's own strength is a sure recipe for defeat. Without God's strength, our weaknesses will overpower us, and we will lack the fortitude to endure. Depending on works to maintain salvation is a flawed basis for having assurance of salvation. The only basis for the assurance of salvation must be solely trusting in God's grace.

The idea that Christians needed to keep the law to remain saved was an issue that caused great controversy in the early church. This was such an important issue that it was brought before the Jerusalem Council for resolution (Acts 15:1–29). Important questions needed to be answered before this issue could be resolved. Some were saying that both Jewish Christians and the new Gentile Christians had to follow the law to maintain their salvation. Were Jewish Christians just a new sect of Judaism or something different? Some wrongly concluded that Christianity was just a new form of Judaism because all the initial Christians were Jewish. Were Gentile converts proselytes of Judaism or Christianity? If Christianity were merely a new sect of Judaism, then observance of the Law was mandatory for Gentile converts as well. Since converts to Judaism were required to be circumcised, some at the Jerusalem Council insisted that all male converts to Christianity be circumcised. Some of the sect of the Pharisees who believed rose up, saying, "It is necessary to circumcise them, and to command *them* to keep the law of Moses" (Acts 15:5 NKJV).

After much debate, Peter stood up at the Jerusalem Council and made some very important remarks concerning the issue of requiring Gentile believers to observe the Law of Moses. First, Peter reminded them of how Gentiles had been saved under his ministry just as the Jews were saved (Acts 10:34–48). Peter rightly stated that they were testing God by trying to put the yoke of the law upon the necks of Gentile believers which they themselves, as Jews, had failed to fully obey: "Now therefore why do you put God to the test by placing upon the neck of the disciples a yoke which neither our fathers nor we have been able to bear?" (Acts 15:10). Peter concluded his comments by declaring that both Gentiles and Jews were saved by grace: "But we believe that we are saved through the grace of the Lord Jesus, in the same way as they also are" (Acts 15:11). The debate was not just about the issue of how a person is initially saved but similarly how he would maintain salvation. The issue was settled by only requiring Gentiles to abstain from practicing a few things (Acts 15:20). Keeping the law is not what saves a person; neither is it what keeps him saved.

The apostle Paul addressed the issue of trying to maintain salvation through works in his epistle to the Galatians. There were false teachers in the churches of Galatia who taught that Christians must maintain their salvation through keeping the law. Apparently, many in the church were deceived by this false teaching, so much so that Paul had to confront it head on in his letter to the Galatians. Paul was amazed that so many had been deceived into believing a distortion of the true gospel which he had originally given to them. Paul had to remind them that no one is justified (declared forgiven and righteous by God) by keeping the law but only through his faith in Christ: "nevertheless knowing that a man is not justified by the works of the Law but through faith in Christ Jesus, even we have believed in Christ Jesus, so that we may be justified by faith in Christ and not by the works of the Law; since by the works of the Law no flesh will be justified" (Gal. 2:16).

What was the false gospel taught by some in the Galatian church? Paul pressed his point by asking several questions of the Galatian church. Were they saved by receiving the Spirit by keeping the law or by hearing the gospel by faith? (Gal. 3:2). Were they so foolish to believe that they could begin their salvation through receiving the Spirit of God but then be perfected by keeping the law in the strength of the flesh? (Gal. 3:2–3). This is the point of distortion from the true gospel; people cannot begin by being born of the Spirit but subsequently complete their salvation through efforts of the flesh. All believers are saved by grace, and only by God's grace are they made complete in their salvation. Paul declared that he was not going to nullify the grace of God by teaching that righteousness could be gained through keeping the law (Gal. 2:21). If receiving and maintaining salvation depends on keeping the law, then Christ died in vain: "I do not nullify the grace of God, for if righteousness *comes* through the Law, then Christ died needlessly" (Gal. 2:21). The grace of God has not been nullified, nor did Christ die in vain! Believers in Christ must solely trust in God's grace for salvation and be kept by God's grace.

Salvation is just the beginning of what God does by His grace in the life of a believer. Salvation opens the doors of heaven for God's blessings to flow. When we contemplate the wonders of God's grace, we need to realize that it is more than grace, God's unmerited favor for salvation, and it is grace in every area of the believer's life which gives him power to live out his salvation. There are far more Scriptures that speak of the grace of God as His power or enablement than there are those that speak about God's unmerited favor for salvation.

> *God's grace does so much more for us than just save us. God's grace is also the power and favor of God to help us throughout our Christian lives.*

When we reflect on the meaning of God's grace, we need to equate it with God's power. Remember, God's grace is always given as a gift. God's grace is not some abstract concept of God's power; it is the power of God given to a person as an unmerited gift. God's grace gives believers gifts of power to enable them to accomplish whatever God calls them to accomplish. God's grace empowers believers to live victorious Christian lives and to serve proficiently in ministry. When we realize that God's grace is the power of God working in us, we should also realize that God's grace is limitless. God is omnipotent in His expressions of grace.

God's grace is always more than what is needed for any specific occasion. It is not that God gives believers just a little bit of grace and then they are expected to make up the difference with their works. God's grace supplies all that is needed for salvation. Believers do not have to add anything to it. One needs to have faith alone to receive it. God's grace is more than sufficient to save completely and more than sufficient to help the believer live out his salvation. God's grace supplies all that is needed to empower the believer to overcome whatever he may encounter from the time of salvation until the day he is ushered into heavenly glory.

God's grace is sufficient for all areas of one's life. Second Corinthians 9:8 proclaims the sufficiency of God's grace: "And God is able to make all grace abound to you, so that always having all sufficiency in everything, you may have an abundance for every good deed." God's grace abounds by giving far more than what is needed at all times and in everything. Because of God's unlimited love and power, He can do more than we could ever imagine. "Now to Him who is able to do far more abundantly beyond all that we ask or think, according to the power that works within us" (Eph. 3:20).

In addition to being more than sufficient in everything, God's grace is also diverse. God can offer grace in unique ways depending on what is needed. God gives different gifts of grace to all believers in Christ. First Peter 4:10 states, "As each one has received a *special* gift, employ it in serving one another as good stewards of the manifold grace of God." Peter described God's grace as being "manifold," meaning it is multifaceted with many diverse components. This means that God's grace can be distributed as many differing kinds of gifts to each individual. In other words, God can tailor-make His gifts of grace to fit each individual in his specific needs or requirements.

Since God's grace is diverse, it is not "one size fits all." Each person is unique in his own needs and weaknesses. Just as a tailor adjusts the size of a garment to conform to the shape of a person's body, so God adjusts His gifts of grace specifically for what is necessary. God gives His enablement to fit each person's exact needs. Each believer is granted special gifts that will enable him to overcome his challenges and to serve others.

What are some ways that the grace of God enables every person who is saved? Asking what the grace of God can do is the same as asking what God's power can do. God's power can do anything that does not violate His moral nature or disregard the infinite wisdom of His divine plan. Because God's power is limitless, so is His grace. Through grace, God makes His power available to all those who have been born again. It is by the indwelling of the Holy Spirit at salvation that a person is given gifts of grace (God's specific enablement). God's grace begins with salvation and then continues to work in believers' lives by strengthening, sustaining, sanctifying, serving through them, and, finally, securing them.

God's Grace Strengthens a Believer in His Weaknesses

How does the grace of God strengthen those who believe in Christ? One of the reasons God's grace is available to believers is to help strengthen them in their weaknesses. By weaknesses, I am referring to areas of a person's life where there is a noticeable lack of capability to learn or develop certain skills. The concept of weaknesses also includes a person's areas of vulnerability where he has a predisposition for failure. When God created us, He made us with both strengths and weaknesses. Everyone is born with some proficiencies; however, each person is also born with areas where he is deficient in ability. Some people are born with natural capacities to excel in such things as music, art, math, language, and athletics. A person can be endowed with abilities in one or more of these areas but be woefully lacking in others.

The problem with being especially gifted in some areas is that it can lead to pride. When we compare ourselves with others, we may observe that many do not have our level of ability. We can become prideful about our capabilities. The apostle Paul warned believers not to become prideful regarding the gifts of grace that God had given them: "For through the grace given to me I say to everyone among you not to think more highly of himself than he ought to think; but to think so as to have sound judgment, as God has allotted to each a measure of faith" (Rom. 12:3). In His divine wisdom, God knew that He could not create us with competencies without any deficiencies. In order to prevent pride, God allowed all of us to have areas where we lack ability. God's grace can help reinforce those very areas of insufficiency.

In addition to having strengths and weaknesses in our natural abilities, we can also have areas of strength and weakness in our physical bodies. Some people have better health because of their genetics. Likewise, some people are more prone to sickness because of genetic flaws. Even though we cannot improve our genetics, we should do all we can to take care of our physical health. Some have ill health that comes from living sinful lifestyles. Many have made poor choices and abused their bodies with alcoholism, smoking, misuse of drugs, or promiscuous sexual activity. No matter what the cause of our physical infirmities, we should access all the help we need to deal with our physical frailties. These physical frailties can come at birth, by an accident, or through being wounded in battle. There are many who struggle with physical abnormalities. God's grace can help a person deal with these physical challenges.

Even if we had great health when we were young, that can change as we age. Sooner or later, everyone will experience the physical degeneration that comes with age, becoming weaker and more prone to ill health. When we experience life-threatening sicknesses or malignancy, God's grace can sustain us. I can speak from my own experience about how God's grace helped me through times when I could have lost my life. I almost died from a pulmonary embolism but God's grace kept me alive. When I contracted Covid and was afflicted with double pneumonia, God spared my life, and God's grace was with me each of the five different times the doctor told me I had more cancer. I know what it is like to have overwhelming fears concerning my health. I have learned to trust in God's unfailing grace to overcome those fears. It was during those times of illness that I was brought nearer to God. If one turns to the Lord during his times of vulnerability, God's grace will supersede his frailties.

We all have strengths and shortcomings in our character. All personality types exhibit strengths and deficiencies. A person can be very outgoing and friendly but lack personal discipline. Some are very disciplined but lack social skills. One personality type can be meticulous about details but prone to melancholy. Each personality is like two sides of a coin; one side stands for positive aspects of that personality while the other side represents the negative aspects. The positive aspects of one's personality can lead one to become prideful; meanwhile, one can struggle with the negative aspects of his personality. We will find it quite difficult to change the negative aspects of our personality. Through the indwelling of the Holy Spirit, God's grace can transform our character by turning those flaws into our greatest strengths.

There is one area in which everyone is utterly feeble; every human is born with a certain infirmity. What is this infirmity? All humanity is born with a fallen, sinful nature. This sinful nature is an innate propensity to sin. We are all powerless to resist the domination of our sinful nature. The apostle Paul describes this human frailty that plagues us: "For I know that nothing good dwells in me, that is, in my flesh; for the willing is present in me, but the doing of the good *is* not. For the good that I want, I do not do, but I practice the very evil that I do not want" (Rom. 7:18–19). Humanity has attempted to change this aspect of its nature but continues to fail. Apart from the intervention of God's grace, we are all hopelessly enslaved to our sinful nature.

It is in man's battle with his fallen nature that God's grace abounds: "The Law came in so that the transgression would increase; but where sin increased, grace abounded all the more" (Rom. 5:20). This verse is not suggesting, as some have falsely interpreted, that as one sins more, the more God will show His grace. God's grace will never cause us to sin more. The opposite is true. God's grace will give power to overcome the pull of the sinful nature. Paul addressed this way of thinking in Romans 6:1–2, "What shall we say then? Are we to continue in sin so that grace may increase? May it never be! How shall we who died to sin still live in it?" God provides abundant grace when a person humbles himself by recognizing his complete vulnerability to sin.

We can become blind to our limitations when we focus only on our strengths. Pride deceives us into believing that we have no insufficiencies. The more we honestly evaluate our lives over time, the more we should recognize our limitations. Limitations do not readily reveal themselves. It is only through testing by adverse circumstances that vulnerabilities are revealed. It is only when a metal is heated to certain temperatures that impurities in the metal surface. It is only through the heated testing of difficulties that our deficiencies will surface. When the strength of a metal chain is tested, the weakest link will break first. Everyone will experience weaknesses, inadequacies, infirmities, deficiencies, and inabilities; that is part of being human. A person's pride either keeps him from seeing his limitations or he will attempt to conceal them. Pride is one of the greatest hindrances to receiving God's grace. As long as we believe we are without personal limitations, the flow of God's grace in our lives will be greatly hindered.

God purposely allows difficulties in the believer's life to expose weaknesses. Why would God do such a thing? If we do not acknowledge our deficiencies, we will never seek God's help. The more we realize our desperate need for help, the more we will turn to God for help. Everyone needs to humble himself before God by acknowledging his debilities and his total dependance on God. God gives us His grace when we humble ourselves. Thus, our deficiencies serve a significant purpose by causing us to turn to God. When we understand the importance of having limitations and how they can bring more of God's grace into our lives, we will not despise them but realize that they have a redemptive purpose.

The apostle Paul learned the lesson of valuing infirmities in his life. Paul, in writing to the church of Corinth, described his struggles as a "thorn in the flesh" (2 Cor. 12:7). Paul did not say exactly what this "thorn in the flesh" was, but it was some type of infirmity. Paul earnestly prayed three times for God to remove this "thorn in the flesh," but God did not remove it. God revealed the reason He was not removing the problem. The Lord did not want Paul to be tempted with pride because of the great revelation that he had received (2 Cor. 12:7). To prevent Paul from becoming prideful, God was allowing him to be humbled by his malady.

God comforted Paul by reassuring him that His grace would give Paul more than enough strength to endure this ailment: "And He has said to me, "My grace is sufficient for you, for power is perfected in weakness. Most gladly, therefore, I will rather boast about my weaknesses, so that the power of Christ may dwell in me" (2 Cor. 12:9). Paul continued by revealing one of the greatest paradoxical revelations he ever had, "for when I am weak, then I am strong" (2 Cor. 12:10). We all need to discover this supreme truth about our weaknesses. For it is when we realize just how weak we are that we become dependent on God's grace. When people are prideful, they will trust in their own strength which, in reality, is very weak and woefully inadequate. Recognizing our limitations causes us to humble ourselves and to rely on God's grace. We are strongest when we rely on God's grace.

Application

1. What are some of your natural strengths?

2. Have your natural strengths caused you to be prideful?

3. Have you come to the place where you recognize your limitations?

4. What are some of your shortcomings?

5. What is your greatest weakness?

6. Have your limitations brought you to the point of humbling yourself before God and relying on His grace to strengthen you?

God's Grace Strengthens a Believer's Relationship with God

Have you ever done something a certain way for a long time and then discovered a much better way of doing it? When we discover a new way of doing things that is much easier, we think, *I wish I had known about this sooner.* This has happened to me numerous times. One example comes from my time as a school bus driver. Before a driver can go on his route, he is required to do a pre-trip inspection of the bus. For a long time, I did my pre-trip inspection a certain way as a routine. I would test each item on the checklist separately to be sure everything was functioning properly. It would take me ten or fifteen minutes to check the whole bus. One day, another driver came over to my newly assigned bus while I was doing my pre-trip inspection and showed me a much simpler way of doing the inspection; she showed me a button on the dashboard to push for pre-trip inspections of all the lights. All the lights on the bus would flash on and off and would be shown on a screen on the dashboard. I just had to make one trip around the bus to check all the lights at one time. Wow! That was so much easier!

Another example of finding a better method of doing something comes from my recent discovery of a new way to drive screws. People who have experience in construction have most likely used screws to secure materials and can relate to my frustration in using old power tools. It is often difficult to drive screws all the way into thick boards. When the screw stops going in, I often would strip the head, making it impossible to screw it in all the way. I would then drill bigger holes for the screws, but, even then, this would happen again. I recently purchased a new power tool that makes driving screws in so much easier. The new tool is called an "impact driver."

With the impact driver, I can easily drive screws all the way into pieces of wood. I am sure you have discovered things that make your work much easier. Discovering how God's grace continues to work in our lives after salvation is much like discovering a better way of doing things, only on a much more significant level. We do not have to try to serve God in our own strength or try to maintain our salvation through our own efforts. There is a "new and living way" to have access to God through the sacrificial death of Christ. When believers understand just how God's grace enables them after their salvation, it will cause them to say, "Wow! I wish I knew about this sooner!"

Believers are made right in their relationship with God because of His grace. Believers in Christ now have a new, wonderful relationship with God. Those who are "in Christ" have access to God through the atoning work of Christ. However, if believers do not understand how God's grace continues to work in their lives, they will be hindered in maintaining their relationship with God. Once believers begin to comprehend how God's grace continues to work in their lives, their relationship with God will be greatly improved. Understanding God's continuing work of grace will significantly enhance a believer's prayer life and his faith. People do not have to struggle with condemnation and feelings of unworthiness that keep them from praying because of God's grace. Likewise, His grace frees them from struggling with doubts about having His favor to answer their prayers.

There are several detrimental consequences of not understanding how God's grace continues to work after salvation. One of the consequences is that it can negatively affect a believer's relationship with God. Believers can struggle with condemnation and feelings of being unworthy of God's favor. This lack of understanding of God's grace can lead to a lack of desire for prayer. People tend to stay away from those to whom they owe something or with whom they have unresolved issues. This is how many relate to God. Some people avoid God by avoiding prayer, devotions, and church because they have unresolved issues with sin.

Another consequence of not understanding the grace of God is that it can lead to a lack of faith. Over my fifty-plus years of working with people, I have discovered a common thread of doubt that vexes many Christians when they pray for themselves. What is this thread of doubt that is interwoven into so many Christians' fabric of thinking? Christians can have great faith when praying for others, but not when they pray for themselves. Why is that? People doubt that God will do anything for them because they feel undeserving. Many Christians believe God will not answer prayer for themselves because of some sin in their lives, and because of that sin, they believe that they have lost favor with God. When we believe that we are in a state of disfavor with God, it causes us to doubt that God will show any goodness toward us. Praying in faith is essential for God to answer our prayers. Doubting that God will answer prayer for ourselves undermines our faith and the likelihood of God answering our prayers — "But he must ask in faith without any doubting, for the one who doubts is like the surf of the sea, driven and tossed by the wind. For that man ought not to expect that he will receive anything from the Lord" (James 1:6–7).

A lack of understanding of God's grace can cause many believers to have a wrong basis for gaining access to, and favor with, God in prayer. Some believers mistakenly think they need to approach God on the basis of their worthiness. Some think they must have perfect performance for God to look favorably upon them. Granted, some days we can feel our spiritual performance is better than others. Some days are better than others when it comes to living a holy life. On our good days we can think, *I was pretty good today, so God will answer my prayers.* In contrast, on our not-so-good days, we feel God will not listen to our prayers.

This causes us to either not pray or pray doubting God will answer our prayers. This is incorrect thinking. No one ever has a perfect day. Thinking that our righteousness can ever gain us access to God is a totally futile basis for approaching God in prayer. The Bible clearly states, "There is none righteous, not even one" (Rom. 3:10). Everyone must come to the full realization that he or she will never be worthy to approach God in prayer.

Some believers think they can earn access and favor with God. Some have the audacity to believe that God owes them for what they have done or sacrificed for Him. Some foolishly make bargains with God. If they uphold their end of the bargain, then God is obligated to uphold His end. Some Christians mistakenly think that they have earned God's favor by being faithful in serving Him. Yes, God is pleased with a person's faithful service, and He will reward him greatly during this life and especially in his next life in heaven. However, a person cannot use his faithfulness as a basis for expecting God to answer prayer. We cannot think that God is indebted to us. God owes no one anything and, conversely, all of humanity owes Him everything. What God does for people is not based on merit but on their faith in His grace to answer their prayers.

Within some Christian circles, there is the belief that gaining access to God requires great struggle and great sacrifice. Some think that it is through much effort on their part that they earn God's favor and answers to their prayers. This kind of thinking comes out of the monastic movement of the Middle Ages. The monastic movement promoted the idea that for anyone to really know God, he would need to become a monk or nun. Monks or nuns were required to live in a monastery or nunnery where they were required to live secluded and ascetic lives. Some believe that the more sacrificial a person was in his personal life, the better the chances were for him to experience God's favor. Many monks or nuns would take vows of poverty or vows of silence, thinking that asceticism would please God and enable them to earn His approval. It is true that God wants people to diligently seek Him, but that does not mean that closeness to God is gained through human effort. Just as we are saved by grace through faith and not by our works, so it is the same with drawing close to God. We can only come close to God because He allows it only on the basis of His grace. It is because of God's grace that He gives the gift of His presence and His unmerited favor.

There is a way of approaching God for answers to prayer that I consider preposterous. Some believe they can demand that God answer their prayers by quoting Scriptures. It is appropriate to humbly appeal to God on the basis of His Word but never to demand God to do what we want Him to do because we quoted Scripture verses. Some preachers proclaim to their followers what I consider "name and claim it." They tell us to name what we want, quote the right Scripture, and then claim possession of whatever we want. God is not some cosmic slot machine where one can quote Scriptures as if they are tokens thrown into heaven's prayer answering machine. God is an almighty sovereign God who answers to no one. God cannot be coerced into doing anything. God cannot be manipulated into doing anything—not even by quoting Scriptures.

It is only on the basis of God's grace that believers can freely come to God in prayer. Hebrews 10:19-20 describes this new and living way of having access to God: "Therefore, brethren, since we have confidence to enter the holy place by the blood of Jesus, by a new and living way which He inaugurated for us through the veil, that is, His flesh." The writer of Hebrews goes on to encourage believers to come near to God in full assurance of faith: "Let us draw near with a sincere heart in full assurance of faith, having our hearts sprinkled *clean* from an evil conscience and our bodies washed with pure water" (Heb. 10:22). The phrase, "having our hearts sprinkled *clean* from an evil conscience," is important for every believer to understand. It is because we do not have a clear conscience that we avoid approaching God in prayer. We know that we are not sinless and are not worthy to come before God in prayer, so we do not pray as we should.

Having a clear conscience does not mean that we have never sinned. Having a clear conscience means we have asked God's forgiveness and have confidence through faith in Christ's atoning work that we are completely forgiven. We must understand that we cannot ever come before God on the basis of our own righteousness or worthiness. We have access to God only because of His grace. The blood of Christ cleanses us from sin so that we can freely come before God in prayer. How do we "sprinkle" our hearts with the blood of Christ? It is through humbling ourselves by confessing our sins and trusting fully in the grace of God that we are welcomed into God's presence. Because of God's grace, one day all those who put their faith in Christ will be embraced by God's love as they are welcomed into His glorious presence in heaven.

Hebrews 10:22 states that believers can draw near to God "with a sincere heart in full assurance of faith." How can believers have full assurance of faith when they come to God in prayer? Understanding how God's grace continues to work after salvation will help us have full assurance of faith when we pray. God does not answer prayer because we are worthy or sinless. Instead, He answers prayer because of His grace. If we base our faith for answered prayer on our worthiness then we will either come before God with pride, thinking we have earned God's favorable response or be full of doubt knowing we do not deserve God's favor.

Every person must come to the full realization that he will never be qualified to approach God in prayer without God's grace. God's answers to prayer are not based on human worthiness. God answers prayer on the basis of His grace because of the petitioner's faith in Christ. Because a person is in Christ through his faith in Christ, he is in a constant state of having God's unmerited favor. If there is sin in our lives, we must come humbly before God seeking forgiveness based on our faith in the atoning work of Christ.

The result of knowing that the only way to come to God in prayer is on the basis of God's grace encourages us to come to God more freely. God's grace covers all our debt of sin and resolves any issues that alienate us from God. As we better appreciate God's grace, we will draw closer to Him and have faith that God will answer prayers both for ourselves and others. As we pray in this frame of mind, we will have greater faith; with greater faith will come greater answers to prayer. As we spend more time in prayer, we will experience God's power working in boundless measure. Isaiah described how spending time in prayer (waiting on the Lord), immensely increases our strength:

> He gives power to the weak, and to *those who have* no might He increases strength. Even the youths shall faint and be weary, And the young men shall utterly fall, but those who wait on the Lord Shall renew *their* strength; They shall mount up with wings like eagles, They shall run and not be weary, They shall walk and not faint. (Isa. 40:29–31, NKJV)

We can enjoy a stronger prayer life because of God's grace. A more consistent prayer life will enhance our relationship with God. As we wait on God in prayer, we will gain new strength from God's all sufficient grace.

Application

1. Do you struggle with feeling condemned by God?

2. Do you believe that God is not smiling upon you but frowning on you because of your failures?

3. Do you struggle with the feeling of being unworthy to approach God in prayer?

4. Have you avoided prayer or do you feel free to come to God at any time?

5. When you pray, do you pray in faith for your own needs or do you have doubts that God will answer because you are unworthy?

6. Have you come to the place where you totally trust in God's grace when you approach God in prayer?

CHAPTER 9

The Grace of God That Sustains

In this life we will experience hardships, difficulties, setbacks, failures, trials, suffering, sickness, grief, sorrows and various other problems. Life is like a battle; it seems like so many things come against us that we have to fight back every day. Life can seem like a long uphill climb where there seems to be no end in sight. This is especially true concerning what we have experienced during the Covid pandemic. Many have died or have lost a loved one. Many have been adversely affected financially through a loss of employment or business. Our lives have been so greatly disrupted that more people are turning to drugs or committing suicide. School-age children are suffering mentally and socially because of the disruption in their education. However, God's grace can sustain us through this pandemic or anything else that may come our way. God has an abundance of grace to sustain all those who call on Him.

Being a Christian will not exempt a person from the tribulations of life. While everyone will experience difficulties, those who call on the Lord will have His help to endure through even the most difficult circumstances. The apostle Paul openly shared how God's power helped him to endure his own intense and relentless struggles, "But we have this treasure in earthen vessels, so that the surpassing greatness of the power will be of God and not from ourselves; *we are* afflicted in every way, but not crushed; perplexed, but not despairing; persecuted, but not forsaken; struck down, but not destroyed" (2 Cor. 4:7–9).

Paul made it clear that this power to overcome the most difficult adversities is from God and not of ourselves. How does one access this power from God? In order to have this power working in us to strengthen us, we must come to know God through faith in Jesus Christ. When a person is born again, the Holy Spirit indwells and empowers him. This inner strength from God is the power of God's grace working in the believer. God's grace is not only what saves people but also what empowers them to be overcomers. It is by God's grace that a person stands, "through whom also we have obtained our introduction by faith into this grace in which we stand; and we exult in hope of the glory of God" (Rom. 5:2). God's grace sustains believers to enable them to stand, persevere, and endure.

God's grace will sustain us through all the difficulties of this life and will motivate believers to persevere. God's grace is the power that He gives as a gift to people of faith in order to sustain them. The definition of "sustain" is: "1. To give support or relief, 2. to supply with sustenance, 3. keep up, prolong, 4. to support the weight of, 5. To buoy up."[52] Examining these various definitions can give us a fuller understanding of how the grace of God *sustains* us. Each of these definitions offers a different perspective of how God's grace enables us. The first definition, "to give support or relief," applies to God's grace helping people by supporting them through difficult times. God's grace can give you *relief* during your struggles. Even though you may be going through a storm in your life, God can give you a peace that is beyond understanding. The winds of adversity may be blowing ever so severely, but God's Spirit can send peace to your spirit.

The second definition, "to supply with sustenance," speaks to how the grace of God gives believers sufficiency for every need: "And God is able to make all grace abound to you, so that always having all sufficiency in everything, you may have an abundance for every good deed" (2 Cor. 9:8). The third definition, "keep up, prolong," addresses how God's grace enables people to keep going, to persevere, and to endure. The fourth definition, "to support the weight," means to hold up under weight or pressure. God's grace can hold you up no matter how heavy the troubles are that weigh upon you. The next definition, "to buoy up," gives a picture of being kept above water. God's grace is like a lifejacket to support and hold you up above your problems and circumstances.

God's grace sustains people so that they are able to persevere through life's greatest difficulties. To persevere means "to persist in a state, enterprise, or undertaking in spite of counterinfluence, opposition or discouragement."[53] The Scriptures emphasize the need to persevere under trials, as in, "Blessed is a man who perseveres under trial; for once he has been approved, he will receive the crown of life which *the Lord* has promised to those who love Him" (James 1:12). Scriptures speak of the need for endurance. Life is like a marathon; everyone has to run to finish. In order to finish, one must be able to endure. "Therefore, since we have so great a cloud of witnesses surrounding us, let us also lay aside every encumbrance and the sin which so easily entangles us, and let us run with endurance the race that is set before us" (Hebrews 12:1).

When I was in my early thirties, I signed up to participate in a ten-mile Teen Challenge walk-a-thon. Instead of walking, I decided to run the whole distance. Even though I was accustomed to jogging about two to four miles a day, I had never run ten miles before, so I knew that I needed to pace myself. I simply jogged at a steady pace. The first five miles were pretty easy, but with each new mile, it became more difficult. My body was telling me to stop and rest, but I was determined to run the whole distance. I came up with a strategy to help me reach my goal. I purposed not to dwell on how much further I had to go, so I would just think about completing one block at a time. I told myself that I could at least make it one more block. After that block, I told myself I could do the next block. Toward the end of the ten miles, I got down to just thinking about one step at a time. Just one more step, just one more step, just one more step! I finally made it.

This is so very much like the function of God's grace. God gives us His grace one day at a time. God does not give us His grace in advance for everything we will face in our future. Many have the tendency to worry about what lies ahead in their lives. People think of all that could go wrong and become anxious. Jesus encouraged people not to be anxious but to trust in God's providential care, instructing them to just take one day at a time: "So do not worry about tomorrow; for tomorrow will care for itself. Each day has enough trouble of its own" (Matt. 6:34). God gives His supply of grace for each day. God does not give you grace for all the things you might worry about in your future. You must believe God's grace will help you through each day.

Examining a definition of the word *endure* will give us more insight into its meaning: "To undergo (as a hardship) esp. without giving in... to remain firm under suffering or misfortune without yielding."[54] Does God leave it to people to have the power to endure by their own will and determination? We can only go so far with our own inner strength. We will reach a point where we cannot continue. We will eventually give up the fight if we rely on our own strength. God will allow difficulties in our lives to bring us to the point of giving up; however, God does not want us to give up but to give up trying to make it in our own strength. God does not want us to trust in our own strength but to trust in the power of His grace to sustain us. The sooner we realize how truly weak we are, the sooner we will learn to trust in God's grace: "My grace is sufficient for you, for power is perfected in weakness. Most gladly, therefore, I will rather boast about my weaknesses, so that the power of Christ may dwell in me" (2 Cor. 12:9).

Do you feel overwhelmed? Have your problems become so overwhelming that you feel you cannot go on? Are you at the point of giving up? Do not give up the race; give the struggle to God. Humble yourself before God and call on Him for His help. After you ask God for help, believe that He will give you more than enough strength to be an overcomer one day at a time.

Grace That Sustains Believers Through Trials

One of the inescapable facts of life is that everyone experiences trials. We might do everything we can to avoid trials, yet, they have a way finding us. Christians are not exempt from experiencing trials, but what are they? Trials are difficulties that everyone goes through. For Christians, trials are difficulties that test their faith and test the limit of their patience. Why does God allow trials in the Christian's life? God wants to work something beneficial in their lives through the trials that they endure. Trials can make or break us. The Bible teaches that trials are difficulties that can develop endurance and character, "And not only this, but we also exult in our tribulations, knowing that tribulation brings about perseverance; and perseverance, proven character; and proven character, hope" (Rom. 5:3–4).

Trials come in many forms. Many of the trials we experience are relational. We can have problems with our spouse, children, parents, friends, coworkers, boss, teachers, or anyone else with whom we may have social contact. Some of our trials may be financial. We can experience a loss of income, unexpected expenses, foreclosure, bankruptcy, and loss of property. Trials may come concerning our physical health. We can experience sicknesses, disabilities, life-threatening illnesses, or addictions. Trials can emerge in our spiritual lives, such as very strong temptations, periods of spiritual dryness, doubts, and backsliding. Trials can rise in any of these ways or any combination of these areas of our lives. When we experience trials in several areas of our lives at one time it can seem overwhelming and debilitating.

Even though troubles may seem too heavy to bear, there is good news for everyone. God wants to help us through the trials we experience and welcomes everyone to call upon Him for that support. Those who do not know Christ as their Savior need to turn to God and call upon Him for help. God uses trials in the life of the unbeliever to urge him to the point of crying out to Him. When people run out of options, many turn to God for help. When a person humbles himself by asking for assistance, he needs to also humble himself by asking God's forgiveness for his sins and confess his faith in Christ. God does not just answer the prayers of those who are born again. Out of His grace, God sometimes answers certain prayers of those who are not saved. Yes, the unredeemed may not deserve answers to prayer, but that is what God's grace is all about! God's grace flows to both unredeemed sinners and redeemed sinners as answers to their prayers. God can answer the prayers of sinners to show that He is real and that He cares for them. He responds to their cries for salvation and deliverance.

Once a person comes to know Christ as his Savior, he can freely come to God in prayer. Through having faith in Christ, a person has open access to God. Through Christ's death, God's throne of judgment turned into a throne of grace. By coming to God in prayer, people receive God's mercy and His grace: "Therefore let us draw near with confidence to the throne of grace, so that we may receive mercy and find grace to help in time of need" (Heb. 4:16). Take courage because God's grace will help you through the all the trials that you will ever face.

God's presence will always be with the child of God regardless of the severity of his distress. Some tribulations are not too difficult for us to endure while there are some trials that threaten to completely destroy us. One of my favorite Scriptures about God being with us when we are suffering is Isaiah 43:2: "When you pass through the waters, I will be with you; And through the rivers, they will not overflow you. When you walk through the fire, you will not be scorched, Nor will the flame burn you. (Isa. 43:2)

As you read through this verse, you will see that there are three levels of difficulties mentioned by Isaiah: (1) "through the waters"; (2) "through the rivers"; and (3) "through the fire." This verse first mentions going "through the waters." Going through the "waters" suggests shallow waters that are challenging but not life threatening. This seems to refer to problems that challenge us on a daily basis. God promises to be with us even through our ordinary problems. The next level is "through the rivers"; the "rivers" are deeper and can sweep us away by strong currents. The "rivers" are difficult problems that can overwhelm us, and, if we do not deal with them properly, they can destroy us. God promises that these more severe trials will not overflow or overcome the one who trusts in Him. "Through the fire" refers to the most severe problems that threaten to bring destruction in our lives. Fortunately, most people will not be continually going "through the fire" of severe problems; however, everyone can expect to experience some severe trials in his life. Again, God promises that even the most severe trials will not scorch or burn us if we learn to trust in Him.

Application

1. Do you feel overwhelmed?

2. What do you feel is overwhelming you?

3. Have your problems become so severe that you feel you cannot go on?

4. Are you at the point of giving up?

5. Are you going through trials right now?

6. Are you going through severe trials that threaten to destroy you?

7. Have you called upon God to give you His grace to make it through your troubles?

8. Do you believe that God's grace is "more than sufficient" to help you not only through trials but to triumph over them?

Grace That Sustains Believers Through Times of Discouragement

We often experience times of discouragement when going through tribulation. Perhaps certain hopes and expectations did not turn out the way we wanted. We can certainly experience all kinds of disappointments in life. We may be hoping for a promotion at work, but someone less qualified gets the promotion. We are sure that we will get a job, but then someone else gets the job. We may be hoping to get a scholarship for college, but our request is denied. We may be hoping to be accepted into a certain college, but we are turned down. We may be wishing that a new relationship will develop into something more serious, but then the person breaks up with us. We trust our marriages will last a lifetime, but some do not. You may be expecting that your job will last a long time, but, without any warning, you get laid off. You may have prayed that your cancer would never will come back, but it does. Many people have been praying for something for a long time but nothing seems to be happening. When we experience a string of disappointments, we are especially vulnerable to discouragement.

Disappointments can occur in varying degrees of severity. If one possesses a high level of expectation, there will be a corresponding high level of disappointment if it is not fulfilled. If one has a low concern regarding an expectation, there will be a low level of discouragement if it is not fulfilled. If we do not deal with all levels of disappointment correctly, they can turn into discouragement. The Bible describes discouragement as "losing heart." When a person loses heart, he loses hope and may lose the will to continue. Proverbs 13:12 tells us the effect of losing hope: "Hope deferred makes the heart sick, but desire fulfilled is a tree of life." When we become discouraged, we feel like giving up. The Bible tells us not to lose heart: "Let us not lose heart in doing good, for in due time we will reap if we do not grow weary" (Gal. 6:9). Second Corinthians 4:16 states: "Therefore we do not lose heart, but though our outer man is decaying, yet our inner man is being renewed day by day."

How can we avoid becoming discouraged? If we are already discouraged, how do we keep from losing hope? We need to know that we cannot expect to be exempt from disappointments; they are an unavoidable part of life. Whenever we experience disappointments, we need to turn them into appointments with God in prayer. Whenever we are tempted to lose heart, we need to approach God's throne of grace to receive mercy and find the help we need.

At the time that I was writing this section about disappointments, I experienced a loss of a long-time friendship. This loss of a good friend was so disappointing to me, I was becoming exceedingly discouraged; I was tempted to just give in to despair. While driving on an expressway, I came up behind a car that had a bumper sticker I had never seen before that somehow drew my attention. It read, "Prayer Not Despair." I felt God was speaking to me with this message, "Prayer Not Despair." I believe God was urging me to spend more time in prayer. When we spend time in prayer, God will give us grace to help in our time of need. God's grace will strengthen our hearts: "Do not be carried away by varied and strange teachings; for it is good for the heart to be strengthened by grace, not by foods, through which those who were so occupied were not benefited" (Heb. 13:9). We receive God's grace when we humble ourselves before Him. We can receive additional grace when we likewise humble ourselves before others and ask for their help and prayers.

Hope for God's help springs from God's grace. If we rely on our merit to earn God's help, our grounds for hope are entirely unjustified. Everyone must rely solely on God's grace as his grounds for unshakable hope. The believer's hope must be completely fixed on the grace to be brought to him throughout life. God's grace will abound in those who believe: "And God is able to make all grace abound to you, so that always having all sufficiency in everything, you may have an abundance for every good deed" (2 Cor. 9:8). Enough grace is provided each day so the believer can obey God. God's grace is not just to help believers through every day; grace also offers believers hope for the future. Believers can enjoy a future hope of receiving God's grace at Christ's return, "Therefore, prepare your minds for action, keep sober *in spirit,* fix your hope completely on the grace to be brought to you at the revelation of Jesus Christ" (1 Pet. 1:13).

Application

1. Have you experienced many disappointments?

2. Have you experienced a disappointment or a string of disappointments that has discouraged you?

3. Are you losing your hope because you have experienced so many disappointments?

4. Have you responded to your disappointments by seeking God in prayer?

Grace That Sustains Believers During Times of Personal Failure

Some of the most troublesome times we go through are times of failure. Times of failure include not only our personal failures, but the failures of those close to us. Believers will all experience personal failures of some kind. We are all prone to failure because of the relentless struggle with our carnal nature. For every born-again believer, there is tug-of-war for dominance between the Holy Spirit and the flesh. By God's grace, the Spirit will triumph, although there may be many times when the flesh prevails. What is a person to do if he finds himself fallen into a pit of failure? After a failure of sin everyone must go quickly to the throne of grace to receive God's mercy and grace: "Therefore let us draw near with confidence to the throne of grace, so that we may receive mercy and find grace to help in time of need" (Heb. 4:16). We must humble ourselves and ask forgiveness of God and of those we have failed. It is very important to believe that, because of God's grace, He freely forgives those who seek His forgiveness. A key passage of Scripture we need to know and use during time of failure is 1 John 1:9—2:1:

> If we confess our sins, He is faithful and righteous to forgive us our sins and to cleanse us from all unrighteousness. If we say that we have not sinned, we make Him a liar and His word is not in us.
>
> My little children, I am writing these things to you so that you may not sin. And if anyone sins, we have an Advocate with the Father, Jesus Christ the righteous;

This passage offers crucial points to remember during times of failure. First, we need to confess our sins to God. Second, we need to have confidence that God will be faithful and righteous to forgive our sins as He has promised. Third, God will cleanse us from all unrighteousness. No matter what our failures are, God can cleanse us from all unrighteousness and bring restoration. Fourth, if we have sinned, we have someone who will be our advocate before the Father in heaven. Christ will be our defense attorney before the Supreme Judge. Christ will advocate for our forgiveness on the basis of His atoning death on the cross. Christ has never lost a case because the Father is faithful to keep His promise to forgive those who have faith in Christ.

Believing in God's forgiveness is an essential step in recovering from personal failure. An individual may struggle with frequent condemning thoughts after experiencing a personal failure. Believers must always remember that it is not God who condemns them. Because of God's grace, believers know that God does not condemn them; rather, He freely forgives them. If we struggle with condemnation, we must be aware that the source is either Satan, the condemner, or ourselves. Satan loves to constantly remind us of our failures in order to discourage us to the point of hating ourselves and giving up in our struggle with sin. Believers must resist Satan's condemnation and totally trust in God's grace for His forgiveness.

When a believer's own thoughts condemn him, he must learn to forgive himself. If God can forgive him, who is he to not forgive himself? A real issue with people who cannot forgive themselves is pride. People who cannot forgive themselves believe they are better than others who have failed in similar ways. Pride tells a person that he is essentially a good person, so he must try harder not to fail again. Pride tells us to be hard on ourselves by punishing ourselves with condemnation. In reality, we must humble ourselves and acknowledge that we have no righteousness or goodness in ourselves. Everyone needs to realize that his failures are not just a few mistakes, but, more accurately, a pattern of sinfulness that flows out of his sinful nature.

> *It is only when we acknowledge our total depravity that we will totally rely on the grace of God.*

Our failures reveal our utter weakness and our absolute need for God's grace. Once a person learns to respond to failure correctly, he can humble himself and learn to depend on God's grace all the more. Since we only receive God's grace when we humble ourselves, we need to be in a constant state of humility. It is necessary to allow God to develop an attitude of humility in us. This attitude of humility is a quality of character that remains consistent in times of failure or success. Some mistakenly think humility is only needed when they fail. Humility is required both in receiving God's grace in times of failure and in keeping a person from failure. An attitude of humility takes the position of recognizing our perpetual weakness and our constant need of relying on God's grace. Indeed, we need to begin each day confessing our weakness and reaffirming our total dependence on God's grace.

Application

1. Have you experienced a major failure of your own doing?

2. Have you asked forgiveness from God and those you hurt by your failure?

3. Do you trust that God has forgiven you by His grace?

4. Do you struggle with forgiving yourself?

5. Do you struggle with condemning thoughts?

6. Have you come to the point of realizing your total need of God's grace?

Grace That Sustains Believers Through Times of Grief

One of the most difficult emotional experiences a person will suffer is grief. Grief is a deep sorrow that comes to us when we suffer a loss of someone or something that is very valuable to us. Everyone will experience grief during their lives. During this Covid pandemic, a great number have experienced the loss of a family member. One of the most difficult losses is the loss of a child. We have had several families in our church who have lost an adult child by drug overdose. I have seen just how much grief these families suffered from their loss. I cannot imagine the severity of their emotional pain. Some families have survived the pain by the grace of God while others continue to struggle with debilitating pain from their loss.

When anyone suffers grief, he needs to receive comfort and support. God's grace can give eternal comfort to those who suffer grief: "Now may our Lord Jesus Christ Himself and God our Father, who has loved us and given us eternal comfort and good hope by grace" (2 Thess. 2:16). People often give comfort for a short period of time but soon forget your loss and go on with their lives. The person who suffers the loss remains focused on it for years and, for some, even a lifetime. While comfort from people may only last a short time, God's comfort lasts forever. We have God's eternal comfort by His grace. Like a lifejacket to hold people up above their deep sorrows, God's grace provides the comfort and hope that people need to endure through times of grief. God's grace will give us more than what we need to survive grief, "And God is able to make all grace abound to you, so that always having all sufficiency in everything, you may have an abundance for every good deed" (2 Cor. 9:8).

Application

1. Are you suffering from a loss of someone or something that was very valuable to you?

2. Do you struggle to overcome the grief that debilitates you?

3. Have you turned to God in prayer for His comfort?

4. Have you meditated on Scriptures that bring comfort from God?

5. Do you look for opportunities to comfort those in distress?

CHAPTER 10

The Grace of God That Sanctifies

Up to this point in Part Three: God's Enabling Grace, I have explained how God's grace enables by strengthening and sustaining us. Another important aspect of God's grace is that it works in believers to sanctify them. Sanctification means to be set apart. When God calls us to salvation, He also calls us to live godly lives. God desires for His people to be a witness to the world by reflecting His holy character. Believers are to be "set apart" from a lifestyle of sin and "set apart" unto God to become His holy people. Unfortunately, many Christians do not associate God's grace with sanctification. Some think grace only deals with salvation; this is a misunderstanding. God's grace is required for both salvation and sanctification. God's unmerited favor provides the enablement to live a righteous life.

| *No one can live a godly life without God's grace.* |

Through God's grace, those who put their faith in Christ are immediately set apart to be in Christ. Those who experience salvation are declared righteous through the imputation of Christ's righteousness. God's grace does more than just give the believer good standing with God; it enables him to live out that righteousness in his daily life. A person's righteous standing with God is more of an abstract theological concept that is accepted by faith. However, we need to understand that God's grace extends from the theological to the practical. God's grace can help believers to live a godly life in very practical ways.

There is a sizable percentage of Christians that believe too much teaching on grace will lead Christians to live a lifestyle that is indistinguishable from unbelievers. Many pastors avoid speaking too much about God's grace for fear of some misinterpreting what is said. For some, hearing teaching on grace removes their fear of God, which results in a breakdown of their resistance to sin. Yes, there are some who abuse God's grace by believing that they can sin freely because they are no longer under the law. Anyone who believes God's grace gives him a license to sin is abusing the grace of God. Just because some abuse God's grace does not mean there should be restraint on teaching about grace. Clear, biblically balanced teaching on God's grace actually helps people to sin less. Understanding how God's grace sanctifies assists Christians in living a godly life.

How does God's grace help a believer live a godly life? A key passage of Scripture is found in Titus 2:11–12, "For the grace of God has appeared, bringing salvation to all men, instructing us to deny ungodliness and worldly desires and to live sensibly, righteously and godly in the present age." These verses contain two aspects of the work of God's grace. Verse 11 talks about the grace of God that brings salvation to all men. Verse 12 speaks of how the grace of God instructs believers to live godly in the present age. Verse 11 speaks to the grace of God that saves whereas verse 12 addresses how God's grace sanctifies. Since verse 12 deals with the work of grace in sanctification, I will explain what it has to say about sanctification. The first word in verse 12 which explains the work of grace in sanctification is *instructing*. This word is translated *training* in the ESV, and *teaching* in KJV. Further examination of the word instructing brings a wealth of understanding to just what is meant in the context of the verse. The Greek word the apostle Paul uses in this verse for "instructing" is transliterated *paideuō* (3811), which means to "train children, to chasten, correct, discipline."[55] The word is "used of family discipline, as in Heb. 12:6, 7,10."[56]

What Paul was declaring in this verse is that the grace of God disciplines believers as God's children. Out of His grace, God instructs, trains, corrects, chastens, and disciplines His children. It is only because of God's grace that a person is not condemned for his sin. Because a believer is under God's grace does not mean that God will overlook sin in his life. God is never OK with sin. God never condones sin. Being under God's grace means that God will discipline His children but never condemn them. Being disciplined by God, rather than being condemned, is an act of His grace. Discipline by God is a positive thing while being condemned by God is something we all must avoid. When a person becomes a child of God through faith in Jesus Christ, God's condemnation is removed (Rom. 8:1). Being disciplined by God is a sign of being a child in God's family: "It is for discipline that you endure; God deals with you as with sons; for what son is there whom *his* father does not discipline?" (Heb. 12:7). Being disciplined by God's grace is desirable in a believer's life because it produces godliness, "For they disciplined us for a short time as seemed best to them, but He *disciplines us* for *our* good, so that we may share His holiness" (Heb. 12:10).

There are two essential components in the process of sanctification. There is the negative aspect of turning away from sin and the positive aspect of turning to God. The grace of God disciplines His children to both turn away from sin and turn to God with the goal of becoming like Him in godly character. The first part of the work of God's grace is to instruct, train, or teach believers about how to "deny ungodliness and worldly desires" (Titus 2:11). "Denying" deals with being able to resist temptation when it comes. It is impossible to resist temptation for any length of time without God's help. Through the grace of God, He empowers believers to be able to say "no" to temptation. First Corinthians 10:13 explains how God aids believers in times of temptation: "No temptation has overtaken you but such as is common to man; and God is faithful, who will not allow you to be tempted beyond what you are able, but with the temptation will provide the way of escape also, so that you will be able to endure it." This verse promises believers that God will make a way for them to escape so that they will be able to resist temptation.

What is this "way of escape?" For much of my Christian life, the way of escape was a mystery to me. I would pray, "Lord show me this way of escape." When a believer is being tempted, he needs to find God's way of escape. It is like trying to escape from a room with a number of doors; there are several doors that people have tried, but they did not provide a way of escape from surrendering to temptation. Some of these doors are the door of the Law, the door of self-effort, the door of self-discipline, the door of positive thinking, the door of religion, and so forth. The way of escape is the one door called grace. The door of grace is the only way of escape from yielding to temptation. This door of grace is opened when a person humbles himself and confesses his total weakness in resisting temptation. After a person goes through the door of grace, he must continue to totally depend on God for His help.

Humbling oneself before God also involves humbling himself before others. When a person confesses his weak areas in resisting temptation and is accountable to others, that provides a consistent stream of God's grace. After a person humbles himself, God will provide His grace to enable him to overcome temptation. Each day, the believer needs to keep humble and dependent on God. Because a believer chooses the way of grace, Christ will come to aid him when he is tempted — "For since He Himself was tempted in that which He has suffered, He is able to come to the aid of those who are tempted" (Heb. 2:18). We do not know how to resist temptation, but God knows how to rescue us from temptation, "*then* the Lord knows how to rescue the godly from temptation, and to keep the unrighteous under punishment for the day of judgment" (2 Pet. 2:9). The way of grace is when believers rely on the power of the Spirit of God to overcome: "For the law of the Spirit of life in Christ Jesus has set you free from the law of sin and of death" (Rom. 8:2).

Grace goes beyond just helping a person to resist temptation; God wants to help believers overcome the dominion of sin in their lives. By the grace of God, believers can break the control of the sinful nature in their lives. Before a person experiences Christ at salvation, he is ruled by the tyranny of sin. Apart from the grace of God, everyone is a slave to sin. It is only by God's grace that the power of sin can be broken. Where people once yielded themselves to the dictates of sin, they must now surrender themselves to the discipline of God's grace. The way of grace is the way of the Holy Spirit.

When we yield to the control of the Holy Spirit, we will be set free from the rule of sin and death. When sin reigns uncontrolled, it will ultimately destroy us. When grace reigns through righteousness, it leads to eternal life, "so that, as sin reigned in death, even so grace would reign through righteousness to eternal life through Jesus Christ our Lord" (Rom. 5:21). Believers in Christ should not be under the dominion of sin because they have been set free by God's grace. "For sin shall not be master over you, for you are not under law but under grace" (Rom. 6:14).

Once God's grace begins to enable a person to break free from the dominion of sin, the Holy Spirit begins the work of removing sinful aspects of the believer's sinful nature. Through God's grace, a believer can "put off" the old sinful ways of his past and now "put on" the new ways of righteousness. It is not enough to simply "deny ungodliness and worldly desires." Living a godly life is much more than resisting sin; it is becoming alive with spiritual vitality. It is experiencing the "abundant life" that Christ promised (John 10:10).

The grace of God instructs believers to not only resist sin; it also trains them to grow in Christ-like character "to live sensibly, righteously, and godly" (Titus 2:12). This is the positive aspect of sanctification. God's grace enables believers to live sensibly or soberly. What this means is that by God's grace, believers can have minds that are alert to guide them into wise living. The grace of God can enable believers to live their lives unintoxicated or obsessed by worldly desires. Believers can think clearing and act prudently. Faith in Christ brings an abundance of grace along with the gift of Christ's righteousness. "For if by the transgression of the one, death reigned through the one, much more those who receive the abundance of grace and of the gift of righteousness will reign in life through the One, Jesus Christ" (Rom. 5:17). Through God's grace, believers are given the gift of righteousness and a new godly nature that empowers them to conduct themselves in a godly manner. "For our proud confidence is this: the testimony of our conscience, that in holiness and godly sincerity, not in fleshly wisdom but in the grace of God, we have conducted ourselves in the world, and especially toward you" (2 Cor. 1:12.)

Application

1. How successful have you been in resisting temptations?

2. Have you reached a point of desperation where you are convinced that you are not able to resist temptation on your own?

3. Have you turned to God to trust in His grace to overcome sin?

4. Have you shared your struggles with someone you can trust?

5. Have you become accountable to someone who will help you with your weakness?

CHAPTER 11

The Grace of God that Serves

God's grace assists believers to serve God in various ways. The apostle Paul was a great example of a believer who was empowered by God's grace to serve. Paul made it quite clear what was sustaining him in ministry, "But by the grace of God I am what I am, and His grace toward me did not prove vain; but I labored even more than all of them, yet not I, but the grace of God with me" (1 Cor. 15:10). In this verse, Paul explained that the grace of God enabled him to be the person he was and empowered him to labor more than all the others. In this verse, Paul gives a biblically balanced view of how to do the work of God. Some believe that it is all left up to human effort to do the work of ministry. Others believe all that is needed is to pray and leave it all up to God to do the work of ministry.

The balance is that both man's efforts and God's power are involved in the work of God. God's work of ministry depends on us doing our part. As we do our part, God will do His miraculous part. Additionally, our part in ministry is totally supported by the grace of God. Paul claims that it was the grace of God that empowered him to preach to the Gentiles the unfathomable riches of Christ (Eph. 3:8). Paul had to do his part in preaching, but it was God's grace that enabled him to preach. Doing the work of ministry with the capability of the Holy Spirit is like working a construction job with all the needed power tools. God does not do the work for us, but He empowers us to do His work.

Believers are divinely commissioned by God to serve Him with both natural and spiritual gifts. The primary source of ability for ministry is not a person's natural abilities but that which the Holy Spirit supplies by grace to the believer. The calling to serve is not based solely on human abilities: "For consider your calling, brethren, that there were not many wise according to the flesh, not many mighty, not many noble" (1 Cor. 1:26). This is not to suggest that God does not choose people with any natural talents because God can use those talents. God gives to whom He will both natural and spiritual abilities; however, the spiritual abilities that God supplies are far superior in achieving His purpose.

According to God's grace, specific "gifts" are delegated to believers to enable them to serve in distinctive ways. "But to each one of us grace was given according to the measure of Christ's gift" (Eph. 4:7). First Peter 4:10 tells us that: "each one has received a special gift" that should be employed in serving others. In Romans 12:6, believers are encouraged to use their individual gifts: "Since we have gifts that differ according to the grace given to us, *each of us is to exercise them accordingly*: if prophecy, according to the proportion of his faith."

What are these gifts for service that Paul mentions in several of his writings to different churches? I believe the most complete passage on the grace gifts is Romans 12:3–8:

> For through the grace given to me I say to everyone among you not to think more highly of himself than he ought to think; but to think so as to have sound judgment, as God has allotted to each a measure of faith. For just as we have many members in one body and all the members do not have the same function, so we, who are many, are one body in Christ, and individually members one of another. Since we have gifts that differ according to the grace given to us, *each of us is to exercise them accordingly*: if prophecy, according to the proportion of his faith; if service, in his serving; or he who teaches, in his teaching; or he who exhorts, in his exhortation; he who gives, with liberality; he who leads, with diligence; he who shows mercy, with cheerfulness.

There is a wealth of information concerning grace gifts for service in this passage of Scripture. It is important for Christians to understand grace gifts because that knowledge will increase the effectiveness of their ministries. What can a person learn from this passage in Romans 12:3–8? First, I want to explain how the diverse grace gifts are to be compared with each other. Romans 12:3 tells us how believers are to compare their gifts with the gifts of others. In comparing the various grace gifts of service, no one should become prideful regarding his particular gifts of grace, "not to think more highly of himself than he ought to think." Believers should not be prideful because gifts of grace are not given on the basis of merit. The grace gifts of service that God gives are not earned as rewards. Gifts of grace are free gifts of enablement to serve. God determines what each believer receives. No one can take any credit for the grace gifts he has received from God. All the glory goes to God for any gifts that are received. No one is to elevate himself above others because of his gifts. Believers are not to think that their gifts are more important than other's gifts.

The second thing that can be seen in this passage about grace gifts is that everyone is to think with "sound judgment" concerning the gifts of grace he has received. Sound judgment means to have a realistic view of one's gifts. No one should think too highly or too lowly of himself in regard to the gifts of grace he has received. A person can think too lowly of himself by thinking that he has nothing to offer or what he does have is not important. Believers in Christ are not to deny that they have received a grace gift because this verse declares that "God has allotted to each a measure of faith." It should be clearly understood that all believers have something valuable to use in service to others. It is vital for believers to understand spiritual gifts because that will help them to appreciate the gifts of others and empower them to work together in unity and harmony in the Body of Christ.

In verses 4–5, we see where grace gifts are to operate. Grace gifts are designed to work in the context of a local church. "For just as we have many members in one body." If Christians do not get involved in the ministry of a local church, they will never discover or be able to fully use their grace gifts. When Christians do not get involved in ministry, they weaken the church's ability to minister to people both in and outside the church. One of the greatest needs of churches today is the need for workers. It does not matter if the church is big or small, there is always a need for more workers. Churches are greatly weakened in their ability to minister because there is a large percentage of Christians who are not involved in ministry.

All of the parts of the human body, whether the hands, the feet, the eyes, or other parts, have a specific function. As the human body has functioning parts, so does each local church. The local church is like a body with parts that work together and with parts that have their own specific function because "all the members do not have the same function." It is essential that all Christians use the gifts they have received for the benefit of their local church. Each gift is designed to strengthen and improve the Body of Christ. The local church needs all the grace gifts in order to function properly. Just as the parts of a human body cannot survive and function separately from the body, so it is with the body of Christ; the body parts cannot function by themselves.

In verses 6-8, the apostle Paul explains the various grace gifts. Previously, I mentioned that the grace gifts are given to help us to do our part in the ministry equation. God's part is to do the miraculous, while our part is to do the practical work involved in ministry. God did not leave believers to do their part of ministry all on their own. In fact, God gives believers tremendous resources to do what is delegated to them. Believers need much encouragement as they are doing their part of the work of ministry. Believers need to have the motivation to begin and keep performing their ministry.

It is very difficult to get involved in ministry without having motivation. People have to overcome their fear of starting something new and their fear of failure. Once a person enters ministry, he will find it much more difficult than he anticipated. People will find that ministry involves more time and effort than expected. Those who get involved in ministry will quite often face opposition and criticism. There will be many times a person will feel like giving up. It has been my experience over fifty years of pastoral ministry that a large percentage of people who start out in ministry never endure through difficulties. How is it that some will continue to be motivated throughout their ministry while others drop out? How does a person keep motivated in ministry?

What is the answer to having deficiency of motivation? Worldly motivational techniques may work for businesses and sports, but they will fall woefully short when it comes to ministry because of the spiritual aspect involved. The source of a person's motivation must be from outside of himself. That source outside ourselves is the enabling grace of God. When we look at the ministry of Paul, we see no lack of motivation. Paul must have been extremely motivated to be able to endure all the adversity he experienced. Paul revealed that it was the grace of God that motivated him: "But by the grace of God I am what I am, and

His grace toward me did not prove vain; but I labored even more than all of them, yet not I, but the grace of God with me" (1 Cor. 15:10). The same grace of God that motivated Paul is the same grace that will motivate all believers for ministry.

Church history is replete with examples of men and women who accomplished unbelievable feats of ministry. Thousands of missionaries have served their entire lives to reach certain people groups all over the world. Many missionaries have had to forsake their families, their jobs, their homes, and their comfort to fulfill God's call to serve. Many have served under great persecution and have suffered loss of property and even life. Tens of thousands of pastors have faithfully served in churches where there were insufficient funds to adequately support their family's financial needs. Multitudes of millions of believers have faithfully served in ministry where there was no financial reward or recognition. What has driven believers all over the world and through history to sacrifice themselves in service for God?

> ***It is God's empowering grace that has enabled believers to achieve astonishing acts of service for the glory of God.***

Paul lists the differing grace gifts in Romans 12:6–8. These grace gifts are the motivation that God gives us to serve. The word for "gifts" used in verse 6 is the Greek word *charisma*, (5486) "a gift of grace, a gift involving grace" (*charis*) on the part of God as the donor."[57] This Greek word is used of God's gifts of grace, "of His free bestowments upon sinners and of His endowment upon believers by the operation of the Holy Spirit in the churches."[58] The Greek word *charisma* comes from the word *charis*, meaning grace. This Greek word deals with the basic inward drive or motivation, and power to perform ministry. The English dictionary defines *charisma* as an "extraordinary power given a Christian by the Holy Spirit for the good of the church."[59] Grace gifts are those gifts that produce an inner desire to minister in certain ways. Every believer has at least one motivational gift. Believers can serve in many different ways, but the drive behind *why* they serve usually comes from their primary motivational gift of grace.

I could write a whole chapter just on the motivational grace gifts listed in Romans 12:6–8, but, for the sake of brevity, I will give a short summary of the different motivational gifts of grace. The first motivational gift of grace that is listed is the gift of prophecy. This gift is not to be confused with the gift of prophecy listed in 1 Corinthians 12:10 as one of the "effects" or one of the "manifestation" gifts of the Holy Spirit (1 Cor. 12:6). As a motivational gift, prophecy is the desire to proclaim the truth. "In both the Old Testament and the New Testament, prophecy is not primarily foretelling the future, but proclaiming God's will and exhorting and encouraging God's people to righteousness, faithfulness and endurance."[60] One who has the grace gift of prophecy has a motivation to speak forth the truth or proclaim truth. This motivational gift of prophecy is primarily expressed through preaching and teaching.

The second motivational grace gift that is listed is serving. This gift is the desire to help others, usually by doing something with their hands. This gift motivates Christians to demonstrate love by meeting practical needs. "Serving is the God-given desire, ability, and power to give practical assistance to members and leaders of the church to help them fulfill their responsibilities to God"[61] For example, a person with the gift of serving would choose to assist an individual or the church through cleaning, cooking, doing repairs, building, running errands, driving the church van, ushering, and so on.

The gift of teaching is the third listed. The motivation to teach is the desire to explain the truth. "Teaching" is the God-given desire, ability and power to examine and study God's Word, and to clarify, defend and proclaim its truth in such a way that others grow in grace and godliness."[62] A believer who possesses this grace gift desires to search out and validate truth. A person with this gift enjoys research and pays much attention to the details and facts of his own and others' presentations. A person with this gift is very concerned that any presentation of God's Word is accurate. For example, this gift can be expressed by being in a position as a teacher in an adult Bible class, college professor, or pastor who teaches Bible classes and has a teaching style of preaching. I see the difference between preaching and teaching is that preaching proclaims God's Word, whereas teaching focuses more on explaining the truth of God's Word.

The fourth motivational gift is the gift of exhortation. One who has the gift of exhortation (encouraging) demonstrates love by doing or saying things to encourage others. "Encouraging is the God-given desire, ability and power to proclaim God's Word in such a way that it touches the heart, conscience and will of the hearers, stimulates faith, and produces a deeper commitment to Christ and a more thorough separation from the world"[63] This gift can express itself in many ways. It can be the motivation behind many types of ministries, such as preaching, teaching, serving, and giving, all with the goal of encouraging others.

The fifth motivational gift of grace is giving. All believers are instructed to give to the work of God and to the needs of others. Those with the gift of giving make it the focus of their ministry. Those with this gift truly enjoy giving. "'Contributing' is the God-given desire, ability, and power because one has resources above life's basic needs, to give freely of one's personal possessions to the needs of God's work or people."[64] Those with this gift of giving can be a tremendous help in supplying resources for the work of God and demonstrating God's love to those in need.

The sixth motivational gift of grace is leading. The gift of leading is the desire to coordinate activities or projects. A person with this gift excels in administration. "'Leadership' is the God-given desire, ability and power to guide and oversee the various activities of the church for the spiritual good of all."[65] People with this gift tend to be well organized and are task- and goal-oriented. People with this gift are very disturbed when things are done in a chaotic manner. They greatly enjoy turning chaos into order. Those with the gift of ruling are the ideal people for administrative positions in the church or for organizing people for certain projects and tasks.

The final motivational gift listed is the gift of mercy. The gift of mercy is the desire to comfort those who suffer. People with this gift tend to be very sensitive to the feelings and needs of others. They empathize with the misfortunes and misery of others. Those motivated by this gift relate to those in need both mentally and emotionally. People with this gift enjoy being involved in ministries that reach out to those in need, such as a ministry to the homeless, soup kitchens, and benevolent ministries of all sorts.

Application

1. Have you responded to God's call to receive salvation?

2. Have you responded to God's call to serve?

3. Has God given you a desire to serve?

4. Are you committed to getting involved in a church?

5. What are some of your natural talents?

6. As you read through the description of the motivational gifts of grace, did you see any gifts with which you can identify?

7. What do you believe might be your strongest motivational gift?

8. Do you feel that God has called you to serve Him in a specific way?

   If so, what are you doing about it?

CHAPTER 12

The Grace of God That Secures

So many Christians make the mistake of believing that after they are saved, they are essentially left on their own without any help from God. Many Christians believe that they are saved by grace but then have to maintain their salvation through works. Unfortunately, many Christians believe that if they commit sins after they are saved, they need to be resaved. When I was growing up, our family attended several different types of churches. Some of the churches we attended would have regular altar calls for people to come forward for salvation. When the pastor would have an altar call, I noticed many of the same people coming forward each week. Even as a child I thought something was not right. Why would people need to be saved over and over again? It was not until later that I understood why people think they needed repeated salvations.

People who believe they need to be resaved presume that every time they sin, they lose their salvation. This line of thinking leads to the erroneous belief that God only shows His grace and mercy at the time of salvation. So, with this thinking, if a believer sins, the only way to receive God's grace and mercy is to be resaved. However, the grace of God is not just for salvation; it is also for living out the Christian life day by day. God's grace is available every day from the time of salvation to the day the believer is called home to heaven. If Christians base maintaining their salvation on their performance, they are doomed to living with doubts and uncertainty about their salvation. Not only will Christians struggle with doubts about their salvation, but they will also live with a consciousness of God's condemnation hanging over them. This is not how God wants His children to live. God's grace has freed those who are in Christ from His condemnation (Rom. 8:1).

Once a person bases his continuing salvation on God's grace and not his performance, he will enjoy a much greater sense of security. Earlier in this book, I explained that God's grace sanctifies the believer. There are two ways that God's grace sanctifies the believer. There is an instantaneous sanctification at the moment of salvation where God declares a person righteous in Christ. Those who believe in Christ are considered righteous in their standing before God. It is through faith that a person is declared righteous before God, "Even so Abraham believed God, and it was reckoned to him as righteousness" (Gal. 3:6). Believers have a righteousness that comes through faith and not of works. Believers are declared justified by their faith in Christ (Rom. 5:1; Gal. 3:24). As a believer continues to have faith in Christ, he will continue in this state of being considered righteous by faith. Believers are in a constant state of grace because they are united with Christ; they are not under the law but under grace (Rom. 6:14).

The second type of sanctification is a progressive development over the lifetime of the believer. With progressive sanctification, God keeps working in a believer's life in the areas that have not yet been conformed to the image of Christ. Being secure in God's grace does not mean that God just overlooks sin in a believer's life. God is always grieved by sin in a person's life and is constantly working to help him remove anything that is displeasing to Him. God lets believers know when they do something that displeases Him by convicting them. This conviction is a godly sorrow that makes a person feel terrible about his sins. Conviction is not the same as condemnation. Conviction causes one to feel bad about sin, whereas condemnation makes one feel bad about oneself.

Conviction is from God and leads people to repentance. Condemnation is not from God and leads to despair and defeat. As a person humbles himself in repentance, God will freely forgive him by His grace. Trusting God's grace does not mean a believer can overlook sin in his life. Whenever a believer becomes aware of sin in his life he must immediately repent and reject sin. The conviction–repentance cycle will continue throughout a Christian's life. Believers in Christ will always be "works in progress" until they are glorified in heaven.

Our development as a "work in progress" should not be what determines our security in our salvation. It is not as though we have to reach a certain level of spiritual maturity before we can be secure in our salvation.

> ***Our level of spiritual maturity is not what determines our salvation nor should it be the basis of our security in our salvation.***

The process of transformation is not always a steady increase in godliness. There will be times of notable progress and times of regress. We will feel insecure in times of relapse if we base our security on our spiritual progress. Whether we are making momentous improvements in our spiritual life or experiencing setbacks, we can be secure in our salvation if we base that confidence on God's grace. It is only by God's grace that we are saved and it is only by the grace of God that we continue to be saved.

As a believer in Christ, one can be secure in God's grace because God's enabling grace strengthens one in his weaknesses: "Now to Him who is able to keep you from stumbling, and to make you stand in the presence of His glory blameless with great joy" (Jude 24). God's grace will sustain believers through trials, times of discouragement, times of failure, and times of grief. No matter what a believer may go through, nothing will separate him from God's love and grace. "For I am convinced that neither death, nor life, nor angels, nor principalities, nor things present, nor things to come, nor powers, nor height, nor depth, nor any other created thing, will be able to separate us from the love of God, which is in Christ Jesus our Lord" (Rom. 8:38–39).

God's grace sanctifies the believer by enabling him to live a godly life, "so that, as sin reigned in death, even so grace would reign through righteousness to eternal life through Jesus Christ our Lord" (Rom. 5:21). A believer can be secure in his salvation because God is able to keep him. Believers are secure because God will complete the work He has begun in them: "*For I am* confident of this very thing, that He who began a good work in you will perfect it until the day of Christ Jesus" (Phil. 1:6). Believers can experience assurance because God's power will protect them, "who are protected by the power of God through faith for a salvation ready to be revealed in the last time" (1 Pet. 1:5).

Application

1. If you consider yourself to be a Christian, on what do you base your salvation? Your works or God's grace?

2. Do you believe that you need to get resaved every time you sin?

3. Do you believe that after you are saved, you are on your own to live the Christian life?

4. Do you believe that God's grace continues to work in a person's life after he is saved? If so, in what ways?

5. In what ways do you believe that God's grace can help you after salvation?

Trophy of Grace: Marsha Thomas

The earliest memories I have are when I was about four or five years old, going to my grandmother's house for the weekends. I can remember attending church with my grandmother. My grandmother and I always sat in the front row of the First Baptist Church in Olean, New York. Grandma sang the church hymns the loudest of everyone in the church. Though I attended church with my grandma for many years until I was in my teenage years, I did so only to please my grandma.

During my teenage years my parents moved from Olean to Batavia, New York. I was not able to continue attending church with my grandmother, but I did continue to attend church with my mother. Even though I was baptized, I was not living as I should nor did I have a personal relationship with Jesus. Through most of my early adult life, I went to church, but I pretty much lived another life outside the church. It was a real disappointment for my parents and grandmother when at seventeen I became pregnant. I was forced to leave home and was sent to a Christian home for unwed mothers. The Christian agency cared for me until I completed my pregnancy and gave birth to a son.

It was very difficult for me to determine what was the right thing to do. I knew at seventeen that I was not capable of caring for my son. I felt that if I tried to raise my son, I would not have been a very good mother. I wanted to do what was best for my son. I was worried that if I would put my son up for adoption that he was would not be placed in a good Christian home. I was assured by the Christian adoption agency that if I put my son up for adaption, they would find a good Christian home for my son. Even with their assurance it was difficult to give up my child. To this day I have never seen my son again. I pray for him all the time and hope he is doing well. I hope someday that he will try to find me.

At eighteen I got married to my first husband. Not long after we were married, my husband was drafted by the army to go fight in the

Vietnam. After being in Vietnam for just thirteen months, he was able to come home for a short time. I was happy to have him home, but I soon found out that he came home a different man. The war had left my husband with emotional and mental scars. My husband became very controlling and suspicious of everything I did. He would not allow me to get rides from work with anyone other than him. Whenever I would go shopping, he would limit the time I could be in the store. He wouldn't allow me to have any friends.

During my first marriage, I had two children. After seven years of marriage, I divorced my husband. After my divorce, I went through a number of relationships with men. I lived with a man who was an alcoholic. This man would beat me up nearly every time he was drunk, which was often. At times he would choke me almost to death. I suffered this abuse for six years. The only thing that enabled me to endure through all the abuse was knowing that Jesus loved me. During all that I was going through I still continued to work two jobs and faithfully attend church. After years of suffering abuse, I finally got an order of protection.

After we separated, I began to live with another man for several years with whom I had two children. This relationship did not last very long, and I again moved on to another relationship and, years later, I was remarried, but during my second marriage, I experienced an unexpected loss of custody of my two youngest children. The two little children that I had with the man I lived with were taken from me when they went to stay with their father for supposedly a short visit. When I went to pick the two children up where he lived with his girlfriend, I was hit with a custody battle. I was not even allowed to see my two children who were three and five years old for about ten months. Because I loved my children so much this was a horrifying time for me.

It was during this extremely difficult time that I began to cry out to the Lord. During my walks to work I began to pray a lot. I would walk about a mile to work in the early morning while it was still dark. I would pray and cry out to God in desperation for my children as I walked. One morning as I was walking through a parking lot on my way to work, I heard a very strong voice say to me "No weapon formed against you shall prosper." I looked around and there was no one in sight, so I then realized that God had spoken to me. A peace came over me like I had never experienced before. Two weeks later my children came home to me. Glory be to God! After that, God became so real to me. I know for a fact that God is real.

Raising my youngest boy, Jason, without a father was quite a challenge; he was always hard to handle. I taught my youngest son about Jesus, and when he was older, he was baptized in August of 2001. After the terrorist attack on 9/11, he wanted to sign up for military service. He wanted to fight the terrorists for his country but never got the chance. On November 15, 2001, my son was killed when he was shot at point blank range in the stomach while being robbed. After he was shot, he ran for his life several blocks away where he died, bleeding out in front of neighborhood drugstore. He was in the wrong place at the wrong time. I was beside myself with grief for the loss of my son. It is extremely difficult to lose a child but to lose a child by murder is beyond any grief that you can imagine. It was only through the grace of God that I have been able to endure.

During my overwhelming grief, I learned to lean on Jesus. Through my storms, Jesus has given me much peace. Jesus walked with me through all my struggles. God has guided me all the way through my sorrow. I know that God was with me through this agony of the loss of my son. I can declare to you from my personal experience that if you turn to the Lord, He will give you peace. God's grace has sustained me through my loss. Sometimes I will break down and cry, but Jesus is always there to comfort me. I felt Jesus comforting me as He whispered into my ear how my son had died, that he was shot straight through and died without much suffering. I was comforted in knowing that my son had accepted Jesus when he was young. Jesus reminded me that when my son was a little baby he would stand on my lap and praise God with open arms and was full of joy.

One of the things that comforts me is knowing that I cannot live in my past but have a wonderful future. God sees what lies ahead of us; He knows our future. I know that God has a plan and a purpose for me. I purpose to give my life in service to the Lord. Since the death of my son, I have given my life in service in many ways. Through all my struggles, I have found Jesus to be real. Jesus is wonderful, and He loves all of us. It is beautiful how God lifts us up through our struggles if we will just trust in Him. I wish everyone could feel the grace of God that I have felt. Where hurt abounds, God's grace abounds more. Where loss abounds, God's grace abounds more.

PART FOUR

THE AGENT OF GRACE

CHAPTER 13

The Agent of Salvation

A number of years ago I wanted to do some remodeling in my basement to make an additional bedroom. Before I could start this project, I needed to have several water supply lines rerouted through a different part of the basement. I tried calling plumbing companies to come and give me an estimate, but none was interested in my small job. I finally found someone who would come to give me an estimate. When the plumber came to my house, he gave me an estimate that I thought was reasonable, so I agreed to have him do the job. He requested $500 in cash to buy the supplies. I thought it was a little strange to ask that much for a down payment (more than the cost of supplies), but I agreed because I could not find anyone else to do the job. After I came up with the money, I gave it to him and waited a week for him to show up for the job. I kept calling him, and he would always give some kind of excuse as to why he could not come. Even though I called him repeatedly for weeks in a row, he eventually stopped answering my calls.

I decided to take my case to the Small Claims Court because this plumber refused to return my calls for several months. The Small Claims Court accepted my case and scheduled the court date a couple months out, but when the time for the hearing came, the plumber never showed up. I then made another court date months later that was almost two years since I had heard from the plumber. When the next court hearing came, again, he again did not show up, so the judge ruled in my favor because the plumber never showed up for the second time. I asked the judge how was I supposed to collect the money. What the judge said shocked me; he told me it was my responsibility to collect the money. I told the judge that I had earnestly tried to collect the money for two years without any results. The judge said that all he could recommend was for me to contact the marshal in the area where this plumber lived. I contacted the marshal, and he agreed to do what he could to get my money returned. A few months later, I finally received the $500.

I was not able to collect the money on my own, but with the intervention of the marshal, I was successful. The marshal was my agent to help collect the money. An agent is one who acts or exerts power to produce a desired effect.

Just like the marshal who helped me to accomplish what I was not able to do, the Holy Spirit is our agent of grace. The Holy Spirit is the one who supplies us the grace we need to do what we cannot do. The Holy Spirit is called the Spirit of Grace (Heb. 10:29). The Holy Spirit actively works through grace to save, strengthen, sustain, sanctify, serve, and secure us. The objective of the Holy Spirit is to bring people to Christ and then conform them into the image of Christ. The work of grace by the Holy Spirit in the believer is multifaceted. There are many ways the Holy Spirit aids in bringing a person to salvation and then assists in the person's spiritual development.

> *True transformation of character can only occur with God's intervention.*

The work of the Holy Spirit plays a prominent role in the miracle of transformation. Apart from the work of grace by the Holy Spirit, there are no real transformations or miracles of grace. The believer's transformation is a primary task of the Holy Spirit. The Holy Spirit's work of transformation begins even before a person's salvation and continues until a person is glorified. The Holy Spirit works to convince and convict a person to bring him to a point of calling on the Lord for salvation. After a person is saved, the Holy Spirit is constantly working in each believer to make him more like Christ.

Jesus Christ promised to ask the Father to give His followers another Helper, "And I will ask the Father, and He will give you another Helper, that He may be with you forever" (John 14:16). John 16:7 states that Jesus promised His disciples a Helper (NASB, ESV). The Holy Spirit is

The Agent of Salvation

our helper who comes alongside of us to lift us up and aid us through our lifelong journey of transformation.

The manner in which the Holy Spirit works in a believer is the result of God's grace. Because of God's grace, the Holy Spirit is patient with us; He will not force us against our will. The Holy Spirit will demonstrate a great amount of mercy and forgiveness. God's grace will be persistent with each believer, and He will not give up on any believer even though the believer fails Him many times. Through grace, God is committed to working in each believer throughout his life. God promises believers that He will complete the work of grace He has begun in them. "And I am sure of this, that he who began a good work in you will bring it to completion at the day of Jesus Christ" (Phil. 1:6, ESV).

Jesus Christ promised believers that the Holy Spirit would come alongside to strengthen and uphold him. The Holy Spirit serves as the dispenser of God's grace in three major ways: (1) Through God's grace the Spirit is the agent of salvation; (2) Through God's grace the Spirit is the agent of sanctification; and (3) Through God's grace the Spirit is the agent of service.

The salvation of humanity is a cooperative effort of the Godhead—God the Father, Jesus Christ the Son of God, and God the Holy Spirit. The Trinity works in perfect harmony as one, with each performing His task perfectly. In God's plan for salvation, the Father is the one who initiates and authorizes the plan. The Father plays an active part during a person's salvation as the one who officiates the transactions of grace.

In the design of salvation, the Son of God fulfills the requirements of the plan. Christ's purpose in coming to earth was to do the will of the Father and to complete what was required to make possible the salvation of all humanity. It was through the atoning work of Christ's sacrificial death that God's judgment of sin was satisfied (Rom. 5:8–9). Christ became the Lamb of God to take away the sins of the world (John 1:29). Through faith in Christ, the wall of separation between God and man is demolished. Christ's work made it possible for humanity to be restored to a right relationship with God. God's grace enacted His plan to be a bridge between man and God.

The work of the Holy Spirit is to manifest God's grace by implementing the plan of salvation. By implement, I am referring to the dictionary definition: "to carry out, accomplish; esp.: to give practical effect to and ensure of actual fulfillment by concrete measures."[66] Simply put, the Holy Spirit's task is to manifest the grace of God through bringing people to believe and receive Christ for salvation. There are various aspects of how the Holy Spirit manifests God's grace to bring people to salvation.

The Holy Spirit's Work of Grace in Calling People to Salvation

What is the call of the Holy Spirit? There are many definitions of the word *call* that can be found in an English dictionary. The definitions that best describe the biblical meaning are these: as a verb, "to summon to a particular activity,"[67] as a noun, "a divine vocation or strong inner prompting to particular course of action." [68] A common Greek verb used in the New Testament for the word *call* is transliterated from Greek to English as *kaleō* (2564). This Greek word "is used particularly of the divine call to partake of the blessings of redemption, (Romans 8:30, 1 Corinthians 1:9, 1 Thessalonians 2:12, Hebrews 9:15)."[69] Hebrews 9:15 states, "For this reason He is the mediator of a new covenant, so that, since a death has taken place for the redemption of the transgressions that were *committed* under the first covenant, those who have been called may receive the promise of the eternal inheritance.

One of the Greek nouns used for "calling" is transliterated from Greek to English as *klōsis*. This Greek word "is always used in the New Testament of that "calling" the origin, nature and destiny of which are heavenly (the idea of invitation being implied) it is used especially of God's invitation to man to accept the benefits of salvation."[70] This "calling" is described in various ways: "the hope of His calling" (Eph. 1:18); "the upward call of God" (Phil. 3:14); "your calling" (2 Thess. 1:11); "His calling" (2 Pet. 1:10); "holy calling" (2 Tim. 1:9); and the "heavenly calling" (Heb. 3:1).

This call of God is a universal call to receive salvation. God desires everyone to be saved, "who desires all men to be saved and to come to the knowledge of the truth" (1 Tim. 2:4). Salvation is offered to everyone who believes in Christ, "so that whoever believes will in Him have eternal life" (John 3:15). "For God so loved the world, that He gave His only begotten Son, that whoever believes in Him shall not perish, but have eternal life" (John 3:15–16), "and everyone who lives and believes in Me will never die. Do you believe this?" (John 11:26). In the book of

Revelation, we see the universal call to salvation by the Spirit's and the bride's call to all who will hear and to those who are thirsty, "The Spirit and the bride say, "Come." And let the one who hears say, "Come." And let the one who is thirsty come; let the one who wishes take the water of life without cost" (Rev. 22:17).

There are two components of the call to salvation: the call to believe, and the call to repentance. The call to believe is seen in numerous verses of Scripture. The apostle John explains that the purpose of his gospel's recording of some of the miracles of Christ was to help people come to believe in Christ — "Therefore many other signs Jesus also performed in the presence of the disciples, which are not written in this book; but these have been written so that you may believe that Jesus is the Christ, the Son of God; and that believing you may have life in His name" (John 20:30–31). The apostle Paul and Silas responded to the Philippian jailer's question of how to be saved with these words: "Believe in the Lord Jesus, and you shall be saved" (Acts 16:31). Romans 10:9 states, "that if you confess with your mouth Jesus *as* Lord and believe in your heart that God raised Him from the dead, you will be saved." Christ spoke about the importance of believing in Him in order to receive eternal life (John 3:15–16; 11:26).

The second component of the call of salvation is the universal call to repentance. In his sermon on Mars Hill in Athens, the apostle Paul told the Athenians that God required all people everywhere to repent, "Therefore having overlooked the times of ignorance, God is now declaring to men that all *people* everywhere should repent" (Acts 17:30). Peter declared that it is not the will of God that any should perish but that all come to repentance: "The Lord is not slow about His promise, as some count slowness, but is patient toward you, not wishing for any to perish but for all to come to repentance" (2 Pet. 3:9). Jesus Christ made numerous calls to repentance (Matt. 3:2; 4:17; Mark 1:14–15).

The Holy Spirit calls all people to believe in Christ and to repent of their sins; however, not all respond correctly to the call. Jesus gave a parable that illustrated how so few will respond correctly to the invitation to receive the blessings of salvation. In Christ's parable of the wedding feast (Matt. 22:1–14), He spoke about a king who invited many to a wedding feast. The king prepared a great feast and desired for his banquet hall to be full. He invited many guests on several occasions. Despite all the king's efforts to fill the hall with guests, only a few responded to his invitation. In the king's desperation, he sent out his servants to go into the streets and alleys to bring people in.

This parable illustrates how God has invited all to come to the marriage supper of the Lamb, but only a fraction respond favorably to the call. The call to salvation goes out to all but the results depend on man's response to the gospel invitation. "Man's will is the only obstacle to the salvation of anyone. God does not give one man the will to do good and leave the other without all help in this respect."[71] The call to receive salvation comes primarily through the Spirit, using people to proclaim the gospel message (Rom. 10:16–17; 2 Thess. 2:14).

The Holy Spirit's Work of Grace in Convincing People

One of the first works of the Holy Spirit in an unbeliever is the effort to convince him of the truth. To convince means, "to bring to belief, consent, or course of action, to persuade."[72] The Holy Spirit has a very difficult task in persuading unbelievers of the truth because of the condition of their carnal minds, which are not at all receptive to the truth. The Bible addresses the issue of the mind by describing the human mind in its fallen state: (1) defiled (Titus 1:15); (2) depraved (Rom. 1:28); (3) futile (Eph. 4:17); (4) fleshly (Col. 2:18); (5) hostile toward God; and (6) not subject to the laws of God (Rom. 8:7). Man's fallen sinful nature causes his mindset to naturally gravitate to the desires of that sinful nature: "For those who are according to the flesh set their minds on the things of the flesh, but those who are according to the Spirit, the things of the Spirit" (Rom. 8:5).

In addition to man's carnal mind being hostile toward God and the truth, a very powerful influence by the powers of darkness hinders mankind's ability to understand the truth. There is a battle between the powers of darkness and the Holy Spirit to convince people to believe a certain way. The Bible states that the god of this world (Satan) has blinded the minds of the unbelieving so that they are not able to see the light of the gospel of Christ (2 Cor. 4:4). Satan effectively deceives, hardens, and blinds the hearts of people from seeing the truth. One of Satan's tactics is to use false religion and the philosophies of men to keep people from the truth. Colossians 2:8 states, "See to it that no one takes you captive through philosophy and empty deception, according to the tradition of men, according to the elementary principles of the world, rather than according to Christ."

"The Spirit of truth" is one of the names of the Holy Spirit. John 16:13 declares, "But when He, the Spirit of truth, comes, He will guide you into all the truth; for He will not speak on His own initiative, but whatever He hears, He will speak; and He will disclose to you what is to come." It is an essential ministry of the Holy Spirit to work in the minds and hearts of people to reveal truth. The Spirit of God will lead people into all truth.

The Spirit works to convince us of the reality of God's existence by various means. The Holy Spirit can use the order, beauty, and wonder of the world around us to give evidence of a Creator. Romans 1:19–20 proclaims, "because that which is known about God is evident within them; for God made it evident to them. For since the creation of the world His invisible attributes, His eternal power and divine nature, have been clearly seen, being understood through what has been made, so that they are without excuse." The Spirit of God can use man's conscience to convince him of the reality of God's existence. Romans 2:14–15 speaks about the conscience of man bearing witness: "For when Gentiles who do not have the Law do instinctively the things of the Law, these, not having the Law, are a law to themselves, in that they show the work of the Law written in their hearts, their conscience bearing witness and their thoughts alternately accusing or else defending them."

The Spirit of God can use miracles to convince people of God's existence. In his sermon on the day of Pentecost, Peter spoke of how Jesus was attested to people by the miracles, wonders and signs which God performed through Him in their midst (Acts 2:22). Acts 14:3 speaks about how signs and wonders performed by the Holy Spirit gave evidence of God's power. "Therefore, they spent a long time *there* speaking boldly *with reliance* upon the Lord, who was testifying to the word of His grace, granting that signs and wonders be done by their hands." The Spirit works to convince the world of the truth about Jesus Christ, "When the Helper comes, whom I will send to you from the Father, *that is* the Spirit of truth who proceeds from the Father, He will testify about Me" (John 15:26). How does the Holy Spirit speak to the unbeliever about Christ? The Spirit of God uses believers to deliver the message about Christ to the world. God enables believers to be witnesses of

Christ. "For you will be a witness for Him to all men of what you have seen and heard" (Acts. 22:15).

Christ promised that believers would receive power from the Holy Spirit to be witnesses to all the world: "but you shall receive power when the Holy Spirit has come upon you; and you shall be My witnesses both in Jerusalem, and in all Judea and Samaria, and even to the remotest part of the earth" (Acts 1:8). The Holy Spirit anoints believers to preach the Word of God. When this Word is preached, the Spirit illuminates that Word, which produces faith (Rom. 10:17). "So, faith *comes* from hearing, and hearing by the word of Christ." There are several essentials which convince a person about salvation. A person must believe the gospel, believe that Jesus Christ is Lord and that He is risen from the dead. Romans 10:9 states, "that if you confess with our mouth Jesus is Lord, and believe in your heart that God raised Him from the dead, you shall be saved."

The Holy Spirit's Work of Grace in Convicting People

Once the Holy Spirit begins to convince a person of the truth, that truth should also begin to have an impact on his heart. The Holy Spirit moves from convincing to convicting. Conviction is an awakened realization of a person's sinfulness. The Holy Spirit awakens people to the fact that they are sinners and are sinful by nature. The difference between convincing and conviction is that convincing is in the mind and conviction is in the heart. After Peter preached his sermon on the day of Pentecost, the Bible tells us that the hearers were convicted in their hearts, "pierced to the heart" (Acts 2:37). An illustration of the difference between convincing and convicting occurs when you are driving down a highway and see a speed limit sign. You are convinced of what the speed limit is because you know what the sign says. However, when you see a patrol car parked on the side of the highway and you know you were speeding, you will have an emotional reaction in your heart of guilt and a dreaded expectation of punishment.

The Holy Spirit brings sorrow in our hearts (conviction) for the purpose of bringing us to repentance: "For the sorrow that is according to *the will of* God produces a repentance without regret, *leading* to salvation, but the sorrow of the world produces death" (2 Cor. 7:10). The Holy Spirit brings godly sorrow through the human conscience. God has given all humans a conscience, which gives them warnings when they do something wrong. Romans 2:15 describes the conscience as the law written on human hearts. Yet, man's conscience can be desensitized, "seared in their own conscience," through sin and deception (1 Tim. 4:2). When the Holy Spirit begins to work in a person's heart, He revives the conscience so as to open up the possibility for a positive response to conviction. Because of man's fallen nature, no one has the ability, apart from the working of the Holy Spirit, to respond positively to God's conviction. However, with the assistance of the Holy Spirit, a person is freed to choose to respond correctly to conviction, thus being freed to choose to turn to God for forgiveness or to turn away from God with a sense of guilt and condemnation.

In the gospel of John 16:8–11, Christ describes three ways that the Holy Spirit brings conviction into the world, "And He, when He comes, will convict the world concerning sin and righteousness and judgment; concerning sin, because they do not believe in Me; and concerning righteousness, because I go to the Father and you no longer see Me; and concerning judgment, because the ruler of this world has been judged." The Holy Spirit will convict the world of sin, righteousness, and judgment. The Holy Spirit will convict the world of sin, "concerning sin, because they do not believe in Me" (John 16:9). One of the most important tasks that the Holy Spirit has is to bring people to a saving faith in Christ. To do this, He must first convict them of their unbelief in Christ and their need for repentance, which leads to faith in Christ. Many will not repent of their unbelief because of the hardness of their hearts. The Holy Spirit convicts of righteousness, "because I go to the Father and you no longer behold Me" (John 16:10).

The Holy Spirit not only convicts of sin but also of God's righteousness and holiness. Whenever a person experiences the presence of God, he will have an overwhelming sense of God's holiness and his own sinfulness (Isa. 6:5). The Holy Spirit will also convict of judgment: "and concerning judgment, because the ruler of this world has been judged" (John 16:11). In order to convict of judgment, the Holy Spirit stirs up a godly fear in one's heart. One aspect of the fear of the Lord is to fear His judgment. Being convicted of judgment means that one knows that sin and all that is evil will be punished. A person knows in his heart that Satan will be judged along with all those who follow him. When a person is convicted, he will recognize that God is perfectly justified in His judgment of sin and evil.

Conviction is an uncomfortable feeling that demands some kind of response to find relief. People try to find relief from a guilty conscience in ways that only make them feel worse. They can try to drown their guilt through the use of alcohol or drugs. Some try to forget their guilt through preoccupation with entertainment or with an obsession with material things. These approaches to dealing with the conviction of sin only cover the problem like a band-aid.

Our cars have warning lights on the dash that come on when there is a problem with the car. One of the most serious warning lights is the check engine light. If a person does not do something right away about a check engine light, it could result in a ruined engine. It is not a good idea to ignore the light. The warning light is not the problem but is indicator of something wrong. How foolish it would be to just cover the warning light with a piece of tape, thinking it solved the problem. God gave people a warning light called the conscience. We should not ignore our conscience when it is warning us.

Feelings of guilt are not the problem; the cause of the guilt is the problem. It is the desire of the Holy Spirit to use conviction to move people toward a point where they cry out in repentance for God's mercy and forgiveness. It is important not to confuse conviction and condemnation. Conviction makes people feel bad about their sin; whereas, condemnation makes people feel bad about themselves.

The Holy Spirit's Work of Grace in a Person's Conversion

Once a person has experienced the convincing and the conviction of the Holy Spirit, there comes a point when he must make a decision. A person can decide to yield to the Spirit's work in him or choose to resist the Spirit's work. The Holy Spirit will not violate a person's will by making him choose to yield or to resist. A person can choose to yield to or resist God's grace. If a person initially chooses to resist the Holy Spirit, the Spirit will continue with repeated attempts to convince and to convict. The Holy Spirit will be persistent in His efforts to gently encourage a person to turn to the Lord. However, each time a person resists the working of the Holy Spirit, his heart is further hardened.

In most cases, there is not just one instance when a person has the opportunity to respond correctly to the work of the Holy Spirit. There are some exceptions when a person never gets another opportunity, especially those who are near death. There is no opportunity for salvation after a person dies. The Bible declares that, "today is the day of salvation" (2 Cor. 6:2). It is of the utmost importance for people to yield quickly to the work of the Spirit to receive salvation because they do not have any guarantee of continued opportunities to respond correctly.

The moment of conversion occurs when a person comes to the point where he is willing to turn to God as a result of the Spirit's work of convincing and convicting. The Greek verb used for "to convert," *epistrephō*, (1994), means "to turn towards, to turn oneself around."[73] The Holy Spirit is not the one who is doing the turning or changing; He is there to assist the person in turning to God. The Holy Spirit frees the sinner to make a choice to turn to God or not. Conversion, specifically, turning to God, is a voluntary act in response to the presentation of the gospel. When this Greek verb, *convert*, is used to express action in the past (aorist tense), it indicates, "an immediate and decisive change, consequently upon a deliberate choice; conversion is a voluntary act in response to the presentation of truth."[74] The exhortations in Scripture to turn to God imply that a person is free to make that choice (Matt. 18:3; Acts 3:19). Conversion is the essential part that one plays in his salvation; however, this does not mean that a positive response in any way earns merit to receive God's grace. When a person turns to God, he demonstrates his willingness to receive God's grace.

As part of a person's turning to God in his conversion, he will verbalize what is on his heart and mind by calling out to the Lord for salvation. When Peter preached his sermon to the crowds gathered in the temple area on the day of Pentecost, he quoted a passage from the Old Testament: "And it shall be that everyone who calls on the name of the Lord will be saved" (Acts 2:21). When the apostle Paul wrote to the church in Rome, he explained the importance of calling on the Lord for salvation, "For there is no distinction between Jew and Greek; for the same *Lord* is Lord of all, abounding in riches for all who call on Him; for "Whoever will call on the name of the Lord will be saved." How then will they call on Him in whom they have not believed? How will they believe in Him whom they have not heard? And how will they hear without a preacher?" (Rom. 10:12–14).

Paul describes how a person comes to be saved in Romans 10:12–14. Paul moves in reverse order by starting with a person's salvation and working back from that point. Before a person can be saved, he needs to call on the Lord; before he can call on the Lord, he must believe. Before a person believes, he must hear the Word of God; people hear the Word of God as a result of someone preaching it. In these verses, we can observe that belief comes before someone calls on the Lord. The act of calling on the Lord is an outward expression of belief.

The Holy Spirit's Work of Grace in a Person's Confession

Confession is a critical part of salvation. The Holy Spirit brings a person to the point of confession as He assists in each step of salvation. After a person is convicted of his sins, the proper response is to acknowledge those sins first to himself and then to God. Confession is to admit or acknowledge something to be true; it moves one beyond thinking to expression. The Scriptures declare that there are two aspects of verbally confessing or acknowledging sin. The first is that a person must verbally acknowledge his sins. The tendency of human nature is to conceal sins from God and others. The thinking behind concealment of sin is that as long as sin is hidden, there are no consequences. Proverbs 28:11 tells us that concealing sins does not prevent adverse consequences, "He who conceals his transgressions will not prosper, but he who confesses and forsakes them will find compassion."

People resist admitting their sins because to do so is to take responsibility for them. Most often, people will deny their wrongdoing or put blame on someone or something else. Today, it is popular to even deny the existence of sin. Today's postmodern thinking proports that the concept of sin is just a social construct developed by Christianity to gain control over others. In postmodern thinking, the concept of right and wrong is purely a cultural thing, and every cultural group can develop its own standards of right or wrong. According to Postmodernists, no one cultural group can impose its cultural norms on others outside their group. All the standards held by each cultural group are considered equal to any other.

Postmodernists do not believe that there is a universal standard that applies to everyone. In other words, there is no such thing as sin but rather just different cultural views. The Postmodernists are wrong because there is a holy God who rules over all with His standard of holiness. All will be judged by God's standard, not the standards of men. As long as people will not take responsibility for their sins, they will not find forgiveness from God. Everyone is required to confess his sins in order to receive God's forgiveness. First John 1:9 assures a person of forgiveness when he confesses his sins: "If we confess our sins, He is faithful and righteous to forgive us our sins and to cleanse us from all unrighteousness."

Second, the Bible requires an open confession of Christ as Lord, "that if you confess with your mouth Jesus *as* Lord, and believe in your heart that God raised Him from the dead, you will be saved; for with the heart man believes, resulting in righteousness, and with the mouth he confesses, resulting in salvation" (Rom. 10:9–10). First Corinthians 12:3 explains that apart from the working of the Holy Spirit, no one can confess Jesus is Lord, "Therefore I make known to you that no one speaking by the Spirit of God says, 'Jesus is accursed'; and no one can say, 'Jesus is Lord,' except by the Holy Spirit."

The Holy Spirit's Work of Grace in a Believer's Spiritual Conception

Mankind is separated from God, and all are spiritually dead. Ephesians 2:1 declares, "And you were dead in your trespasses and sins." People are excluded from the life of God because of ignorance and the hardness of their hearts according to Ephesians 4:18, "being darkened in their understanding, excluded from the life of God because of the ignorance that is in them, because of the hardness of their heart." There is no spiritual life in a person apart from the working of the Holy Spirit. Colossians 2:13 describes the spiritual condition of man, "When you were dead in your transgressions and the uncircumcision of your flesh, He made you alive together with Him, having forgiven us all our transgressions."

When a person hears and receives God's Word in faith, the new (*zoe*) abundant life is implanted by the Holy Spirit. It is the Spirit of God that gives people life. "It is the Spirit who gives life; the flesh profits nothing; the words that I have spoken to you are spirit and are life" (John 6:63). Spiritual conception happens when the Holy Spirit implants the seed of God's Word into a person's heart. From the indwelling of the Holy Spirit, a new spiritual life is conceived in the believer, "for you have been born again not of seed which is perishable but imperishable, *that is,* through the living and enduring word of God" (1 Pet. 1:23).

The work of the Holy Spirit is to bring people to Jesus Christ who is the source of new spiritual life. Christ is the life as in John 11:25, "Jesus said to her, "I am the resurrection and the life; he who believes in Me will live even if he dies." First John 5:12 declares, "He who has the Son has the life; he who does not have the Son of God does not have the life." This new life is secured through faith in Christ, "so that whoever believes will in Him have eternal life" (John 3:15). Eternal life is the present possession of believers because of their relationship with Christ, "Truly, truly, I say to you, he who hears My word, and believes Him who sent Me, has eternal life, and does not come into judgment, but has passed out of death into life" (John 5:24).

As an agent of salvation, the Holy Spirit does the miraculous work of convincing, convicting, converting, enabling a person to call on the Lord for salvation, help in confession of sins, acknowledgment of Christ's lordship, and creation of a new spiritual life in a repentant, new believer. Apart from the work of the Holy Spirit, no one would experience salvation. No one is able to be saved on his own. It is only as a person responds correctly to the working of the Holy Spirit that he becomes a born-again child of God.

It is important to understand the position of the Spirit of God after a person experiences salvation. Before salvation, the Holy Spirit works with the person to bring him to Christ. Once a person accepts Christ and is born again, the Holy Spirit now resides within him. Once the Holy Spirit dwells within a person, He can begin His work of transformation. There is a wonderful and tremendous difference in a person's life once he has the Spirit of God dwelling in him. The indwelling Spirit of God will make incredible changes in the life of the born-again believer.

The Holy Spirit's Work of Grace in Confirming Believers

One of the greatest struggles a new believer has is the struggle with doubts. As the Spirit of God does His work of convincing believers of the truth, many doubts will subside and eventually be replaced with confident faith. There is one doubt that must be overcome in every believer's life. This one doubt can cause a great amount of consternation in a believer's spiritual walk. A person will remain destabilized and inconsistent in all aspects of his faith if he doubts his salvation. The person who doubts will be like a roller-coaster Christian whose spiritual life is up and down. James 1:6–8 describes the instability of a person who struggles with doubts: "But he must ask in faith without any doubting, for the one who doubts is like the surf of the sea, driven and tossed by the wind. For that man ought not to expect that he will receive anything from the Lord, *being* a double-minded man, unstable in all his ways."

At some point in time, every believer must come to a place of confidence about his salvation. If a believer does not come to a place of confident faith in his salvation, he will be held back from growing in Christ. Without the assurance of salvation, a believer will not progress in experiencing transformation. Doubt about one's salvation substantially hinders the working of the Spirit of God in the work of sanctification.

How does the Holy Spirit help a believer in Christ have confidence about being saved?

There are specific ways that the Spirit of God confirms a believer's faith concerning salvation. It is essential to possess a clear understanding of what is meant by "confirm." There are two Greek words used in the New Testament for "confirm" or "establish" that are relevant to this commentary on the Spirit's confirming work. One of the Greek words used for "confirm" is *bebaioō* (950), "to make firm, establish, make secure."[75] This word is used in 1 Corinthians 1:8 as confirming the saints, "who will also confirm you to the end, blameless in the day of our Lord Jesus Christ." This same Greek word is used in 2 Corinthians 1:21 where it is translated "establishes"; "Now He who establishes us with you in Christ and anointed us is God." This verse speaks about God establishing or confirming believers in Christ. The same Greek word (950) is used in a key verse concerning confirming of faith in Colossians 2:7, "having been firmly rooted *and now* being built up in Him and established in your faith, just as you were instructed, *and* overflowing with gratitude." Believers who are established in faith are those who are assured of their salvation.

The second Greek word used that is similar in meaning to "confirm" is *stērizō* (4741). *Vines Complete Expository Dictionary of Old and New Testament Words* describes the meaning of this Greek word as: "'to fix, make fast, to set" is used of "establishing" or "stablishing" (that is, the confirmation) of persons."[76] This Greek word is found in 1 Peter 5:10: "After you have suffered for a little while, the God of all grace, who called you to His eternal glory in Christ, will Himself perfect, confirm, strengthen *and* establish you." Another key verse using this term is Romans 16:25, "Now to Him who is able to establish you according to my gospel and the preaching of Jesus Christ, according to the revelation of the mystery which has been kept secret for long ages past."

These Greek words are used to describe the concept of being established or strengthened. Several versions of the Bible translate the same word as confirmed, established, or strengthened. To *confirm* or *establish* a believer's faith regarding salvation makes it secure, or established as a certainty. When a person's faith about his salvation is confirmed, such as in Colossians 2:7, he will possess a new assurance of the certainty of his salvation.

The dictionary definition of confirm that best aligns with its biblical meaning is: "to give new assurance of the validity of, removal of doubt by an authoritative statement or indisputable fact."[77] The second part of this definition, "removal of doubt by an authoritative statement or indisputable fact," describes exactly how the Holy Spirit works to confirm a believer's faith concerning his salvation. A new assurance comes through the Holy Spirit using authoritative statements of the Word of God to confirm a person's salvation. There are many authoritative Scriptures concerning how to be saved (Rom. 10:9–10; John 3:15; 5:24; 20:31; 1 Cor. 1:21). When a person hears and responds appropriately in faith and repentance to receive God's forgiveness, he can be assured that God will fulfill what He has promised. God is faithful to perform His Word; what He has promised He most assuredly will perform.

As a believer develops faith in God's trustworthy Word, the Holy Spirit will begin to remove doubts about salvation. What indisputable fact will help remove uncertainty about a person's salvation? When a person is born again, the Holy Spirit indwells him. When a person experiences this indwelling of the Spirit of God, he knows that something profound has happened to him. Romans 8:16 speaks about the witness of the Spirit that a person is a child of God, "The Spirit Himself bears witness with our spirit that we are children of God." The witness of the Spirit confirms that a person is a child of God. Second Corinthians

1:22 explains that the indwelling Spirit is God's down payment, guaranteeing all that God has promised to those who believe, "who also sealed us and gave *us* the Spirit in our hearts as a pledge." The presence of the Holy Spirit indwelling a person is the indisputable evidence that should remove all doubt about his salvation. Once a believer is established in his faith and assured of his salvation, the Spirit of God will be released to begin His work of sanctification.

Personal Application Concerning Salvation

1. Do you believe that God is calling you to receive salvation?

2. Have you been convinced of God's existence?

3. Do you believe in the truth of God's Word?

4. Do you believe that Jesus Christ is the Son of God and is risen from the dead?

5. Have you experienced conviction of sin in your life?

6. Have you ever confessed your sins to God?

7. Have you confessed Jesus Christ as your Lord?

8. Have you experienced a spiritual change in your life? If so, in what way has your life changed?

9. Have you repented of your sins? If you have, do you believe that God has forgiven you?

10. How would you describe your relationship with God?

11. Do you sense that the Spirit of God indwells you?

12. Do you have confidence in your salvation?

CHAPTER 14

The Agent of Sanctification

The Holy Spirit's work of grace in salvation is only the beginning of what grace can do in a believer's life. People often think that God's grace has more to do with their salvation than with how they live out their Christian lives. People must realize the grace of God is not just the unmerited favor of God; it is also power of God to live a godly life. Titus 2:11–12 affirms that God's grace helps people to deny ungodliness and worldly desires and live a righteous and godly life: "For the grace of God has appeared, bringing salvation to all men, instructing us to deny ungodliness and worldly desires and to live sensibly, righteously and godly in the present age."

The apostle Paul told the Corinthian church that God is able to make all grace abound to them. The result of God's grace abounding in them is that the Corinthians would experience sufficiency in everything and that they would have an abundance of power to perform every good deed: "And God is able to make all grace abound to you, so that always having all sufficiency in everything, you may have an abundance for every good deed" (2 Cor. 9:8). Do you grasp the magnitude of what Paul is saying? Second Corinthians 9:8 declares that God's grace will always give believers sufficiency in everything. The grace of God enables believers to have all the power necessary to live a godly, sanctified life. A person is saved by God's grace and is likewise sanctified by God's grace.

From the very moment that a person is saved, the Holy Spirit initiates the work of sanctification. The work of sanctification is attributed to the Holy Spirit (1 Pet. 1:2). Through the working of grace, the Holy Spirit is the agent of sanctification. The Holy Spirit's work of grace in sanctification differs from His work of grace in salvation as sanctification is distinct from salvation. Even though there are some similarities between salvation and sanctification, there are many more distinctions than similarities.

It is important to understand the meaning of sanctification so a person can better comprehend this distinguishing work of the Spirit of God. It is of utmost importance to have a full understanding of sanctification because that is key to understanding how transformation occurs in a believer. Studying the scriptural usage of the term *sanctification* is key to understanding its meaning. First, the term sanctification can be used to describe a separation. Sanctification means to separate from something and then be dedicated to something. Sanctification is being set apart for sacred use. In the Old Testament, certain items were set apart to be used solely for the temple (Exod. 40:10, 11; Num. 7:1, 2). Sanctified items were considered holy and could not be used for common use outside the temple. This concept of being set apart for sacred use or for a dedicated purpose is very similar to the concept of consecration. To consecrate something is to make or declare sacred. To consecrate something is, "to make or declare sacred; esp. to devote irrevocably to the worship of God."[78] An individual is set aside for God's purposes at the moment of salvation.

The second element of sanctification used in Scripture is the impartation of Christ's holiness at salvation. At salvation, Jesus Christ imputes His righteousness to the new believer. Second Corinthians 1:30 states, "But by His doing you are in Christ Jesus, who became to us wisdom from God, and righteousness and sanctification, and redemption." At the beginning of Paul's letter to the Corinthians, he addressed the believers as those who have been sanctified in Christ, "To the church of God which is at Corinth, to those who have been sanctified in Christ Jesus, saints by calling, with all who in every place call on the name of our Lord Jesus Christ, their *Lord* and ours" (1 Cor. 1:2). This righteousness is obtained by grace through faith in Christ, "to open their eyes so that they may turn from darkness to light and from the dominion of Satan to God, that they may receive forgiveness of sins and an inheritance among those who have been sanctified by faith in Me'" (Acts 26:18).

There is an immediate act of sanctification when a person is set apart unto God by the Holy Spirit through his personal faith in Christ. The believer is sanctified through the blood of Christ (Heb. 13:12). The sanctified believer is reckoned holy by God (Rom. 4:24). God looks upon those who are in Christ as covered by the righteousness of Christ because of grace. This initial type of sanctification is described by some as positional sanctification. A believer is considered holy before God when he is in Christ. This is evident in the naming of all born-again believers as saints (Rom. 1:7; 1 Cor. 1:2; Eph. 1:1; Phil. 1:1; Col. 1:1).

The third use of the word *sanctification* is the concept that sanctification involves purification from all that is evil. Sanctification, in this case, incorporates the idea of separating from evil. Thus, there is both a negative and positive aspect of sanctification. The negative aspect is the removal of evil; the positive side of sanctification is the development of Christlike character. This third use of the word involves the negative aspect of sanctification. The separation is an act of obedience of the believer. This is not something God does but something the believer must do. An example of this is when Old Testament priests were required to sanctify themselves before approaching God (Exod. 19:22). Similarly, believers are not to be bound together with unbelievers (2 Cor. 6:14) but are to separate themselves from the ungodly (2 Cor. 6:17). Believers are to separate themselves from their former way of life as Ephesians 4:22 declares: "that, in reference to your former manner of life, you lay aside the old self, which is being corrupted in accordance with the lusts of deceit." Believers are to separate themselves from evil practices, "Therefore, if anyone cleanses himself from these *things,* he will be a vessel for honor, sanctified, useful to the Master, prepared for every good work" (2 Tim. 2:21).

Since this aspect of sanctification requires the believer's obedience, it necessitates a great amount of assistance from the Holy Spirit. Even though obedience is required, God's grace will always be sufficient. God's grace will enable a person to be obedient. This type of sanctification is not a one-time act of obedience but an ongoing, developing practice of obedience through the help of the Holy Spirit. This kind of sanctification is a lifelong process that requires the Spirit's constant help. Cleansing from evil by the grace of God is an integral part of the process of transformation.

The fourth use of the word sanctification deals with the concept of being conformed to the image of Christ (Rom. 8:29), "For whom He foreknew, He also predestined to become conformed to the image of His Son, that He might be the first-born, among many brethren." This type of sanctification is a lifelong process of becoming more like Christ every day. This is the positive aspect of sanctification. The initial act of sanctification at salvation dealt with the believer's standing before God. Through faith in Christ, a believer is declared righteous in Christ. This fourth aspect of sanctification focuses on the development of the believer into Christlikeness or the believer's actual spiritual condition. One type of sanctification deals with the believer's standing with God while the other type of sanctification deals with his walk with God. God the Father views believers as holy through Christ's righteousness. The Holy Spirit's work of grace in sanctification enables believers to live out that righteousness. Galatians 5:22–23 lists the fruit of the Spirit: love, joy, peace, patience, kindness, goodness, faithfulness, gentleness, and self-control, which are a result of the Spirit's work of grace in the believer's process of growth. Notice that these character traits of the Holy Spirit are called "fruit." Fruit is a result of gradual growth in contrast to the gifts of the Spirit that can be given immediately.

The third and fourth usages of the word sanctification involve a lifelong process, as a lifelong work of grace. This does not mean that a believer will reach a point of sinless perfection anytime in this life. As long as a person is alive, he will still be a work in progress. Only when the believer meets Christ face to face will the Holy Spirit's work of sanctification be complete. Many of the sanctifying works of grace may occur simultaneously. Ideally, it is best to have all these functions of the Spirit in sanctification working simultaneously throughout the life of the believer.

The Holy Spirit's Work of Grace in Counseling Believers

In Isaiah 11:2, the Holy Spirit is called a number of names: Spirit of wisdom, Spirit of understanding, Spirit of counsel, the Spirit of strength, and the Spirit of knowledge. As the Spirit of counsel, the Holy Spirit teaches knowledge, understanding, and wisdom. As the Spirit of counsel, the Spirit of God instructs and guides believers. John 14:26 reveals that the Holy Spirit will teach believers all things, "But the Helper, the Holy Spirit, whom the Father will send in My name, He will teach you all things, and bring to your remembrance all that I said to you." The Holy Spirit teaches a believer in various ways. The Holy Spirit can teach directly when one reads the Word of God or indirectly when one hears a sermon. The teaching of the Holy Spirit goes beyond just helping mental comprehension. The Spirit of God will illuminate a believer's understanding of Scriptures and open up a whole new understanding of them. Believers will have a much greater insight not only into the meaning of Scripture but also into its application in daily life. It is very important to rely on the Spirit whenever the Scriptures are read or studied.

The Spirit can teach through Spirit-anointed preaching and teaching. The Spirit of God can anoint a person to preach or teach beyond his natural or intellectual ability. The apostle Paul spoke about reliance on the Holy Spirit in his preaching and teaching:

> And when I came to you, brethren, I did not come with superiority of speech or of wisdom, proclaiming to you the testimony of God. For I determined to know nothing among you except Jesus Christ, and Him crucified. I was with you in weakness and in fear and in much trembling, and my message and my preaching were not in persuasive words of wisdom, but in demonstration of the Spirit and of power. (1 Cor. 2:1–4)

The Spirit of God teaches both through anointing the preacher/teacher and through illuminating the comprehension of the listener. The teaching of the Spirit works in both aspects of communication both in the one who transmits the message and the one who receives the message. It is important that those who are listening to preaching/teaching always be tuned into what the Spirit is saying to them during a message or lesson. Whenever the Word of God is presented, the Spirit desires to help a person understand its meaning and personal application to his life.

In addition to teaching, the Holy Spirit counsels by giving guidance to believers. There is a great need for guidance in people's lives. So many voices clamor to give guidance. There are many who claim to be the right way or in the truth. How is a person to know the truth? The Scriptures are God's primary source of guidance. The Spirit of God will give believers guidance through the Word of God. The Psalmist declared that God's Word was, "a lamp unto his feet and the light unto his path" (Ps. 119:105).

Jesus Christ stated in John 16:13 that the Spirit will guide us into all truth, "But when He, the Spirit of truth, comes, He will guide you into all the truth; for He will not speak on His own initiative, but whatever He hears, He will speak; and He will disclose to you what is to come." The Holy Spirit will reveal truth to people so they can understand it; and, even more importantly, the Spirit helps the believer to know the truth by helping him experience the truth. To experience the truth, one must have more than intellectual understanding; one will experience the truth when he obeys it. The Holy Spirit will not continue to reveal truth if there is no obedience to what has already been revealed. As a believer puts into practice the truth he has learned, the Spirit will continue to reveal more truth.

The Holy Spirit gives counsel by helping believers to understand God's ways. The apostle Paul explained to the Corinthians how necessary the Holy Spirit is in comprehending God's ways (1 Cor. 2:10–14). Paul explained that the natural mind cannot understand spiritual things (1 Cor. 2:14). It is only through the Spirit that spiritual things are revealed (1 Cor. 2:12–13). Believers must be totally dependent on the Spirit to reveal the truth of God's ways.

On a more personal level, the Holy Spirit can guide a believer though the witness of the Spirit to his human spirit. When a believer walks in obedience to God's will, he will sense a peace in his spirit. When a believer is out of God's will, he will be grieved in his spirit. Over the fifty-seven years of being saved, I have learned how the Spirit of God leads me when I am searching for His direction. I seek God's direction in many things, but the one thing I seek every week is for God's direction in my sermon preparation. I always preach from God's Word and when I preach, I incorporate numerous Scriptures. I seek God for what topic or book of the Bible He wants me to speak on for a particular sermon series.

There have been times when I did not know what God wanted me to preach about, so I sought God in prayer. Sometimes the answer came to me while I was praying and other times when I was studying. Every time I believed that God had shown me the answer, I felt an excitement in my spirit. It was the witness of the Spirit of God within me letting me know that I was on target. God has given me direction in many other matters through the witness of His Spirit.

I want to caution people to always confirm personal direction with Scripture and guidance from mature spiritual leaders, and not to solely trust the witness of the Spirit on major decisions. This personal level of guidance must always be in agreement with God's Word. The Holy Spirit will not contradict Himself; the written Word and His personal word as a witness to a person's spirit will be in agreement.

Application

1. Do you ask for the Holy Spirit's help when reading the Bible?

2. Do you ask the Holy Spirit to show personal applications whenever you read or study God's Word?

3. If you preach or teach God's Word, do you ask God for the anointing of the Holy Spirit?

4. Do you ask for God's guidance when you are making important decisions?

5. Are you obeying the truth that you have learned from the Bible?

    If not, what are some areas in which you need God's help to be obedient?

The Holy Spirit's Work of Grace in Helping Believers Communicate with God

Learning how to pray with the assistance of the Holy Spirit is essential for having a strong and effective prayer life. There is a lot of prayer in religion but most is without any power. Prayer can be just the empty repetition of words having no ability to have an impact on a person's spiritual life. Learning how to pray with the assistance of the Holy Spirit opens up many ways for the Spirit to work in one's life. If a person does not know how to hear from the Spirit of God, he will not be able to benefit from all that the Spirit wants to do in him. The more a person is able to hear what the Spirit of God is saying to him, the more he will be able to cooperate with the Spirit's work of sanctification.

Without the assistance of the Holy Spirit, believers will struggle to pray effectively. Believers face various challenges in prayer. One of those challenges is not knowing what to pray about. Many Christians run out of things to pray for after a few minutes. There will be times that believers will not know what to pray for because they do not know the will of God in a particular situation. Besides not knowing what to pray about, there are physical and mental limitations when believers pray.

When Christ was praying through the night in the Garden of Gethsemane, He was disappointed with His disciples' failure to pray. Time after time, Christ would find the disciples asleep after He had spent an hour in prayer. Christ told the disciples that their spirits were willing, but their flesh was weak, or a hindrance to prayer, "Keep watching and praying, that you may not enter into temptation; the spirit is willing, but the flesh is weak" (Matt. 26:41). Physical limitations due to tiredness can certainly hinder prayer. One of the most significant struggles in prayer is mental distraction. It is a common occurrence that when one begins to pray, a parade of distracting thoughts comes flooding in. This parade of thoughts will not be things one should be praying about but all sorts of other things with which people's minds are preoccupied. My problem is usually thoughts about things I need to do for that day or for an entire week. My mind keeps making a list.

The Holy Spirit can help believers to overcome these obstacles so they can be effective in prayer. With the Holy Spirit's help, believers can experience dynamic prayer in numerous ways. The Holy Spirit can help believers know what to pray for by putting thoughts in their minds regarding people and situations. A believer who is in tune with the leading of the Spirit will be directed by the Spirit in intercession. I have found it so much easier to rely on the Spirit in prayer. An experienced intercessor can pray for hours at times without running out of prayer needs due to the Spirit's enablement. We do not always know what the will of God is in certain situations, but the Holy Spirit will direct us to pray according to God's will.

First Corinthians 14:2 explains how the Spirit of God enables the believer to pray to God from his spirit, "For he who speaks in a tongue does not speak to men but to God, for no one understands *him;* however, in the spirit he speaks mysteries" (1 Cor. 14:2, NKJV). Being empowered by the Spirit of God to pray from one's own spirit opens up a whole new dimension of prayer. Being able to pray from one's spirit directly to God helps one overcome the hindrances of the weakness of the flesh and mind. The apostle Paul explained to the church at Rome how the Spirit helps believers in their weaknesses in prayer, "Likewise the Spirit also helps in our weaknesses. For we do not know what we should pray for as we ought, but the Spirit Himself makes intercession for us with groanings which cannot be uttered. Now He who searches the hearts knows what the mind of the Spirit *is*, because He makes intercession for the saints according to *the will of* God" (Rom. 8:26–27, NKJV).

I can give personal testimony to how the Holy Spirit has grown my prayer life. Throughout each day, I pray from my mind and my spirit. Frequently, through each day, I pray for things that are on my mind and, at other times, I just pray in the Spirit, not knowing exactly what I am praying about. I may know for whom I am praying in the Spirit but not the details of what I am praying. I try to put into practice praying without ceasing. I strive to be in constant communication with God daily.

Another challenge to praying is being motivated to pray. When a person has struggled with weaknesses in his prayer life, he can get discouraged and lose his motivation to pray. One can ask God to motivate him by the Spirit. The Holy Spirit will help believers to be more motivated to pray. If believers rely on their flesh to motivate them to pray, they will continually lack motivation. The flesh will always prefer to do something else like watch TV, play computer games, go on Facebook, or just get busy doing things that need to get done. When a person learns to rely on the leading of the Spirit of God for motivation, he will indeed be praying more often and with greater passion.

Communication with God is not just talking to God; it includes God communicating with us. Prayer is two-way communication. The Holy Spirit not only helps the believer to talk to God but also to hear from God. The Holy Spirit can converse with the born-again believer, whom He indwells. The Spirit of God can speak to the believer's mind and his spirit. Romans 8:16 states, "The Spirit Himself bears witness with our spirit that we are the children of God." "Bearing witness" is a form of communication between the Spirit of God and a person's spirit.

How are believers to know when the Spirit of God is speaking to them? Every believer must learn to distinguish between various thoughts that come into his mind. Thoughts can come from oneself, from other people, from Satan, or from God. How can the believer discern the source of his thoughts? Over many years of pastoral ministry, I have had quite a few people come to me and claim that the Lord was telling them to do something. If the person was a mature Christian, I would give more credibility to his claim. However, when immature Christians make this claim, I tend to receive it with caution and with some people even skepticism. Immature Christians usually do not yet possess the needed discernment to differentiate the source of their thoughts.

There are principles that one can use to know the voice of God in one's thoughts. First, and most importantly, the Holy Spirit will never contradict Himself nor will He contradict the written Word of God. Believers must immediately reject anything that is contrary to Scripture since those thoughts are from another source. Second, when the Spirit of God is speaking to a person, He is comforting rather than condemning. Who is the condemner of believers? It is not God; He does not condemn those who have faith in Christ, "There is therefore now no condemnation for those who are in Christ Jesus" (Rom. 8:2). Satan is the condemner (Rev. 12:10). When one hears condemning thoughts, it is not God speaking and must therefore be rejected. When the Holy Spirit speaks into our thoughts, He is not harsh, but gentle. The Holy Spirit softly reminds believers of what He desires for them to do or not do.

Third, there will a peace or a witness in a believer's spirit that this is the Holy Spirit speaking. When a believer is sensitive to the Spirit, he will pay attention to what he senses in his spirit. If his spirit is uncomfortable or ill at ease, he knows that something is wrong or is not in agreement with the Spirit of God. If there is an excitement in a believer's spirit, that can be an indication of what God wants.

The fourth criterion for discerning God's leading is that the Spirit of God will give confirmation in several ways. God's leading can come when a Scripture just jumps off the page and speaks to his spirit. Confirmation can come through consulting one's spiritual leaders. Confirmation can come through specific circumstances as when God opens and closes doors of opportunity. There will be an accumulation of confirmations from a number of sources that will bring surety to the right decision. The believer must be assured that if he is sincerely seeking to do God's will, the Holy Spirit will bring him to a point of being convinced that he is being led by God.

Application

1. Is your prayer life all that it should be?

2. Are you struggling with weaknesses in prayer?

3. What are some of the struggles you have in prayer?

4. Have you asked God to help you pray more effectively?

5. Have you ever prayed in the Spirit? If not, do you want to be able to pray in the Spirit?

The Holy Spirit's Work of Grace in Consecrating Believers

What is the meaning of being consecrated to God? I selected several definitions from Webster's dictionary similar to the biblical definition of consecration: (1) "To make or declare sacred, dedicated to the service of a deity;" (2) To devote or dedicate to some cause or purpose"[79]; (3) "To devote to a purpose with or as if with deep solemnity of dedication."[80] Synonyms for consecration include full devotion or full commitment.

The scriptural meaning of consecration is similar to the concept of sanctification. With both consecration and sanctification, there is a separation from all that displeases God and being set apart for the exclusive service and purpose of God. Sanctification is mainly what God does in a believer; whereas, consecration is what a believer does for God. In the Old Testament, God instructed the Israelites to consecrate every firstborn male (Exod. 13:2), all the furnishings of the temple (Exod. 40:9), and themselves (Lev. 20:7; 1 Chron. 15:12).

When one consecrates himself to God, he purposes to turn from all else and to give himself exclusively and wholeheartedly to love and serve God. This type of dedication is what the Lord desires for all those who believe in Him. Deuteronomy 6:5 clearly states the Lord's expectation from those who are His people: "You shall love the Lord your God with all your heart and with all your soul and with all your might." Deuteronomy 10:12 also states, "Now, Israel, what does the Lord your God require from you, but to fear the Lord your God, to walk in all His ways and love Him, and to serve the Lord your God with all your heart and with all your soul." From these Scriptures, we clearly see that the Lord God expects full devotion to Him. God is very displeased with half-hearted commitment. A work of grace that the Holy Spirit desires to complete in each believer is to bring him to the point of full surrender to Christ.

Apart from religious connotations, this type of full devotion or commitment to some purpose or cause is actually quite common. In order for anyone to achieve excellence, he must become fully devoted to that purpose. Athletes who desire to be the best give full dedication to their physical training. I was involved in sports during my junior high and high school years. I was on the varsity basketball team, track team, football team, and tennis team. All my coaches expected every team member to give his best effort or be taken off the team. My football coach was the most demanding of all. He demanded that each player give 110 percent effort. I believe what the coach meant was for each of us to give his very best effort and then go beyond that. If the football coach ever thought you were not giving your best, he would have you sit on the bench and not be allowed to play in that game. We can see the same kind of dedication in education. A student who desires to excel in his field of study must fully commit to studying and doing all that is required to achieve the desired degree. Likewise, a business person who desires to excel fully commits himself to do whatever it takes to achieve success in his business.

A couple must make at least two decisions about their relationship before they decide to get married. First, they must purpose to love each other with all their hearts. Second, they have to turn from any affection for anyone else. The love of a married couple must be exclusive and wholehearted. This is exactly what should happen when a person comes to know Christ as his Savior. Jesus Christ is to become the love of a believer's life by loving Him with all his heart, soul, mind, and strength. Believers are to be exclusive in their level of devotion to Christ. Believers in Christ must come to a decision to pursue loving and serving God with all their heart and to stop loving the things of this world.

The Holy Spirit works in the believer's heart to bring him to a point where he is willing to consecrate himself to Christ.

> *For full transformation to happen in a believer's life, he must come to the point of surrendering to the lordship of Christ.*

First Peter 3:15 admonishes believers to set apart Christ in their hearts as Lord of their lives, "But sanctify Christ as Lord in your hearts, always *being* ready to make a defense to everyone who asks you to give an account for the hope that is in you, yet with gentleness and reverence."

The Holy Spirit does a great amount of work in assisting believers in their struggle to become and remain fully consecrated to Christ. One of the problems that believers struggle with is double-mindedness.

Believers struggle with whom they will love; they struggle to either love and serve self or to love and serve Christ. Believers in Christ must decide to either pursue what pleases the flesh or pursue what pleases Christ. A person will either love God, or he will love what the world loves. "Do not love the world nor the things in the world. If anyone loves the world, the love of the Father is not in him. For all that is in the world, the lust of the flesh and the lust of the eyes and the boastful pride of life, is not from the Father, but is from the world" (1 John 2:15–16).

Another cause of struggling to fully surrender to Christ is the problem with doubt and lack of trust in God. If a believer is not fully convinced that God is capable of caring for him, he will be reluctant to yield to God. A good example of being reluctant to surrender because of lack of trust happened to me when I was in the hospital a number of years ago. While I was in the hospital for over a week, I had numerous nurses draw blood from me. After a week of drawing my blood, it became more difficult to find a vein from which to draw blood. Most of the nurses were pretty good at drawing blood, but there was one nurse who had great difficulty finding a vein in my arm. I hate needles to start with, so I was very reluctant to allow that nurse to draw blood from me. As she kept trying and made several misses, I realized that this was not an experienced nurse but a nurse in training who was being supervised by a veteran nurse. I asked the supervising nurse if she would draw the blood instead; I was much more confident in yielding my arm to the experienced nurse than I was to the trainee. This is how it is with trusting in God; if one does not trust Him, he will be reluctant to surrender to Him. Believers must come to the point in their lives where they trust Christ enough to surrender fully to Him.

The Holy Spirit works to create the desire for consecration in each believer. Consecration is never forced on anyone. Even though God is fully worthy of all of humanity's full devotion, God wants it to be a person's choice to consecrate himself. The Holy Spirit will not violate a person's will. There will, however, come a time in the future where everyone will be forced to acknowledge Christ is Lord, "So that at the name of Jesus every knee will bow, of those who are in heaven and on earth and under the earth, and that every tongue will confess that Jesus Christ is Lord, to the glory of God the Father" (Phil. 2:10–11). It much better to willingly acknowledge Christ as Lord now in this life than to be forced to acknowledge Him in the next life.

The Holy Spirit helps create the desire for consecration in the believer in several ways. First, the Holy Spirit helps believers develop a distaste for sin. The Spirit opens believers' eyes to see the destructiveness of sin and how their sin grieves God. The Holy Spirit gives believers a godly sorrow, which should lead them to repentance. The Holy Spirit helps turn the believer away from sin and to God. As part of His turning believers to God, He helps develop believers' love for God. The Spirit of God brings believers to the place where they want to surrender to God in their love for Him.

A good example of this kind of devotion is found in the practice of becoming a bond servant. In biblical times, a bond servant was a person who once served as a slave by force, but when he gained his freedom, willingly chose to remain a servant of his master. Believers who once were slaves to sin now can choose to willingly serve their new master. "*Act* as free men, and do not use your freedom as a covering for evil but *use it* as bondslaves of God" (1 Pet. 2:16).

Application

1. Are you torn between your love for God and your love for the things of this world?

2. Does a lack of trust in God cause you to hold back from fully surrendering to Him?

3. If you have a lack of trust in God, what do you think is the cause of this lack of trust?

4. Do you have a growing distaste for sin?

5. Have you come to the place where you can fully surrender to Christ as your Lord? If not, what is holding you back?

The Holy Spirit's Work of Grace in Connecting Believers

Being connected to a local church is an essential part of how the Holy Spirit supplies God's grace to believers. I have previously shown how gifts of service operate in the context of the local church. A lack of connection to a local church greatly diminishes the benefits a person can receive from the gifts of service. The Holy Spirit connects believers by drawing them together in the spirit of unity: "Being diligent to preserve the unity of the Spirit in the bond of peace" (Eph. 4:3). Believers are baptized into the body of Christ at the point of salvation. "For by one Spirit we were all baptized into one body, whether Jews or Greeks, whether slaves or free, and we were all made to drink of one Spirit" (1 Cor. 12:13). This refers to a person becoming part of the spiritual body of Jesus Christ (the Church) through his faith in Christ. A believer's connection to the body of Christ must go beyond what he knows by faith to what he experiences in a more practical connection with the body of Christ. The Holy Spirit works to draw believers into becoming part of the expression of the body of Christ, which is a local church.

When I write about being connected with other believers, I mean developing close relationships with believers who come together regularly to hear God's Word, worship, pray, fellowship, and serve one another. Some think that being connected to a church is synonymous with being a member of a church. In many cases, membership does help a person become more committed to local church but not necessarily. In some churches, being a member means no more than having one's name on the membership roll. The Holy Spirit wants to connect believers to a body of believers, not to a building. The church is people who are committed to each other wherever they may meet. Being connected to a body of believers means that believers come to know each other, love each other, help each other, and serve together in ministry. The Holy Spirit wants to bond believers together like parts of a body.

A major strategy of Satan is to prevent believers from connecting together with other believers. Satan does everything he can to divide and scatter believers. First, Satan does all he can to keep Christians from coming to church. There is a growing trend in America to be unchurched, even among those who consider themselves Christians.

People have developed an aversion to "organized religion." Many who call themselves Christians are convinced that they have no need of church.

Satan uses various tactics to keep people from church. A primary tactic that Satan uses is to cause offenses to happen between church members so they will never come to church again. People may go to several churches and find that there are imperfect people in all of them. Rather than learning to forgive and grow in love, many give up going to church. The work of the Holy Spirit enables believers to act in love rather than out of the flesh. Believers have an opportunity to grow in love and patience when they allow the Holy Spirit to work in them when offenses come.

Staying connected with other believers requires growth in godly character. Many will never grow in godly character because they will not try to work out their conflicts with others in the church. Getting to know other believers is like looking into a mirror. The more people get to know each other, the more they discover both their strengths and weaknesses. When people get to know each other, they see each other's deficiencies of character. Conflict in a church is usually due to a lack to character qualities such as love, patience, kindness, and gentleness. The problem comes when the persons involved in the conflict only see the character deficiencies of the other person or persons. It is the intent of the Holy Spirit to use this mirror to show believers where they need to grow in character. Character qualities, such as humility, gentleness, tolerance, and patience, are needed to have unity in a church. "With all humility and gentleness, with patience, showing tolerance for one another in love, being diligent to preserve the unity of the Spirit in the bond of peace" (Eph. 4:2–3). These character qualities build unity through the inner working of the Spirit. Nevertheless, believers must cooperate with the Holy Spirit by being diligent to preserve the unity of the Spirit.

Any Christian who is staying away from church is resisting the Spirit and is falling prey to Satan's tactics. If a person has been offended in some way, he will need to forgive the offender. Believers are to forgive each other just as God has forgiven them. "And do not grieve the Holy Spirit of God, by whom you were sealed for the day of redemption. Let all bitterness, and wrath, and anger and clamor and slander be put away from you, along with all malice. And be kind to one another, tender-hearted, forgiving each other, just as God in Christ also has forgiven you" (Eph. 4:30–32).

The Spirit of God is grieved when believers do not dwell together in unity. It is the task of the Spirit to bring believers together in lasting relationships in a local church. Believers are not to continually jump from church to church because this hinders them from developing close relationships with other Christians. The Spirit wants to use close and lasting relationships with other believers to strengthen and help transform believers. The Spirit is grieved when believers are divided or avoid getting close to other believers. It is when believers bind together that they can most effectively help each other grow in Christ and be transformed into Christ's likeness.

Application

1. Are you connected to a group of Christian believers?

2. Have you been offended by someone in a church?

3. How did you respond to that offense? Did you just leave the church or did you go in love to be reconciled to your fellow believers?

4. If you are connected to a church, are you doing all you can to preserve the unity of the Spirit?

The Holy Spirit's Work of Grace in Correcting Believers

My experience has been that most people do not respond well to correction or criticism. Many times, as a pastor, I have gone in love and gentleness to people attending the church to correct something. Even this gentle approach does not always lead to the proper response to correction. In some cases, people took offense and left the church. None of us likes correction or criticism, and we feel that our lives would be just fine without them. I must admit that there were times in my early years of pastoring that I was not very receptive to criticism either. Most people become defensive and withdraw when they are corrected or criticized. Some take any correction as a personal attack and retaliate by going on the offensive to protect themselves.

Some years ago, I drove a school bus route that followed another bus for several blocks. The bus driver picked up a certain student and moved up the block to pick up other students. Almost every day, a student would throw a banana peel out of the back window of the bus. So, one day I mentioned to the bus driver what was happening. I thought she might not know what was going on. I was surprised by her response. She yelled at me and told me off, asserting that there was nothing wrong with one of her students throwing out a banana peel because it was biodegradable. As believers in Christ, we are not to react to correction or criticism in this way. We need to understand that God can use correction and even criticism for our good.

To correct implies taking actions to remove errors, faults, deviations, and defects. Correction is being shown the need to change or to correct something. The definition of correction is: "a bringing into conformity with a standard "[81] Correction usually comes from someone who is an authority in our lives or a person to whom we give permission to speak into our lives. To criticize implies finding fault with something or someone. Criticism often comes from our peers or those under our authority.

What does the Holy Spirit want to correct in believers? The definition: "to alter or adjust so to bring to some standard or required condition" is exactly what the Spirit of God desires to do in each believer. There are no exceptions; every believer will go through a lifelong process of correction. Do not think of it as a negative thing, but rather as something uniquely positive for spiritual growth. The Spirit works is to alter (sanctify) by removing everything that is not according to God's standard of holiness in every believer. The Spirit works to sanctify by helping each believer to remove sin from his life.

The Holy Spirit corrects believers regarding their sin by first exposing it. Many new believers are shocked by an unaccustomed awareness of sin in their lives. Recent believers may feel that they must not be saved if they have so much sin in their lives. The sin that they now see was there before their salvation, but they are just now recognizing it. Why does this happen? What has happened is that the Holy Spirit that now resides in them is a light that exposes sin. Before salvation, each person's soul is like a dark room full of trash. The unbeliever does not see the trash (sin) because he is blinded by spiritual darkness. But when the Holy Spirit comes into a person's life, the light of righteousness is turned on and consequently a person sees his true spiritual condition.

Exposure of sin is just the first part of the Spirit's correction. After exposure of sin, the Holy Spirit brings a godly sorrow so believers can repent of any sins that are brought to their attention. In order for correction to be beneficial, it is absolutely necessary for the believer to repent of the sins that have been exposed. When a believer does not repent when the Spirit exposes sin, this grieves the Spirit and hinders His work of sanctification. If a believer does not repent after being corrected of sin, his heart will eventually become hardened through the deceitfulness of sin, "But encourage one another day after day, as long as it is still called "Today," lest anyone of you be hardened by the deceitfulness of sin" (Heb. 3:13).

In addition to the removal of sin, the Holy Spirit desires for believers to experience spiritual growth in godly character. The Spirit's work of developing Christlike character is the positive aspect of sanctification. Remember, sanctification is not just the removal of sin; it is also the development of godly character. The Holy Spirit is concerned about more than just the removal of sin. The Holy Spirit desires to correct deficiencies in character. Everyone has areas of character that need to be improved. Unless flaws are exposed, they will never be corrected. How does the Holy Spirit expose these areas of personal weakness?

Weaknesses are revealed in times of testing. A person can believe that he is strong in certain character qualities, but he can never really know until he is tested. The Holy Spirit will expose deficiencies of character through trying circumstances. It is only when gold is tested by fire that the impurities come to the surface. Likewise, it is true that when fiery trails come into believers' lives that impurities surface. For example, a person may believe that he has a lot of patience until he is put into circumstances that require a great amount of patience. A person may believe that he has a great amount of love for people, but when the Holy Spirit puts people who are difficult to love in his life, he will realize just how little love he possesses.

After the Spirit of God exposes weak areas in character development, He encourages the believer to cooperate by getting help in improving those deficiencies. There will always be areas in one's character that need more development or refining. The result of the work of the Holy Spirit in changing a person's character is described as the "fruit of the Spirit." Galatians 5:22-23 lists the fruit of the Spirit: love, joy, peace, patience, kindness, goodness, faithfulness, gentleness, and self-control. Change in character does not come as a result of receiving a gift from God but, rather, as a gradual development through cooperation with the correction of the Holy Spirit. When one is receptive to the correction of the Holy Spirit, he will keep becoming more like Christ until he meets Christ in heaven.

The Holy Spirit can use various methods for correcting believers. The Holy Spirit can speak to us through conviction as the Spirit speaks directly to our spirit. When we are doing something wrong, the Holy Spirit is grieved, and so is our spirit. The Holy Spirit brings conviction from learning God's standards that are presented in the Word of God. Hearing and responding to the preaching of God's Word can be great sources of correction.

Even with all the ways the Holy Spirit can convict us, there are times when we may not be listening to what the Spirit is saying. When one ignores the Spirit's conviction, the Holy Spirit will need to resort to other means of correction. Sometimes the Holy Spirit will use adverse circumstances to get our attention. When we are all wrapped up in our cares and responsibilities, we tend to neglect God and pay little attention to what God is wanting to do in our lives. When we allow sin to return in our lives through small compromises, we are turning a deaf ear to what the Spirit of God is speaking to us. When difficult times come, we return to God and seek Him for help.

As we seek Him for help, God will bring to our attention the changes we need to make in our lives. We must understand that the Holy Spirit

The Agent of Sanctification

also can use people to bring correction if needed. Quite often, God will use those who are in authority or have great influence in our lives to bring correction. The correction may come from our parents, our spouse, our boss, our coach, a spiritual leader, our pastor, our mentor, a teacher, or a close friend.

We must learn to respond correctly to correction and criticism in order to benefit from the Holy Spirit's correction. When being corrected by someone, we must humbly listen to what is being said and then to what the Spirit of God is saying. We must not reject any correction or criticism outright but rather consider that the Holy Spirit may be saying something to us in the correction. When we are corrected or criticized, we should take the matter to God in prayer and see what He may say to us about the criticism. Maybe a person is only one percent right in his criticism. We should take that one percent and let God make corrections there. Responding to correction or criticism properly will only make us better. We can become bitter if we react to criticism incorrectly. Believers must learn to trust the Spirit's correction and not react in negative ways to the good that the Spirit is endeavoring to do. The Holy Spirit's correction must be looked at as a positive thing for spiritual development.

The Spirit's correction is never done in a harsh way. The Holy Spirit will always be gentle and bring correction solely for the benefit of the believer. The Holy Spirit's correction is never done as a put down but always done to strengthen and improve the believer (Heb. 12:5–7). Believers must never think of the Spirit's correction as something condemning but as an encouragement to grow in righteousness and spiritual maturity. Furthermore, the Holy Spirit will not overwhelm a believer with all that needs to change at one time; He will patiently introduce personal improvement projects one at a time. We all need to put a sign on us saying, "Please forgive the mess; I am still a work in progress."

A good analogy of how the Spirit works is to compare the Spirit to a master sculptor who works on a huge piece of stone. At first, the sculptor must chisel off big chunks of stone; later, he will just be chiseling off small pieces. The more he chisels, the more the image of what the sculptor imagined becomes a reality. Eventually, when the sculptor is finished, a beautiful image has been created according to the sculptor's design. This is how the Holy Spirit works in correcting each believer. At first, the Spirit chisels off big chunks of sin. Eventually, the Spirit of God begins working on removing small pieces while refining a person's character into the image of Christ.

Application

1. How open are you to correction?

2. How do you react to criticism?

3. Do you believe that you can learn from correction?

4. Have you become more aware of sin in your life?

5. Have you become more aware of some aspects of your character that need improvement? What are some ways you could improve?

The Holy Spirit's Work of Grace in Cleansing Believers

During my teen years, I worked for three summers at Kansas University in dormitory maintenance. The pay was good and I gained experience doing such practical work, such as mowing grass, painting, moving furniture, and so forth. I enjoyed most of our jobs, but there was one that I did not like at all. The job I dreaded the most was cleaning out the dormitory grease traps. These grease traps had to be cleaned out at least once a year. Because no one wanted to do the job, those with the least amount of seniority, or summer workers, were assigned the job. Those who were not very fortunate were assigned this task and dropped off at the various dormitories. I would go with another worker into the kitchen and open up a floor plate to get to the grease trap. The grease traps were filled with grease and garbage that had rotted over the year. The foulest smell you can imagine was released when we opened the grease trap. Many of the workers could not stand doing the job. Many would feel like throwing up and could not be in the room. I was one of the few who could tolerate the job. I guess I could do it because I do not have a strong sense of smell. The grease traps had to be cleaned out so that the sinks could drain properly; it was an unpleasant but necessary task.

There is a comparison to these grease traps in our lives. Our hearts and minds can be just like those grease traps—filled with many defiling things. We all have allowed sinful things into our minds and hearts. Before anyone comes to know Christ, every part of his life is defiled by the filth of sin. Once a person comes to know Christ and is born again, he will have the Holy Spirit residing in him. The Holy Spirit will then begin the work of continual cleansing to remove the filth of sin. Believers in Christ must cooperate with the Holy Spirit by not allowing this filth of sin to continue in their lives. They must cry out to God not only for forgiveness but also for repeated spiritual cleansing.

We find the example of a person who committed the sin of adultery in the Old Testament. King David committed adultery with another man's wife and then had the husband killed in battle so he could cover up his sin. David thought he would get away with the sin. Instead, he was sharply confronted by the prophet Nathan about his actions. David cried out to God in repentance after his sin was exposed. David petitioned God to forgive him and blot out his transgression because he knew God is compassionate (Ps. 51:1). David was not content to just have forgiveness; he also wanted cleansing from his sins, "Wash me thoroughly from my iniquity, and cleanse me from my sin...Purify me with hyssop, and I shall be clean; Wash me, and I shall be whiter than snow" (Ps. 51:2, 7). One of the first works of the Holy Spirit is to bring a person to belief in Christ and to repentance which removes the penalty for sins. The proper response to conviction of sin by the Holy Spirit is confession and repentance. The believer can have confidence that God is merciful and compassionate and will forgive him. One must seek not only the removal of the penalty of sin but also the removal of the defilement of sin.

What is spiritual cleansing? The definition of cleanse is, "to purify, to rid of impurities."[82] Applying this definition to spiritual cleansing would mean to purify, purge, and remove everything sinful. To cleanse "in a moral sense, from the defilement of sin, Acts 15:9; 2 Corinthians 7:1; Hebrews 9:14; James 4:8."[83] To be cleansed from sin is of absolute importance because sin defiles or contaminates a person. Sin is filth, a deadly poison, and a carcinogen. Sin is deadly (Rom. 6:23). Because sin is deadly, it must be thoroughly removed as soon as possible. The removal or cleansing for sin is a vital work of the Holy Spirit in our lives.

We use water purifiers to remove contaminates from the water we drink. We use air filters to remove airborne materials. We use oil and air filters for our cars. Haz-mat crews come in and remove hazardous materials from contaminated areas. Since cleansing is a very important practice in many aspects of our lives, should it not as well be a vital part of our spiritual lives? What type of things need to be removed from a believer's life? There are things that defile our thoughts, our flesh, our spirit, our conscience, our speech and our relationships. Titus 1:15 speaks about the defilement of a person's thoughts and conscience, "To the pure, all things are pure; but to those who are defiled and unbelieving, nothing is pure, but both their mind and their conscience are defiled."

A person's mind can be defiled by worldly concepts and ideas, unbiblical worldviews, falsehoods, lustful thoughts, lies, and deceptions. Second Corinthians 7:1 speaks about cleansing oneself from the defilement of the flesh and spirit: "Therefore, having these promises, beloved, let us cleanse ourselves from all defilement of flesh and spirit, perfecting holiness in the fear of God." What kind of things defile the flesh? Galatians 5:19–21 presents a list of the works of the flesh: "Now the deeds of the flesh are evident, which are: immorality, impurity, sensuality, idolatry, sorcery, enmities, strife, jealousy, outbursts of anger, disputes, dissensions, factions, envying, drunkenness, carousing, and things like these, of which I forewarn you, just as I have forewarned you, that those who practice such things will not inherit the kingdom of God."

One notices from this list that some things that are a defilement of the flesh: immorality, sexual impurity, sensuality, and addictions (drunkenness or drugs). In this list, one can spot things that defile the spirit: idolatry, sorcery, jealousy, anger, wrath, and envy. Hebrews 12:15 reveals how bitterness defiles many — "See to it that no one comes short of the grace of God; that no root of bitterness springing up causes trouble, and by it many be defiled." The apostle Paul admonished the church in Ephesus to put off bitterness, wrath, anger, clamor, slander, and malice: "Let all bitterness and wrath and anger and clamor and slander be put away from you, along with all malice" (Eph. 4:31).

The Spirit of God desires to cleanse the believer from defilement of speech. Colossians 3:8 states, "But now you also, put them all aside: anger, wrath, malice, slander, *and* abusive speech from your mouth." Defilement of speech includes such things as slander, gossip, abusive speech, and coarse and foul language. In addition to things that defile the flesh and spirit are things that defile the conscience. Hebrews 9:14 speaks about the defilement of the conscience, "How much more will the blood of Christ, who through the eternal Spirit offered Himself without blemish to God, cleanse your conscience from dead works to serve the living God?" The guilt and shame from sin can defile a person's conscience. There are things that defile or destroy relationships. The list in Galatians 5:19–21 contains sins that are destructive to relationships: enmities, strife, jealousy, outbursts of anger, disputes, dissensions, factions, and envy. Since the Spirit of God is the Spirit of unity, He desires to work in the lives of believers to bring unity in their relationships. Removing these works of the flesh will undoubtedly improve relationships in marriages, families, and friendships.

How does the Holy Spirit cleanse a believer? In order for the Holy Spirit to be effective in removing issues of the sinful nature, He will need a believer's full cooperation in this cleansing process. When the Spirit corrects a believer, that person needs to confess his sins and repent. It is through repentance that the Spirit cleanses from sin. If there is no confession and repentance, there will be no cleansing. Each day believers must be sensitive to the correction of the Spirit and be quick to confess and repent. As a follower of Christ, one must daily surrender everything to the Spirit's cleansing. Our lives are like a house with many rooms, which represent manifold aspects of our lives. As a believer and follower of Christ, one must give the Holy Spirit permission to purge every room of his life. There should not be any rooms that are off limits for the Holy Spirit to cleanse. Believers need to surrender their personal, private lives for cleansing; they cannot just offer their spiritual life to God.

Many Christians compartmentalize their lives. They have a church life, and they have the personal life that they live during the week. Many Christians believe that God is only interested in their church life. They believe that how they live their personal lives outside of church is of little importance to God. God does not compartmentalize our lives; He looks at every aspect of our lives as being significant. God desires cleansing in every part of their lives. Isaiah was cleansed of his sins by a coal from the altar while spending time in God's holy presence (Isa. 6:7). Every believer can experience spiritual cleansing through seeking God in prayer at his private altar and at the church altar. Believers can surrender to the Spirit's cleansing during times of worship. Believers can be cleaned by meditating on God's Word (Eph. 5:26; John 15:3).

In addition to what has been mentioned, the Holy Spirit often uses trials to purify believers. Trials will have a cleansing effect in a believer's life if he humbles himself during the trial and uses it to drive him closer to God. Every believer is faced with this choice; he can just keep hiding his sins, or he can have them removed through confession and repentance. It is wonderful to live the Christian life being cleansed from sins, "Come now, and let us reason together," says the Lord, "Though your sins are as scarlet, They shall be white as snow; Though they are red like crimson, They shall be like wool" (Isa. 1:18).

Application

1. Are you allowing the Holy Spirit to cleanse your thoughts from things like:
   Worldly concepts and ideas?
   Unbiblical worldviews?
   Deceptions and lies?
   Lustful thoughts?

2. Are you allowing the Holy Spirit to cleanse your flesh from such things as:
   Immorality?
   Impurity?
   Sensuality?
   Addiction?

3. Are you allowing the Holy Spirit to cleanse your spirit from such things as:
   Idolatry?
   Sorcery?
   Jealousy?
   Anger?
   Wrath?
   Envy?

4. Are you allowing the Holy Spirit to cleanse your speech from such things as:
   Slander?
   Gossip?
   Abusive speech?
   Foul language?

5. Are you allowing the Holy Spirit to cleanse your relationships from such things as:
   Enmity/strife?
   Jealousy?
   Disputes?
   Dissensions and factions?

The Holy Spirit's Work of Grace in Comforting Believers

The journey down the road of transformation can become difficult; it is certainly not the path of least resistance. There will be many times a believer will feel that it is too difficult and consequently want to just give up and go the easy route. Completing the journey will require determination and persistence; it will require one's best effort. Even with a believer's best attempts, he cannot make it on his own. There will be times of sorrow, times of grief, and times of discouragement. There may be times when a believer can become weary, depressed, and feel like giving up. The process of transformation involves moments when a person can feel it is not worth the trouble to become Christlike. Where can a believer find comfort and encouragement to make it through difficult times?

The Scriptures tell us that God provides comfort to those who call on Him. In his letter to the Corinthians, Paul emphasizes the comfort that God provides:

> Blessed *be* the God and Father of our Lord Jesus Christ, the Father of mercies and God of all comfort, who comforts us in all our affliction so that we will be able to comfort those who are in any affliction with the comfort with which we ourselves are comforted by God. (2 Cor. 1:3–4)

> But God, who comforts the depressed, comforted us by the coming of Titus; and not only by his coming, but also by the comfort with which he was comforted in you, as he reported to us your longing, your mourning, your zeal for me; so that I rejoiced even more. (2 Cor. 7:6–7)

These verses reassure believers that God is the God of all comfort, who comforts them in all their affliction, and who comforts the depressed.

The Holy Spirit is a comforter to those who call on Him. Jesus Christ bestowed an important name on the Holy Spirit in John 16:7, "But I tell you the truth, it is to your advantage that I go away; for if I do not go away, the Helper will not come to you; but if I go, I will send Him to you"

(John 16:7). Different translations translate this name differently: NASB and ESV use Helper, NIV uses Counselor, and KJV uses Comforter. The Greek word used for this name of the Holy Spirit is transliterated *Paraklētos* "called to one's side," that is, to one's aid, is primarily a verbal adjective, and suggests the capability or adaptability for giving aid."[84] The meanings of this word as it relates to the Holy Spirit is one who comforts, encourages, exhorts, and consoles. The Holy Spirit is like someone who comes alongside to help lift someone up to help him continue to walk.

The Holy Spirit gives comforting assistance to believers during times of discouragement. Discouragement comes when one experiences disappointment. People will disappoint each other, they can let each other down, not do what they promised, betray, and forsake each other. Believers can get discouraged when certain prayers are not answered right away. People can disappoint themselves by their own failures. The road to transformation is not only an uphill climb; it also has pits of despair that must be avoided. And, if a believer ever finds himself in a pit of despair, he will need help getting out. The Holy Spirit comes alongside the believer when he calls on the Lord for help.

The Holy Spirit can gently guide believers through times of affliction. The Spirit will give strength to endure and overcome to all those who call on Him. The apostle Paul gives an excellent example of how the Spirit helps through difficult times: "But we have this treasure in earthen vessels, so that the surpassing greatness of the power will be of God and not from ourselves; *we are* afflicted in every way, but not crushed; perplexed, but not despairing; persecuted, but not forsaken; struck down, but not destroyed" (2 Cor. 4:7–9). God gives strength to the believer who looks to Him and trusts in Him. "Yet those who wait for the Lord will gain new strength; they will mount up *with* wings like eagles, they will run and not get tired, they will walk and not become weary" (Isaiah 40:31).

The Holy Spirit can heal a person's emotional pain. Believers can experience grief and sorrow from a loss of a loved one through death or the loss of a relationship through divorce. Since believers live in a sinful world, people can do things that wound them physically and/or emotionally and even abuse them sexually. People can develop emotional pain because of these experiences. Some never heal emotionally and remain fixated on their past. Some people go through life, seeing themselves as victims. Believers in Christ do not have to be victims of their circumstances; instead, through the comfort of the Spirit of God, they can be victorious. The Holy Spirit can be one's healing balm. Believers must allow the Spirit to open wounds by forgiving those who have hurt them and then let the Spirit bring healing to those deep wounds of the soul. Believers need to pour out their hearts to the Lord in prayer to let the Spirit of God get out the emotional infection. Emotional healing is necessary because emotional wounds can be like chains that hold people back from progressing in their transformation.

The Holy Spirit can bring emotional healing through believers encouraging each other. That is why the Bible tells believers not to forsake coming together so that they can encourage each other — "Not forsaking our own assembling together, as is the habit of some, but encouraging *one another;* and all the more as you see the day drawing near" (Heb. 10:25). The Holy Spirit can bring comfort and encouragement directly, but most often it comes through believers moved by the Spirit to show compassion and bring restoration to others.

Let us examine 1 Corinthians 1:3–4: "Blessed *be* the God and Father of our Lord Jesus Christ, the Father of mercies and God of all comfort, who comforts us in all our affliction so that we will be able to comfort those who are in any affliction with the comfort with which we ourselves are comforted by God." Look closely to the part of the verse that says, "Who comforts us in all our affliction so that we will be able to comfort those who are in any affliction with the comfort with which we ourselves are comforted by God." The Spirit of God works to bring solace directly to some so that they, in turn, can bring comfort to others with the same comfort they received from God. It is essential to grasp the significance of what is being said here. The Holy Spirit, the "Comforter," will use believers to bring comfort to others. People will not know how to call on the Lord for comfort, so the "Spirit of Comfort" will move believers to show His consolation and encouragement.

Application

1. Have you experienced times of sorrow and grief?

2. What is the one thing that has caused you the most emotional pain?

3. How have you dealt with your emotional pain?

4. Have you turned to the God of all comfort for His comfort?

5. If you have been comforted by God, are you now using that to comfort others?

6. Who among your acquaintances could use some comfort?

The Holy Spirit's Work of Grace in Conforming Believers

What does it mean to conform something? The definition for the verb *to conform* "means to become similar or identical to."[85] The Greek word for *conformed* as an adjective is transliterated *summorphos* (4832), which means: "having the same form as another, conformed to as; of the "conformity" of children of God "to the image of His Son" Romans 8:29."[86]

> 28 And we know that God causes all things to work together for good to those who love God, to those who are called according to *His* purpose. 29 For those whom He foreknew, He also predestined *to become* conformed to the image of His Son, so that He would be the firstborn among many brethren. (Rom. 8:28–29)

Believers in Christ have to choose between two spheres from which they will be influenced. Some Christians try to conform to both the world and to the Holy Spirit. In order for transformation to happen, a believer must choose to be conformed to what the Holy Spirit desires. Romans 12:2 urges believers not to be conformed to the world: "And do not be conformed to this world, but be transformed by the renewing of your mind, so that you may prove what the will of God is, that which is good and acceptable and perfect" (Rom. 12:2).

What does conformity to the world mean? A similar definition to "conformed" is "to make of like form with another person or thing, to render like."[87] To be conformed to the world means to become similar in nature or character as the world. Ephesians 2:1–3 describes in detail the character of the world:

> 1 And you were dead in your trespasses and sins, 2 in which you formerly walked according to the course of this world, according to the prince of the power of the air, of the spirit that is now working in the sons of disobedience. 3 Among them we too all formerly lived in the lusts of our flesh, indulging the desires of the flesh and of the mind, and were by nature children of wrath, even as the rest. (Ephesians 2:1–3)

Being conformed to the world is a state of mind or way of thinking that focuses on what pleases the flesh or the sinful nature. This mindset is held by the vast majority of people.

How does the world conform people? A large majority of people are part of the world's system of living. This puts pressure on everyone to conform to the majority, to go along with the crowd, to fit in, and to belong. Jesus described it as the broad way that leads to destruction: "Enter by the narrow gate; for the gate is wide, and the way is broad that leads to destruction, and many are those who enter by it" (Matt. 7:13). Pressure is applied to conform to the world through rewards and punishments. Those who conform are rewarded through being accepted, liked, praised, made famous or popular. Those who conform are given financial rewards, jobs, promotions, and favors. Those who do not conform are punished by ostracization, ridicule, verbal attacks, slander, and defamation of character. Some who do not conform are persecuted through loss of a job, destruction of property, and even execution in some countries.

Rather than being conformed by the world, believers are to be transformed by the Holy Spirit into the image of Christ (Rom. 8:28-29). Through the indwelling of the Spirit, radical changes should be happening in every believer. Believers are not to continue allowing themselves to be conformed to the world but to be transformed by the renewing of their minds (Rom. 12:2). Believers must choose to cooperate with the Holy Spirit by allowing Him to transform them. It is God's plan and purpose for believers to become like Christ. All believers in Christ must make becoming like Jesus the ultimate goal of their transformation. The goal of every believer should be to think like Jesus, talk like Jesus, love like Jesus, and act like Jesus.

An excellent analogy is the Holy Spirit as the master potter (Jer. 18:1-6). Believers are the clay that God fashions into something beautiful. Believers are raw clay containing a lot of imperfections, rocks, and debris that need to be removed. Imperfections must be removed from clay before it can be used. In the preparation of the clay for making pottery, the clay must be dried out completely and then crushed to powder. The powder must be sifted, removing any rocks or debris. Finally, the clay must be soaked in water for several days. Only after the clay is prepared and processed will it be put on the potter's wheel. The master potter will then shape it into a beautiful vessel. The Holy Spirit is the master potter who will help each willing believer to go through the transformation process to be shaped (conformed) into the image of Christ.

Application

1. Have you been pressured to conform to worldly ways at work or school, and by friends or family?

2. Have you made the choice not to be conformed to the world?

3. Have you chosen to allow the Holy Spirit to transform you into the image of Christ?

CHAPTER 15

The Agent of Service

A change in our attitude about ourselves and others is a sure indicator that God's grace is transforming us. People are selfish by nature; they naturally think that the whole world revolves around them. They are egocentric; everything is about self. People are looking for how others can serve them. People tend to look at how everything will benefit them personally. One of the greatest demonstrations of the transforming work of grace is when a person changes from being self-centered to being Christ-centered. A Christ-centered person is a person who becomes others-centered. In other words, he starts thinking more about others and their needs as he becomes more like Christ. The people that have given their personal testimonies throughout this book have been miraculously transformed by God's grace. They are indeed trophies of God's grace. In each of these testimonies, you will notice that lives were dramatically changed. One of the notable changes was the change from being self-centered to being Christ-centered. You will observe how lives were changed from serving self to being dedicated in service for Christ.

Believers are prepared for service through the sanctifying work of the Holy Spirit. The believer is led into some form of ministry service as part of the process of sanctification. Serving the Lord in ministry is actually part of the transformation process. After the Holy Spirit has worked in us to save and sanctify us, He moves on to work through us in ministry. The last level of transformation is service. It has been my observation that those who get involved in ministry are the ones who mature the fastest. Involvement in ministry accelerates the transformation process. Those who do not get involved in ministry will be stunted in their spiritual growth and will, unfortunately, have limited transformation.

The Holy Spirit's Work of Grace in Calling Believers to Serve

The Spirit calls individuals to service in addition to the call to salvation and sanctification. The call to salvation is the Spirit's invitation to everyone who would believe in Christ and repent of his sins. The call to salvation is a call to come to Christ. The call to sanctification is the call to separate from the world and become like Christ. The call to service is a call to do something for Christ and His kingdom. Every believer has a general call to serve God.

A study of church history shows that a misconception developed that resulted in dividing believers between two groups: the clergy and the laity. The church believed that because the clergy were trained, they were the only ones qualified to perform ministry. The laity were only allowed limited opportunities for ministry. There is no such division between the clergy and the laity found in the New Testament nor in the practices of the early church. The Bible teaches the priesthood of all believers, "You also, as living stones, are being built up as a spiritual house for a holy priesthood, to offer up spiritual sacrifices acceptable to God through Jesus Christ" (1 Pet. 2:5). In God's eyes, every believer has a ministry; in a general sense, all believers are ministers.

Besides the general call of the Holy Spirit to serve God, He calls individual believers to specific ministries. Every believer is created for the purpose of serving in a unique way. Within God's calling to serve, believers are endowed with both natural talents and spiritual gifts to serve according to His plan. The purpose of these God-given talents is greater than merely serving self; they are to be used to glorify God in the fulfillment of His will. The primary source of ability for ministry is not a person's natural abilities but what the Holy Spirit implants in the believer at salvation. First Corinthians 1:26 makes it clear that the Spirit's calling to serve is not based on human abilities: "For consider your calling, brethren, that there were not many wise according to the flesh, not many mighty, not many noble." The Spirit of God provides numerous gifts of ministry to enable believers to serve (Rom. 12:6–8; Eph. 4:11–12).

In the book of Acts, one can observe how the Spirit of God called people into ministry. In Acts 13:2, the Spirit of God called Barnabas and Saul to do missions work. "While they were ministering to the Lord and fasting, the Holy Spirit said, 'Set apart for Me Barnabas and Saul for the work to which I have called them.'" Paul was directed by the Spirit, through a vision, to go and preach the gospel to the Macedonians. "When he had seen the vision, immediately we sought to go into Macedonia, concluding that God had called us to preach the gospel to them" (Acts 16:10).

Believers can best discover their calling through involvement in a local church. Every believer is part of the Body of Christ. Clearly, every member of a body has a distinctive function. The Holy Spirit directs a believer into the specific type of ministry that best utilizes his gifts once he is involved in a local church.

The Holy Spirit's Work of Grace in Compelling Believers to Serve

The Holy Spirit does more than just call people into ministry; He also gives them the motivation to serve. Involvement in ministry comes with many challenges that test the limit of a person's will to continue. There will be many times in ministry when a person becomes weary and feels like giving up. The Holy Spirit can compel believers not only to start serving in ministry but to have the determination to continue until completion. Believers must have the right motivation in order to succeed in ministry. The way the Holy Spirit motivates is in stark contrast to how the world motivates. The world uses fleshly means to motivate.

Worldly methods resort to manipulation through the use of guilt, use of threats and anger, appealing to people's pride through recognition by awards or titles, or offering monetary benefits and positions of power. The use of worldly methods to motivate people in ministry will not endure the test of time. Furthermore, workers will not be blessed by their service. Rather than working with joy, serving is done with a sense of obligation or duty. Work done for the wrong motivation will not be rewarded. Believers can serve God with the wrong motives, such as trying to earn their salvation, trying to compensate for sin, to gain the praise and approval of people, or to gain respect from people. How does the Holy Spirit motivate believers to serve for the right reasons?

Second Corinthians 5:9–15 gives great insight into how the Spirit of God motivated the apostle Paul:

> Therefore, we also have as our ambition, whether at home or absent, to be pleasing to Him. For we must all appear before the judgment seat of Christ, so that each one may be recompensed for his deeds in the body, according to what he has done, whether good or bad. Therefore, knowing the fear of the Lord, we persuade men, but we are made manifest to God; and I hope that we are made manifest also in your consciences. We are not again commending ourselves to you but *are* giving you an occasion to be proud of us, so that you will have *an answer* for those who take pride in appearance and not in heart. For if we are beside ourselves, it is for God; if we are of sound mind, it is for you. For the love of Christ controls us, having concluded this, that one died for all, therefore all died; and He died for all, so that they who live might no longer live for themselves, but for Him who died and rose again on their behalf. (2 Cor. 5:9-15)

There are several phrases that stand out in this passage of Scripture regarding the motivation of the Holy Spirit in service. The phrase, "We also have as our ambition, whether at home of absent, to be pleasing to Him" (v. 9) describes a strong, stirring force for ministry. The Holy Spirit works in believers to create in them a passion to please Christ. The Spirit of God helps transform believers from being focused on pleasing self to pleasing Christ. "So that they who live might no longer live for themselves, but for Him" (v. 15). The foremost reason for serving Christ is that it pleases Him. Another significant phrase is, "We must all appear before the judgment seat of Christ" (v. 10). Knowing that one day all believers will be accountable to Christ for how they have served Him should provide another strong motivation to faithfully serve Christ.

The phrase, "For the love of Christ controls (compels, NKJV) us" (v. 14) is the most important reason for serving Christ in ministry. Through the working of the Holy Spirit, the love of Christ is developed in the hearts of those who serve Him. The love of Christ birthed in believers' hearts through the inner working of the Spirit of God is such a compelling force that it can drive believers to make even the greatest sacrifice of their lives. The love that compelled Christ to give His life on the cross is the same love that compels believers to give themselves sacrificially in their service to God.

The Holy Spirit's Work of Grace in Commissioning Believers in Service

When God calls believers into service, He provides what is needed to accomplish the given task. The gifts of grace will help believers to have the motivation to do their ministry. These motivational gifts compel believers to go forth and complete their mission. God knows that believers need much more than motivation to complete their given responsibilities. In addition to motivating believers, God bestows the authority and power to fulfill their mission. God commissions believers as ambassadors of Christ and gives them the authority to act on His behalf. When an ambassador is sent to a foreign country, he is given the right and the ability to act on behalf of the government of his country. An ambassador is "a diplomatic agent of the highest rank accredited to a foreign government as the resident representative of his own government.... an ambassador is an authorized representative or messenger."[88]

Every believer is an ambassador for Christ (2 Cor. 5:20). Those who are followers of Christ are representatives from another kingdom—the kingdom of heaven. Believers are witnesses or representatives of Christ on earth. All believers have been given a mission to accomplish and the authority to fulfill it. Every believer has been commissioned by the Holy Spirit to serve God in a specific way. Additionally, to be commissioned means that believers are authorized to act in a prescribed manner. To be commissioned means to have authority to act for, in the behalf of, or in place of another. Believers in Christ have been commissioned to serve on His behalf with His authority.

At the conclusion of Christ's ministry on earth, He gave believers a simple but well-defined mission. Christ gave His followers what is called the Great Commission in Matthew 28:18–20:

> And Jesus came up and spoke to them, saying, "All authority has been given to Me in heaven and on earth.

> 19 "Go therefore and make disciples of all the nations, baptizing them in the name of the Father and the Son and the Holy Spirit, 20 teaching them to observe all that I commanded you; and lo, I am with you always, even to the end of the age.

Ambassadors of Christ have been commissioned to go into the whole world and preach the gospel message, and to make disciples. Believers are commissioned to do the ministry of reconciliation. "Now all *these* things are from God, who reconciled us to Himself through Christ and gave us the ministry of reconciliation, namely, that God was in Christ reconciling the world to Himself, not counting their trespasses against them, and He has committed to us the word of reconciliation" (2 Cor. 5:18–19). As ambassadors of Christ, believers bring terms of peace for the world to be reconciled to God through Christ.

Believers have not only been given the authority (the right) but also the power to fulfill the Great Commission. Romans 12:6–8 shows how the Holy Spirit gives motivational gifts for service. These are gifts of grace that motivate believers to serve in particular ways. The gifts of grace are prophecy (the ability to speak for God), service (the ability to do things for God), teaching (the ability to explain the things of God), exhortation (the ability to encourage others), giving (the ability to give on behalf of God), leadership (the ability to administrate the work of God), and mercy (the ability to demonstrate God's compassion).

Believers need God's power because ministry involves engagement in spiritual warfare. "For our struggle is not against flesh and blood, but against the rulers, against the powers, against the world forces of this darkness, against the spiritual *forces* of wickedness in the heavenly *places*" (Eph. 6:12). Those who are involved in ministry face opposition from the powers of darkness. The success of Christian service requires an enormous amount of spiritual power to overcome the powers of darkness. The Holy Spirit has given believers powerful, spiritual weapons to defeat the powers of darkness, "for the weapons of our warfare are not of the flesh, but divinely powerful for the destruction of fortresses" (2 Cor. 10:4). Believers cannot rely on their own strength for the work of ministry because they are engaged in spiritual warfare, "Then he said to me, 'This is the word of the Lord to Zerubbabel saying,

'Not by might nor by power, but by My Spirit,' says the Lord of hosts" (Zech. 4:6). Satanic opposition is overcome by the power of the Spirit.

The Holy Spirit empowers believers for service by equipping them with various gifts. Some people wrongly assume that all of the spiritual gifts belong on a single list. A closer look reveals that there are actually three categories of spiritual gifts. Separate lists provide clarification. Once one understands these distinctions, one will have a much greater appreciation of spiritual gifts. The reason that Scripture lists the gifts in separate groups is because there are distinct categories. Even though these lists may contain similarities, there are important differences. The three major listings of gifts are found in Romans 12:3–8, 1 Corinthians 12:4–11, and Ephesians 4:7–11.

As you study these lists of gifts, you will discover that these three lists are actually three different categories of spiritual gifts. The key passage that clarifies the distinction between the categories of gifts is 1 Corinthians 12:4–6, "Now there are varieties of gifts, but the same Spirit. And there are varieties of ministries, and the same Lord. There are varieties of effects, but the same God who works all things in all *persons*." Notice that these verses mention three different *varieties*.

The three key words in verses 4 through 6 are *gifts, ministries,* and *effects*. A brief explanation of the Greek words will clarify the distinctions. The word for gifts used in verse 4 is *charisma* (5486), "'a gift of grace, a gift involving grace' (*charis*) on the part of God as the donor."[89] This Greek word deals with basic inward drive, or motivation, and the power to perform ministry. The word for "ministries" used in verse 5 is "*diakonia*, (1248), which is derived from *diakonos* (1249) meaning "servant, attendant, minister, deacon."[90] This Greek word emphasizes the diverse avenues of service or ministry in which God can enable one to serve others. The word for "effects" used in verse 6 is *energēma*, (1755) meaning "an effect, operation."[91] This Greek word signifies that these spiritual gifts are a direct operation of the power of God.

These three Greek words reveal the three distinct categories of spiritual gifts. The grace gifts are referred to as the motivational gifts, the gifts of service are referred to as the ministry gifts, and the effects gifts are referred to as the manifestation gifts. These three categories match the three scriptural passages that list the gifts: gifts of grace (or motivation; Rom. 12:3–8), gifts of service (or ministry; Eph. 4:7–11), or gifts of workings of the Spirit (manifestations; 1 Cor. 12:4–11).

The gifts of ministry that are listed in Ephesians 4:11 are: "And He gave some *as* apostles, and some *as* prophets, and some *as* evangelists, and some *as* pastors and teachers." These ministry gifts are people given to the Church for the purpose of equipping the saints for the work of service to build up the body of Christ. There is a calling of individuals to each of these ministry gifts. God calls some to be apostles, some to be prophets, some to be evangelists, some to be pastors, and some to be teachers. God gives special grace to individuals to be one of these ministry gifts to the church. The church is built up when these gifts of ministry are functioning.

The third list, found in 1 Corinthians 12:6–11, presents the manifestation gifts of the Spirit. The manifestation gifts of the Spirit are divine wisdom, knowledge, faith, gifts of healing, effecting miracles, prophecy, discerning of spirits, kinds of tongues, and the interpretation of tongues. It is the Holy Spirit who chooses who receives each gift and at what times these gifts will be manifested. The concept of manifestation gifts implies that they happen at a given time at the Holy Spirit's choosing. Some mistakenly think that these gifts are a permanent possession of an individual who has experienced the effects of these gifts. If a person is given one of these gifts by the Holy Spirit, he can certainly be used again in the gifts, but he should not assume that it is available when he chooses. It is only the Spirit of God who chooses by whom and when these gifts are manifested.

A good illustration of how manifestation gifts work is to compare them to an electrical wire and a light bulb. When a switch is turned on, electricity flows through the line to the bulb, and the bulb lights up. The bulb does not possess the electricity but only shows the effects of the electricity. The bulb does not control when the power flows but only shows when it flows. A believer who receives the flow of God's power will manifest that power at the given time and the way the Holy Spirit determines. These gifts are God's divine enablement for the work of ministry. The Holy Spirit desires to empower believers when they are engaged in ministry; He is looking for willing participants. The apostle Paul teaches the Corinthian church that they should earnestly desire spiritual gifts (1 Cor. 14:1). If a believer shows that he is desiring all that God has available for him, he will be supplied with the power needed to succeed in whatever task God has prepared for him to do.

Application

1. Do you believe that God has called you to serve Him?

2. Have you become involved in a ministry at a local church?

3. How strong is your desire to please Christ by serving Him?

4. Do you believe that God has given you a mission to accomplish?

5. What kind of an ambassador of Christ are you in your home, work, or school?

6. Are there some ways that you can improve in how you represent Christ to others? If so, what should you change?

Trophy of Grace: Ann Winfield

I was brought up in a home with both of my parents. My mom loved me very much, and she showed it when I got sick. She played the very loving nurse when I was sick, but when I was well, she would always criticize me. No matter what I did, it was not good enough. I used to be a competitive roller-skater, but when I came off the skating floor, she would tell me all my mistakes. Even when I won first place, she still had comments of what I did wrong and would not compliment me. She never said she loved me, and she always was telling me of my mistakes and would not compliment me for anything. I can't explain how much that hurt and what low self-esteem I had because of it.

As a child, I had some exposure to church. My mother went to a Christian Science Church when she was a child, so she had my dad drop my sister and me off at a Christian Science Church. My dad considered himself Lutheran even though he never attended church. As I became older, I needed to be at the skating rink on Sundays. I found out from someone else who used to attend the Christian Science Church that there were a lot of questions that did not make sense. For example, a dating or engaged couple were not allowed to live together, but there was no one at the church, who was legally able to marry the couples.

When I attended college, I eventually became what I considered to be an atheist. I did not believe in God. I was a math/science education major at college. I believed that science had all the answers. In science class one day, my cell biology teacher said that science has come so far that if they put one thing from a living cell into a man-made cell, it would become a living cell. That started me thinking and searching for some answers. I used to listen to country music and that started me thinking about the meaning of life. Did I have a purpose here on earth? Did I have a purpose for living?

For about a year, there was a lady that would always come through my line at Loblaws, the grocery store where I worked. She would always hand me a Christian tract. At first, I took them and threw them in the garbage as soon as she left. After a few months, I started to read the front cover out of curiosity and then threw them in the garbage. After about a year, I finally started reading all the tracts that I was given. I went to work on Sundays and when my alarm went off, the radio would play. The music station I used to listen to would play a Christian kids drama story every Sunday at that time. I used to listen to them because I would press the snooze button, but the radio would still play. I am so grateful that God did not give up on me because of how many times I rejected Him.

One day, I was at a boy's house, who I used to date. I was still friends with him and his family. His mom asked if I would like to go to her father's house to a large family picnic on Sunday. The only problem was that it was on Sunday, and they wanted me to go with them to church first. I really wanted to get back together with Gary, and I saw this as an opportunity because the entire extended family would see us together again. I went to church with them. I thought that I would just sit for an hour, but I did not know that the Holy Spirit would start working on me. The service was not a typical service; there was a singing family that did the entire service with testimonies throughout. That service was held at First Assembly of God of Riverside, and later the name was changed to Victory International Assembly of God. I really became confused about my belief that God did not exist. I continued going to that church to learn more about God each week and to meet up with Gary's family there. At that point, I did not realize that it was the Holy Spirit that kept drawing me back.

During this time my grandmother was suffering and dying from colon cancer. I prayed a prayer that went something like this: "God, I hear You are real and that You can heal. If You are real, please heal my grandmother or take her home to be with You soon because she is in so much pain. Please forgive me of anything I have done wrong. I will serve You if you show me You are real by answering my prayer." Minutes later, I received a call from my mom letting me know that the hospital said my grandmother was not going to make it through the night. She passed away that evening, but I had a chance to see her before she passed. A few weeks later, I prayed the salvation prayer with the pastor's wife in the basement of the church on a Sunday evening. When I was going through my grandmother's things, I saw her Bible and found a letter in it. It was a beautiful salvation prayer that she had signed. God did take her home to be with Him! God is so good.

I may not have been a teen who did many things that would have gone against God in other people's eyes, but compared to God's holiness, I was extremely far away. It was God's grace that has given me forgiveness and eternal life Before I accepted Jesus in my heart in September of 1977. I was baptized in water by immersion in January of 1978. After that, I felt that God was calling me into ministry. I loved children, and I had always wanted to be a teacher. I became the Children's Church teacher and director. A year later, I became the Missionette's director and senior teacher. I became involved in the choir, the bus ministry, evangelism, drama, and many other ministries. The Lord had blessed me with many talents and I planned on using them all to honor Him.

Over the following years, I experienced the grace of God during difficulties. A few years later, my dad passed away. He had received Jesus as his Savior before he died. Two years later, I was married, and two years after that, I gave birth to my son, Eric. He was born with a few birth defects. I was in labor for sixty-two hours with him. Most doctors would have given a woman Pitocin by then, but my doctor believed in letting things be as natural as possible. It turned out that my umbilical cord was all shredded but not a single part broke away from the placenta. If I would have been given Pitocin, most likely the threadlike parts of the umbilical cord would have torn away from the placenta, and the baby may have died for lack of oxygen. God knew what He was doing by allowing my labor to be long and by directing me to the right doctor.

God's grace has sustained me through the many difficult challenges I have experienced with my son. Eric almost died a number of times, but the Lord allowed him to live. One of his birth defects was that he was born with just one eye. He has been quite a testimony for the Lord even at a young age in the hospital with all his eye-socket surgeries. At another time, Eric was having abdominal pain, and the doctor thought there was a possibility that it was appendicitis. He sent him to the hospital to have Eric diagnosed.

Eric ended up being diagnosed with Meckel's diverticulum that caused a blockage in his small intestine at the age of ten. He ended up in the hospital, very close to death, and lost about half of his small intestine due to the blockage and the onset of gangrene. We were told that he probably would not have lived another hour without the surgery. He had an ileostomy for about five months and then had surgery to reattach his intestine. Complications occurred after the surgery, and he needed another surgery. We almost lost him again. He has had a total of three surgeries for this. We really needed to rely on God's mercy and grace to make it through those hard times.

We almost lost Eric a few times, but I know God spared his life for a reason. I believe that God has much more for him to do. Eric's life was saved again during a high school science class field trip that included water rafting on a family course. Unfortunately, the raft that we were on tipped over. Everyone was thrown clear of the raft except my son. He was caught underneath the raft by the seat. He was under the water, and there was no air pocket.

I was the closest person to him, and the others were far away. I was still about thirty yards away from the raft. I did not see him anywhere. Finally, I heard his frantic scream. He was by the raft and was heading for a waterfall. I asked the Lord for His help and started swimming as fast as I could toward him. I was grateful that I had lifeguard training. When I reached my son, who was not a swimmer, I put him in a hold that I had learned and swam with him as hard as I could away from the falls. By God's grace, I had the strength to pull him out of danger. One of the rafts came and pulled us aboard. I could share many other stories of how my son almost died, but by God's grace he is still alive.

God has a plan and a purpose for his life. I believe that part of God's purpose for sparing my son's life so many times is his ministry as a member of a Christian worship band called Elmwood Drive. God has used this band to bless many young people at youth camps and conventions. God has used him mightily in this ministry.

Along with the many challenges I faced with my son, Eric, I endured many other difficulties in my life. After my mother's death, I had a lot of problems with my sister regarding my mother's will. Basically, I wanted to buy out my sister's half of my mom's house and my sister did not want me to. I had spent most of my married life taking care of my mother at her house, so I thought it would only be fair for me to be able to keep the house. It was a long ordeal with the attorneys, but by God's grace we got through it.

I thought I would have a lot of time with my husband now that my mom was gone and our children had moved away from the house. We ended up having some time but not what I had hoped. My husband passed away just four years after my mom. His death was very hard to deal with. God's grace is the only thing that helped me and is still helping me deal with the loss. I miss him so much and wish we had more time together, but that is being selfish. I know that he is no longer in pain. He dealt with Crohn's disease, chronic kidney stones, arthritis in his back, and blood clots. I am so grateful for God's grace to help me get through all the things I have experienced.

My son, Eric, was diagnosed with multiple aneurysms in 2020. He found this out when he was going to the doctor for pre-op visits to have an artificial eye permanently put in his left socket. He ended up not having the eye surgery but had surgery for the aneurysm near the eye socket instead. His neurosurgeon told him to tell me to get checked out because aneurysms are hereditary. It turned out that I had multiple aneurysms also. The day after my MRI my general doctor called me to let me know and to set up an appointment with the neurosurgeon for the next day! In less than two weeks after seeing the neurosurgeon in October, I was being operated on.

I had gone to my general doctor in August. She put me on a diet to lower my cholesterol, among a number of other things. My cholesterol level and my blood pressure being lowered definitely helped the surgery's success. It is amazing how God uses so many different circumstances to bring about the outcomes He desires and by His grace He helps us through our circumstances.

In spite of all the problems I have endured, God's grace has enabled me to serve the Lord faithfully at my church for over forty-three years as a youth/leader/minister. I been so blessed to see many teens' lives transformed by God's grace through the years. The teens have gone to weekend Christian events that have taken them out of their normal situations and into a submersion of Jesus Christ. The teens really had a chance to see what Jesus was all about when they were not bombarded by worldly things and were able to experience the life-changing miracles that Jesus has done.

Going back over thirty-seven years ago, I watched as God baptized young girls, who were between the ages of seven and fourteen years, with the Holy Spirit. Some went home so full of the Holy Spirit that it sparked parents who were sending their children to church to come themselves and rededicate themselves to the Lord.

Numerous teens that have gone through the youth group have ended up in ministry. There are those who have become pastors, youth pastors, worship pastors, missionaries, and evangelists. The worship bands, Elmwood Drive and Path Less Chosen, emerged from the youth group. Many were and are still involved with ministry at the church they currently attend. Some of the ministries they are currently doing include drama, sound booth, missions, children's church, Sunday school, and worship. A number of youth have made it to the National Assembly of God Fine Arts Festival in the categories of Short Sermon Jr., Short Sermon Sr., Spoken Word, Song Writing, Two-Dimensional Art, T-Shirt Design, Female Vocal Solo, Vocal Ensemble Small, Urban Dance Solo, and Urban Dance Troupe. What God has done truly amazes me!

What still amazes me is that I was told in school that I was totally tone deaf and that I would never play a musical instrument. Someone at the church wanted to sell me his guitar. I laughed at him because I was tone deaf and politely told him, "No." He told me that God put me on his heart and told me that the musical desire I had was from God, and who cares what it sounds like if I am playing it for the Lord in my room. I bought it. It is by God's grace that after I asked Jesus to come into my heart, I learned to play the guitar, organ, and the piano. What makes it even more amazing is after praying for a number of years for the Lord to bring teens into the youth group, who play instruments so that we could have a youth worship team, He wanted me to teach them. I was able to teach them how to play the guitar, piano, bass, and violin. The Lord provided someone to teach one of the teens how to play the drums. We ended up with a worship team in about six months.

I was praying to find out who the Lord wanted me to choose as the worship leader. He chose someone who I found out later had not sung in many years and just lip-synced in school because someone told him that he could not sing. The worship team went on to become Elmwood Drive, and the worship leader has become the worship pastor at another church.

I currently am on the worship team every other week. I am in charge of the sound booth. I am the youth minister, and I am on the church board as a deaconess. God has been so good to me and His mercies are never ending. He has so much grace to give.

PART FIVE

THE MEANS OF GRACE

CHAPTER 16

Regular Bible Study

In this Part Five, I will explain the different means of grace. By "means," I intend the dictionary's definition, "something useful or helpful to a desired end, and resources available for disposal."[92] The means to a desired end indicates whatever is helpful in reaching an objective. The desired end that I am writing about is the reception of God's grace in its fullest measure. Using this definition, the means of grace would be whatever is biblically useful in helping people receive God's grace. Is there anything that people can do to help them receive God's grace? Why is it that some receive God's grace while others do not? Is the giving of God's grace entirely the result of the work of God, or is there something that man can to do to help him receive God's grace?

The more we understand the working of God's grace, the more we realize it is almost entirely what God does for us. I say almost entirely is because there is a very small, but essential, part that man plays in the working of God's grace. What can a person do that would help him receive God's grace? Let me be perfectly clear when I say that someone can do what is useful in receiving God's grace, but I am not saying that a person can ever earn God's grace. There is nothing a person can do to earn or acquire God's grace; receiving God's grace is never an achievement of man. God chooses to show His grace to whom He will. However, does that mean that God arbitrarily chooses people to receive His grace regardless of their receptivity? Does God force His grace on unwilling people? Is God's grace irresistible?

I explained in Part Four: The Agent of Grace, how the Holy Spirit works as the agent of God's grace. The Spirit of God works in calling all to receive salvation, convincing people of the truth, and convicting them of their unbelief in Christ, their sinfulness, and need of God's grace. The Holy Spirit brings people to the point of conversion where they must decide to receive or reject what the Spirit is endeavoring to complete in them. It is when a person chooses to humble himself and call on the Lord for forgiveness that a person experiences salvation. Apart from the working of the Holy Spirit, no one can receive God's grace, and apart from the work of the Holy Spirit in convincing people of the truth, no one will have faith to believe in Christ. Apart from the work of the Holy Spirit in convicting a person, no one will repent of his sins and turn to God.

In addition to the extensive work of the Holy Spirit in a person's salvation and sanctification, is there a part that a person plays in receiving God's grace? The Bible reveals that there is one key factor on man's part that influences God's impartation of grace. Notice, I said this key factor influences God but does not determine God's choices. God will show mercy and grace to whom He will. No one can force God to show His grace by anything he may do or say. God is never obligated to show His grace because the nature of God's grace is that is freely given.

The Humility Factor

In His Word, God reveals a determining factor in regard to whom He chooses to show His grace. This determining factor has nothing to do with merit, but only with a person's receptivity. What factor of receptivity is God looking for in the giving of His grace?

> *The key human factor for receiving God's grace is humility.*

James 4:6 clearly qualifies to whom God does not and to whom God does give His grace, "But He gives a greater grace. Therefore, *it* says, "God is opposed to the proud, but gives grace to the humble." First Peter 5:5 repeats this same quotation from the Old Testament, "You younger men, likewise, be subject to *your* elders; and all of you, clothe yourselves with humility toward one another, for God is opposed to the proud, but gives grace to the humble." Showing humility is essential in receiving God's grace. God resists the proud but gives His grace to the humble.

If being humble is a key factor in receiving God's grace, then we need to do all we can to be humble. The more we demonstrate true humility before God, the more God will extend to us His grace. True humility is not something a person can feign. A person can put on a pretense of humility through self-deprecation yet that is only false humility. The genuine humility that God is looking for results solely from the inner working of the Spirit of God. A central aspect of man's fallen nature is his pride and self-centeredness. Humans do not easily position themselves in humility before God. Man's pride resists being humbled.

Man's pride is like an unformed piece of steel. The only way for that piece of unformed steel to be shaped into something useful is through being heated to a high temperature and then beaten by a hammer on an anvil. The only way that a prideful person can come to the place of humility is through the Holy Spirit using the hammer of conviction, trials, and failures. A person can choose to yield to God in humility or choose to resist and harden his heart against God. When a person comes to that critical point of humbling himself before God, God will show His grace.

Humility is probably the most misunderstood character trait. The majority of people think of it as a sign of weakness or evidence of a lack of self-confidence. In secular circles, humility is not a valued trait. However, in God's kingdom, humility is a requirement and is highly valued. "And said, "Truly I say to you, unless you are converted and become like children, you will not enter the kingdom of heaven. Whoever then humbles himself as this child, he is the greatest in the kingdom of heaven" (Matt. 18:3–4).

What is humility? It is an attitude that affects nearly everything one does and seriously affects one's relationship with God and others. Humility is a way of thinking about oneself in his relationship with God and others. This character trait comes from recognizing one's dependence on God as well as his interdependent relationship with others.

Humility and Dependence on God

One of the first ways we need to show humility before God is to recognize and confess our absolute dependence on Him. This is especially true when it comes to salvation. A person must recognize his sinfulness and total lack of any ability to earn his salvation. His first act of humility before God must be the confession of sin and a cry for God's forgiveness. A person is most receptive to God's work in his life when he comes to the point of humbling himself before God and seeking His mercy and grace. God will demonstrate His mercy and grace when He sees that a person is humbling himself and has become willing to allow God to work in his life.

After the initial act of humility in trusting God for salvation, believers must learn to continually live humbly before God. Being able to live a life pleasing to God will only come through humbly trusting in God's enabling grace (God's power). God's enabling grace is available to people who have first experienced God's saving grace (God's unmerited favor). Unfortunately, learning to humbly trust in God is something believers will not find easy to do because their pride keeps getting in the way. One can learn to humble himself the easy way or the hard way. Learning the easy way is learning to quickly accept the reality of our sinfulness, weakness, and utter need for God. The hard way is stubbornly thinking that we can do things without God's help. Learning the hard way requires a great deal of personal failure and hardship to break our pride.

Some books that I have read on the grace of God deal briefly with how to receive God's enabling grace. Authors who have written on how believers can receive God's grace use different terms to describe the various ways God's grace flows to a recipient. Some call them avenues, channels, canals, or means of grace. These terms refer to the ways believers can gain access to the grace of God. There are things that a believer can do to help release the flow of God's grace. As believers put into practice the various means of grace, the flow of God's enabling grace will follow.

The most common means of grace are Bible study, prayer, Christian fellowship, and worship. These four means of grace can provide believers with a resource of grace, but only under the right conditions. These means of grace cannot be thought of as ways to earn God's grace. Christians can get into the mentality that they must practice doing what is required to be a good Christian. Subsequently, prayer, Bible study, and going to church are then looked at as ways to earn God's favor and become a duty or obligation rather than being thought of as an opportunity to receive God's grace. These means of grace can become "an ought to" rather than "a want to."

When we turn practicing the means of grace into requirements to earn God's grace, we are putting ourselves back under the Law. When we think we have to work for God's grace, we will not receive it. A Christian can discipline himself in the diligent practice of the means of grace but, for some reason, still not receive much grace from God. I have experienced times when I was doing all the right things but was becoming spiritually dry. In the past, I set up a regimented, daily schedule to pray for a certain amount of time, read so many chapters of the Bible, study and prepare my sermons. You would think that regimenting your day like I was would provide much more of God's grace, but for some unknown reason at the time, the more ordered my day was, the more I became spiritually parched. At first, I thought the reason that I was not getting much out of practicing these means of grace was that I was not doing them enough. So, I would double down and be more regimented in my schedule. This only made things worse. What was I doing wrong? It took me some time to understand what I was doing wrong. I discovered that I was doing the right things but for the wrong reasons. I was more concerned about completing the tasks of prayer and Scripture reading as obligations to be fulfilled rather than in what I was getting spiritually.

Those who have come to know me understand that I am a list person who makes lists of things to do regarding just about everything. I have lists for work to be done for the church, work to do around the house, personal goals (write this book), educational, and spiritual goals. On my lists, I number the things to be done with a little box at the end to check off when done. I get a great amount of satisfaction and a sense of accomplishment when checking off those boxes. Desiring this sense of accomplishment has enabled me to work hard to achieve many things. The problem with this list making is that it does not work very well in receiving God's grace.

Receiving God's grace is not something to be accomplished; it is received freely from God. After being slow to learn this about receiving God's grace, I now take a different approach to receiving God's grace. When practicing the various means of grace, I try to approach them with humility. Rather than taking pride in myself for completing some spiritual practice, I now see them as opportunities to receive more of

God's grace. God gives grace to the humble. It is important that when we partake of the means of grace we do so with humility.

I believe having a schedule to regularly practice the means of grace is very helpful if done with the right attitude and for the right purpose. Believers need to understand and learn to practice the means of receiving God's grace. By nature, people are creatures of habit. After repeating something over a period of time, it becomes a habit. Habits can make or break us. Before a person comes to Christ, he has developed certain habits that reinforced his sinful lifestyle apart from Christ. When a believer commits himself to live a life pleasing to Christ, he will need to develop new habits that will reinforce his new lifestyle in Christ. There are spiritual exercises that can promote believers' growth in grace. If a believer does not practice these means of grace, he will not mature spiritually. It is by practicing these means of grace that God can pour His grace and Spirit into a person's life.

As one studies the book of Acts, he will see how the early Christians devoted themselves to certain practices: "They were continually devoting themselves to the apostles' teaching and to fellowship, to the breaking of bread and to prayer" (Acts 2:42–47). According to this passage from Acts, the early Christians devoted themselves to the following practices: (1) the apostles' teaching (God's Word); (2) fellowship; (3) the breaking of bread (worship); and (4) prayer. By regularly practicing these means of grace, we demonstrate our dependence on God. Why is it so important to regularly study the Word of God? Why have so many devoted their entire lives to studying the Bible?

The Bible is like no other book; it is the most unique book ever written. It is made up of sixty-six individual books written by forty different authors over a span of fifteen centuries, and written in three languages. In spite of this diversity, it is one book, not sixty-six books. Instead of containing conflicting ideas, it is amazingly unified in its content and progression of truth. The Bible is much more than a unique book; it is God's Word to mankind. We must treasure this great revelation from God because it is His Word to all humanity. The Bible is a limitless treasure of knowledge, understanding, wisdom, and insight. Through knowing the Bible, a person can learn about God's character, learn about the nature and fall of humanity, and learn of God's plan of salvation to rescue man from his fallen state. The Bible will give wisdom to those who study and obey it. Wisdom from the Bible will enable us to navigate through life's challenges by making the best choices.

We would not think of going without physical food for a week or more. Food is necessary for physical life. Just as we need food for our bodies, we need spiritual food for our spiritual life. The Word of God is the spiritual food that we need to feed ourselves on a regular basis (1 Pet. 2:2). Some who have been Christians for a while tend to neglect this practice. Some older Christians may think that they know the Bible so well that diligent study of God's Word is no longer necessary. This is a serious mistake. Whatever our level of spiritual maturity we must maintain a healthy diet of God's Word.

There are numerous reasons for learning the contents of the Bible. Learning what is in the Bible can be a substantial means of grace. Grace is God's enablement in many forms. Learning God's Word will help us to grow spiritually (1 Pet. 2:2), help us to overcome sin (Ps. 119:11), and build us up and give us an inheritance (Acts 20:32). Second Timothy 3:14–17 contains a whole list of benefits of learning the Scripture:

> You, however, continue in the things you have learned and become convinced of, knowing from whom you have learned them; and that from childhood you have known the sacred writings which are able to give you the wisdom that leads to salvation through faith which is in Christ Jesus. All Scripture is inspired by God and profitable for teaching, for reproof, for correction, for training in righteousness; so that the man of God may be adequate, equipped for every good work.

The apostle Paul, in his second letter to Timothy, reminded him of how important the Scriptures had been in Timothy's life. Timothy was fortunate to have been taught the Scriptures from his early childhood. Timothy's knowledge of Scripture gave him wisdom that led him to have faith in Christ for his salvation. Paul emphasized that because the Scriptures are inspired by God, they are beneficial for teaching, reproving, correcting, and for training in righteousness. Paul explained to Timothy that knowing the Scripture would help him become a man of God who is adequately equipped to do the good work of ministry. How does a person learn what is in the Bible?

Coming to know the Scriptures is not like reading a book once or twice and then knowing its contents. I laugh to myself when people claim to know the Bible "backwards and forward." Whenever a person boasts about how well he knows the Bible, I know immediately that he does not know the Bible well at all. I have come to the realization, along with a host of others who have studied the Scripture all their lives, that no one will ever completely know and understand all there is to know. Those who think they know the Scripture view the amount of information in the Bible as only a small puddle. In contrast, those who actually understand the depth of knowledge contained in the Bible, view it as a vast ocean of information. Learning God's Word is a great endeavor; it is a lifelong quest. Learning the Bible comes in daily doses and not all at once. Having a schedule of regular Bible study will provide daily sustenance for spiritual growth and also help us make small steps to knowing all we can from Scripture.

The Bible speaks of five ways to know and understand the Scriptures. All five of these ways of learning the Scriptures are important and should be employed in one's pursuit of this knowledge. First, we can learn Scripture through listening to Scriptures being read, "So faith *comes* from hearing, and hearing by the word of Christ" (Rom. 10:17). There are many ways we can listen to Scripture: we can listen to Scripture readings, sermons, Bible lessons, audio recordings of Scriptures, and podcasts. Before the printing press was invented, listening to God's Word was the primary means of learning. People did not have access to the Scriptures to read on their own because there were so few handwritten copies of the Bible and much of the population was illiterate. Those few handwritten copies of the Bible were kept in churches to be brought out and read during services. In his letter to the Colossians, Paul requested that his letter be read aloud in the church along with his letter to the Laodiceans (Col. 4:16).

After the invention of the printing press, copies of the Bible became more plentiful and people eventually were able to own their own personal copy of the Bible. Reading the Bible is the second way of learning the Scriptures. People should make it their goal to read through the entire Bible numerous times. One of my favorite ways to read the Bible is to pick a book of the Bible and read through it many times. I have read some of the shorter New Testament books over a hundred times. I like to read a book of the Bible many times before I look at any commentaries for understanding. Each time you read a passage of Scripture, try to notice things that you did not see in previous readings. If you are reading a book of the Bible, first try to read the whole book through. Try to get an overall picture of what the book is about. After gaining a general idea of the whole book, focus on each chapter and read each chapter many times.

The third way to learn Scripture is by study. Studying Scripture goes much deeper than casual reading. The apostle Paul challenged Timothy to become a good student of Scriptures by studying (KJV) or presenting himself approved: "Be diligent to present yourself approved to God as a workman who does not need to be ashamed, accurately handling the word of truth" (2 Tim. 2:15). We should think of studying God's Word like mining for precious gems and metals. Just reading a passage of Scripture would be like quickly glancing over a patch of ground for anything of value. Some precious gems and metals have been found on the surface but, by far, most have been found after digging into the ground. Studying the Bible is digging under the surface looking for precious gems of truth, knowledge, understanding, and wisdom.

To dig effectively into God's Word, you will need to follow certain steps. There are three basic steps you can follow: (1) observation; (2) interpretation; and (3) application. Study should follow this order to "accurately handle the word of truth" (2 Tim. 2:15). For example, if a person tries to make application before understanding what the passage of Scripture is really saying, he most likely will have a faulty application. Faulty application can lead a person down the wrong path and can bring detrimental results. A person needs to first observe what he is reading. At first, read a passage many times just for observation. As you read portions of Scripture, you should ask yourself, "What is this saying?" Reading a passage several times and in different Bible translations helps you to comprehend what is being said. If you are just studying several verses, you should be sure to read the whole chapter in order to understand how the verses fit into the context and the flow of thought.

After you come to an understanding of what a passage is saying, you need to ask yourself, "What does this passage mean?" This is when you can use the various study tools for assistance. There are many great Scripture mining tools that can help you really dig deeply into God's Word. You can first look up the meaning of certain key words in a dictionary or word study guide. Only after you have done your own study should you consult a commentary. Try to answer the who, what, when, where, and how of the passage. What kind of study tools are helpful in interpreting the Bible? You can start off with several basic tools.

If you are just getting started in Bible study, find a Bible version you can easily understand. The New Living Translation is easy to understand for the person who has never read the Bible before. The King James Version can be difficult for some to understand. If you are not sure, ask your pastor for his recommendation. Most versions come in study or application Bibles that can be very helpful. Next, get a notebook that you will use just for your Bible studies and a pen. Have an English dictionary to start with and, as soon as you can, get a Bible dictionary.

If you really want to get serious about Bible study tools you might consider purchasing: (1) Concordance: *Strong's Exhaustive Concordance* and *Young's Exhaustive Concordance* are the best; (2) Bible Handbooks: *Halley's Bible Handbook, Unger's Bible Dictionary*; (3) Topical Bible: *Nave's Topical Bible*; (4) Commentaries: (do not overly rely on these, let the Scripture speak for itself); and (5) Word studies: *Vine's Complete Expository Dictionary of the Old and New Testament Words*. There are some wonderful computer software programs available for Bible study. The best software that I have found is Logos. I use Logos almost every day. I can do research on biblical topics and specific passages of Scripture in a fraction of the time it would take looking through books.

After you have an understanding of the meaning, you will need to ask yourself and the Holy Spirit, "What does this mean to me, and how should I apply it to my life?" Looking for personal application is the third step in your study process. Here are some good questions to ask: (1) "Are there any sins I need to confess and forsake?" (2) "Are there any ways I need to change my behavior or attitudes?" (3) "What character qualities do I need to grow in?" and (4) "How can I show more love to others?"

The fourth way to learn God's Word is memorization. Memorizing Scripture can be the first part of meditating on it. As a person reads through a verse over and over again contemplating its meaning, he becomes familiar with the words in a passage. Memorizing verses helps a person become so familiar with a certain passage that there is no need to look it up in the Bible. Memorizing Scripture helps a person to be able to readily use a passage of Scripture in witnessing, teaching, or defending oneself against temptation. There will be times when the use of Scripture will be needed immediately at an opportune moment. If a person is not prepared with memorized Scripture, the opportunity can be lost. The Bible describes the Word of God as the Sword of the Spirit (Eph. 6:17). If a soldier cannot get his weapons ready quickly, he could lose his life. If we have Scriptures memorized, we can quickly use the Sword of the Spirit to defend ourselves and defeat the enemy.

Many claim that they cannot memorize anything. Many of these same people who say they cannot memorize have memorized a lot of things: their phone numbers, Social Security number, passwords, and special dates. It is true that some people are more capable than others at memorizing. My wife, Susan, can remember phone numbers for at least fifty people. I do not have that ability; I have to rely on the contact list on my phone.

While memorizing may be more difficult for some, that does not exempt them from trying. Even though memorization requires effort, the reward is worth the effort. There are techniques that aid in memorization. People remember best what they can visualize. We remember pictures far better than words. With this in mind, whenever you try to remember something, you need to put a picture with it. If we can associate words with pictures, it will strengthen memory.

Along with using pictures to assist our memory, repetition is essential for memorization. When a person endeavors to memorize a passage, he needs to break down each verse into small phrases and memorize one phrase at a time. Once a person has a phrase memorized, he can move on to the next phrase. After one has two phrases memorized separately, he then should say them together. A person needs to keep repeating this process until he completes the verse.

Putting words to music is a very effective way to memorize anything. How did we learn the English alphabet as children? We learned it by singing it to a certain tune. I still use that tune to remember the order of letters in the alphabet. That tune is indelibly imprinted on my mind. We can easily remember songs that we have sung many times. I can remember most of the Christian children's songs I learned over sixty years ago. If a person can put Scripture to song, it will be more effective than just the repetition of words alone.

Memory cards can be very helpful. Making memory cards is very simple. Just purchase some 3x5 inch stock cards and write out the verses you want to memorize on separate cards. Start with verses that you are already familiar with and stay with the one version of the Bible that you prefer. Whenever you get some idle time, you can pull memory cards out and review them over and over again. With a little effort you can do it!

The fifth way to learn Scripture is by meditating on verses. The Scriptures put a great amount of importance on meditation on God's Word. God instructs us to meditate on His Word day and night. When Joshua first came into the Promised Land, God instructed him to make meditating on the law a priority, "This book of the law shall not depart from your mouth, but you shall meditate on it day and night, so that you may be careful to do according to all that is written in it; for then you will make your way prosperous, and then you will have success" (Josh. 1:8). Psalm 119 is best known as the longest chapter in the Bible. What most people do not know is that all 176 verses focus on the importance of God's Word. Three times in Psalm 119, there is mention of meditation: meditation on God's precepts (Ps. 119:15), and meditation on God's statutes (Ps. 119:23, 48).

There is a great amount of benefit to meditating on Scripture. God promised Joshua that if he would meditate on God's law, day and night, He would make his ways prosperous and successful (Josh. 1:8). In Psalm 1:2, 3 there is a contrast made between the righteous and the wicked. One of the characteristics of the righteous is that he meditates on God's law day and night. "How blessed is the man who does not walk in the counsel of the wicked, Nor, stand in the path of sinners, Nor, sit in the seat of scoffers! But his delight is in the law of the Lord, And in His law, he meditates day and night" (Ps. 1:1-2).

Meditation on God's Word will make a person wise, "Your commandments make me wiser than my enemies, For, they are ever mine" (Ps. 119:98). Meditation on God's testimonies gives superior insight. "I have more insight than all my teachers, For Your testimonies are my meditation" (Ps. 119:99). Those who love God's law will have great peace and nothing will cause them to stumble (Ps. 119:165).

Just how does a person meditate on God's Word? Notice that often when Scripture speaks about meditation, it mentions meditating "day and night." This gives us a clue as to how meditation on God's Word happens. Meditation on God's Word is the opposite of what Eastern religions mean by meditation. In Eastern religions, meditation is an exercise to "empty the mind," whereas meditation on God's Word means to fill or saturate our minds with Scripture. To meditate on God's Word means to let a passage of Scripture "soak" into your mind throughout the day. Meditating is just like when a person marinates a piece of meat for hours to give it extra flavor when cooked. We are to let a passage of Scripture "marinate" in our minds to change our way of thinking. As the Word of God saturates our minds, it will have a cleansing effect (John 15:3; 17:17). As we meditate on God's Word, the Holy Spirit begins the work of transforming our minds (Rom. 12:2).

Meditation on God's Word does more than just affect the mind. Once the Word of God is saturating your mind, it will begin to permeate your soul and spirit. The Word can cleanse the soul of things that infect one's emotions, such as bitterness, hatred, anger, and worry. Meditating on God's Word can drive away anxiety and replace it with reassuring peace. Meditation can bring healing to the soul like oil being poured on deep emotional wounds. As we meditate, we need to allow the Holy Spirit to redirect our will to conform with His. Our spirit can be strengthened and empowered through meditation on Scripture. When we meditate on God's Word, we are extracting the rich spiritual nutrients held within it. These rich spiritual nutrients bring strength and vitality to our spirit.

A good way to remember the five ways to learn the Bible is to think of them as fingers on a hand. I put hearing the Word as the smallest finger, the next finger as reading the Word, and the longest finger as studying the Word. The first finger represents memorization, and the thumb represents meditation. All these fingers together help us to get a good grip on God's Word. If we only use the small finger (hearing), we will not have a good grip on God's Word. If we hear and read the Word of God, that is better than just one finger, but still not enough to get a good grip. Using three fingers is better, but still does not create a good grip. When you add the fourth finger and the thumb, you will have a full grip. The thumb is essential for getting a good grip with the hand. Think of how difficult it would be to hold anything without a thumb. This is how it is with getting a full grasp of God's Word. It is meditating on the Word that really helps it to have the maximum impact on our lives.

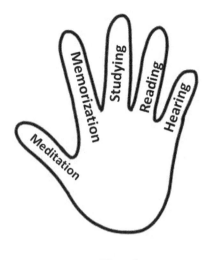

Hand

Humility and Learning God's Word

Some believers have found Bible study to be difficult and seemingly irrelevant. One of the most important factors in understanding Scripture is having God's help. The Holy Spirit is the author of the Bible and, therefore, the most qualified to explain its meaning. Without the aid of the Holy Spirit, a person will not understand much of the Bible or its relevance to his life. Each time one studies or hears God's Word, he needs to show humility by asking for God's help. People cannot approach reading the Word of God as just an intellectual activity. People will not be able to understand with their intellect only because the human mind does not understand the things of the Spirit of God, "But a natural man does not accept the things of the Spirit of God, for they are foolishness to him; and he cannot understand them, because they are spiritually appraised" (1 Cor. 2:14).

A person must be born again to have the Holy Spirit's help in understanding the Bible. An unbeliever will not comprehend the things of God because he simply has his finite intellect to understand the infinite. When we try to learn the Word of God, we show humility by asking for God's help and by our dependence on the Holy Spirit. The Bible states that God will teach the humble His way, "He leads the humble in justice, And He teaches the humble His way" (Ps. 25:9). When a person is trying to learn the Word through hearing, reading, studying, memorizing, and meditating, he must receive it with humility.

"Therefore, putting aside all filthiness and *all* that remains of wickedness, in humility receive the word implanted, which is able to save your souls" (James 1:21). This verse from the book of James mentions that the Word is implanted like a seed into ground. Jesus gave a similar comparison to the implanted Word in His Parable of the Sower (Mark. 4:1–20). A sower drops some seeds on the roadside where the ground is hard; some seeds are thrown onto rocky ground and some are thrown on ground covered with weeds. Finally, the sower throws some seeds onto good soil where they catch root and eventually produce much fruit. The different types of soil represent different conditions of people's hearts. Some people's hearts are like hardened soil which is not receptive to the Word of God and are quickly taken away by Satan. Some people's hearts are like "stony ground" where they do receive the Word but then do not endure when adversity comes. Some people's hearts are like ground full of weeds. The Word does not last because it is choked out by the weeds of the deceitfulness of riches and the lust for things. Jesus described the "good soil" as people who hear the Word of God and accept it. What is this "good soil" where a person is receptive to receive and believe God's Word? This "good soil" is a humble heart which is receptive to the Word.

When we hear the Word of God preached, we can show humility by paying close attention to what is said. It is important to have a humble attitude that acknowledges that there is much more to learn. When we do not pay attention to the preaching of the Word, we show disrespect for God's Word and to the preacher. After preaching for over fifty-three years, I have seen a great amount of disrespect toward God's Word when it is being proclaimed. Some talk to each other during the sermon, some read books, some sleep, and some daydream. The biggest problem I see today is people's addiction to their phones. Texting and scrolling are more of a problem than people talking on their phones during a church service. People will sit through a whole sermon texting the entire time and not paying any attention to the Word being preached. A person shows humility when he comes to receive all he can out of a sermon. The humble person will be listening to not only the preacher, but also to the Holy Spirit. The humble student will take notes to make sure he does not forget what is said.

How does a person show humility when he is reading the Word? A humble person will not assume that he knows much about the passage of Scripture that he is reading. Each time we read a passage of Scripture, we need to approach it as if it were our first time reading it. We can skim over a passage of Scripture, assuming we already know all we need to know. A humble approach will not assume a particular doctrinal interpretation to a passage of Scripture. Each time we read a portion of Scripture, we need to clear our minds of all that we think it says and let it speak to us in a fresh and deeper way.

How does a person show humility in his study of Scripture? The humble student believes that he has just begun to discover all there is to know. It is prideful to assume we already know everything there is to know from a passage of Scripture. The humble student will not be prideful in his use of study tools. By that, I mean a humble student will look for all the help he can by using Bible study tools. Some may think that they do not need any help in studying the Bible. Trying to dig deeply into God's Word without study tools is like trying to dig a hole with your hands. A person can just use his hands, but why not use some tools like a shovel and pick, or better yet, a backhoe digger? There is no glory in taking hours to research something when it can be accomplished in minutes. Using Bible study tools not only helps you work faster, but it also helps you to dig much deeper.

Application

1. Do you recognize your absolute dependence on God?

2. Have you humbled yourself before God by confessing your sins?

3. Do you sometimes feel that prayer, Bible study, and church attendance are more of an obligation than an opportunity?

4. Do you regularly read the Bible?

5. Have you learned to study the Bible?

6. How well do you pay attention when someone is preaching a sermon?

7. Have you memorized any Bible verses?

8. Have you ever meditated on Scripture?

CHAPTER 17

Daily Prayer

If learning God's Word is our spiritual nutrition, then prayer must be the air we breathe. The importance of prayer as a means of grace cannot be overemphasized. Prayer is not complicated to understand; it is simply communicating with God. Prayer is talking with God, not just to God. For many people, prayer is no more than giving God a wish list of things they want Him to do. In contrast, prayer is to be a two-way communication between us and God. Through prayer, a person can keep in constant touch with God. Prayer should be more than just talking to God; prayer should be a spiritual encounter with God. Through prayer, a believer can come to know God and experience His power. Through prayer, a person can have a constant flow of God's grace into his life. It is through the grace of God that we have access to God in prayer. By having this access to God, we can experience God's grace in abundance 24/7.

As we study the Word of God, we will see the importance God has placed on prayer. From the Old Testament to the New Testament, we observe that the great men and women of God knew how to pray and practiced regular prayer. If we are to know God on a personal level, we must do so through having a consistent prayer life. Interestingly, our greatest example of a consistent prayer life is found in Jesus Christ Himself. The Gospels reveal much about the life and ministry of Jesus. One of the things that stands out about Christ is how closely He kept in touch with His Father through prayer. We can see that Jesus made it a priority to communicate with the Father. There were times He would pray all day, and sometimes He would pray all night (Luke 6:12). Jesus was in constant contact with the Father through prayer. Christ's disciples noticed how He prayed and were moved to ask Christ how to pray. Jesus taught them how to pray both through example and teaching.

What is the primary purpose for prayer? Many believe getting God to answer their requests is the obvious answer, but that's not it. God does answer prayer, but that is not His priority; His priority is to have a closer relationship with us. Just as Jesus spent much time in prayer and was one with the Father, God want us to spend time with Him. Our primary purpose of prayer should be to develop a closer relationship with God. We are to have special times in God's presence where we come to know Him. The greatest desire of the apostle Paul was to know Christ, "that I may know Him and the power of His resurrection and the fellowship of His sufferings, being conformed to His death; in order that I may attain to the resurrection from the dead" (Phil. 3:10, 11). Just as Paul's greatest desire was to know Christ, we, too, should have that same passion to know Christ.

The Greek word used for "know" in Philippians 3:10 is *ginosko* (1097). "In the New Testament *ginosko* frequently indicates a relation between the person "knowing" and object known; in this respect, what is "known" is of value or importance to the one who knows, hence the establishment of the relationship."[93] This Greek word speaks of an intimate, growing relationship. It is only through spending time with God in prayer that we really *know* Him.

One of the Hebrew words for "to know" is *yada* (3045). "This verb occurs about 1,400 times (995 in Hebrew and 47 times in Aramaic) in the Bible. Essentially *yada* means: (1) to know by observation and reflection (thinking), and (2) To know by experience."[94] It is the second meaning of *yada* that is used to describe intimate relations as in Genesis 4:1—Adam "knew" Eve. The greater purpose of prayer is to seek to know the Lord for Himself, not for what He can do for us. Prayer is the major way to get to know God and to grow in our love for Him.

God tells us that He wants us to love Him with our whole being, "and you shall love the Lord your God with all your heart, and with all your soul, and with all your mind, and with all your strength" (Mark 12:30). We are to seek God with all our hearts in prayer, "You will seek Me and find *Me* when you search for Me with all your heart" (Jer. 29:13). The primary purposes of prayer are to get to know God, to have fellowship with Him, and to grow in our love for Him. If we pray only to receive something, we are missing deeper reasons and benefits of prayer.

I am not saying that God does not care about answering our prayers; He most surely does. God desires for us to come to Him with our needs because He wants to meet those needs and for us to come to know Him personally. It is in knowing God that we experience His abundant grace.

There are many ways we can pray. A believer should not just pray in the same manner every time he prays. When we pray, we do not have to always pray the same type of prayer. If we always pray the same way, our prayers can become routine and stale. Learning to pray different types of prayer can bring freshness and vitality to our times of prayer. When in prayer, we can pray different types of prayer or any combination of these types of prayer. The different types of prayer that I will explain are: the prayer of adoration, the prayer of thanksgiving, the prayer of confession, the prayer of petition, and the prayer of communion.

A prayer of adoration is the highest form of prayer. Instead of rushing into prayer with our petitions, we should begin with adoration of God. We see this in the way Jesus taught us to pray in what is known as the Lord's Prayer. Jesus started His prayer with, "Father, hallowed be Thy name" (Luke 11:2). Prayer should begin with a focus on the greatness and holiness of God. As we focus on God's greatness at the beginning of our prayers instead of the greatness of our problems, our faith is increased to believe that there is nothing impossible for a great and almighty God. Sometimes when we pray, we spend the whole time just worshiping God. This is my favorite type of prayer. I love to spend time worshiping God while I am listening to worship music. It is when I am worshiping God that I experience my greatest sense of His presence. When I express my love for God in prayer, it becomes a wonderful time of fellowship with God. I feel God's warm embrace of love as I express my love for Him. When I pray in adoration it is an act of sweet surrender to His love. Prayer of adoration is prayer in its finest form.

Another type of prayer is the prayer of thanksgiving. A prayer of thanksgiving is when a person gives thanks to God for what He has done and for what He will do. Every prayer should include some giving of thanks to God. Scripture directs us to offer thanksgiving to God, "Offer to God a sacrifice of thanksgiving" (Ps. 50:14), "always giving thanks for all things in the name of our Lord Jesus Christ to God, even the Father" (Eph. 5:20), "Be anxious for nothing, but in everything by prayer and supplication with thanksgiving let your requests be made known to God" (Phil. 4:6), and "Devote yourselves to prayer, keeping alert in it with *an attitude of* thanksgiving" (Col. 4:2). As we look at the prayers of Christ, we will see Him often giving thanks to the Father. At the gravesite of Lazarus, Christ gave thanks to the Father for answering His prayers (John 11:41). At the Last Supper, Christ gave thanks to the Father as He broke the bread and shared the cup (Mark 14:23).

Another type of prayer is the prayer of confession. There is a real need for confession when we approach a holy God in prayer. One cannot expect God to hear his prayer if he is regarding or cherishing sin in his life. "If I regard wickedness in my heart, The Lord will not hear" (Ps. 66:18). Our confession of sin to God must be sincere and prompted by the conviction of the Holy Spirit. God is not fooled by the false confessions of a person who desires forgiveness but has no desire to turn from his sin through repentance.

What is God looking for in our confession of sin? The Lord is looking for the humility that comes from brokenness: "The Lord is near to the brokenhearted and saves those who are crushed in spirit" (Ps. 34:18). True confession comes from a heart of repentance and produces a release from guilt. With our confession of sin, the barrier of sin is broken down so we then have free access to God in prayer. God responds graciously to true confession. "He who conceals his transgressions will not prosper, but he who confesses and forsakes *them* will find compassion" (Prov. 28:13). A very important verse that every believer should memorize is 1 John 1:9, "If we confess our sins, He is faithful and righteous to forgive us our sins and to cleanse us from all unrighteousness."

The prayer of petition is the most common type of prayer. For many, this is the only type of prayer that they practice. There is nothing wrong with bringing our petitions to God, but that should not be the only type of prayer that we pray. Prayers of petition are requests by the individual who presents his own needs and concerns to God. We are encouraged to bring our needs to God. It is not wrong or selfish to pray for personal needs and concerns. First Peter 5:7 tells us that God desires us to bring our cares to Him, "casting all your anxiety on Him, because He cares for you."

When we pray, we should avoid asking God for things with the wrong motive, "You ask and do not receive, because you ask with wrong motives, so that you may spend *it* on your pleasures" (James 4:3). What this means is that we should not be praying for things that will feed our fleshly sinful nature. For example, it would be wrong to pray for riches and fame.

The prayer of intercession is another form of the prayer of petition. Prayers of petition are generally for one's own needs while prayers of intercession are always for other's needs. Prayers of intercession are requests made to God on behalf of others. Prayers of intercession are the most frequently mentioned in Scripture. When we pray, we should include prayer for others besides ourselves. When we pray for others, we should not limit that to just our own family circle. We all have larger circles of contacts for whom we can pray. While we intercede for those in our inner circle, such as family and close friends, we should also intercede for fellow church members, coworkers, classmates, our neighbors, and for the lost.

In chapter 14, I wrote about how the Holy Spirit helps believers communicate with God in prayer. The Holy Spirit guides us when we pray intercessory prayers. The Holy Spirit can put certain people on our minds as we pray. Intercessory prayer can become a very important ministry. Every church needs intercessory prayer warriors to help the church be successful against the powers of darkness. Churches need to have times of prayer when people from the congregation come together to uphold the leadership and ministries of the church. A praying church is a powerful church. A church that does not come together for prayer will be a powerless and defeated church.

The last type of prayer discussed here is the prayer of communion. The prayer of communion is a type of prayer where one experiences a two-way conversation with God. We understand how we can speak to God but how does God speak to us? God can speak to us through His Word: "Your word is a lamp to my feet and a light to my path" (Ps. 119:105). God can speak to us with an audible voice as He did with Moses (Exod. 3:4). Besides speaking to us from His Word, the most common way that God communicates with us is through our thoughts. Since our thoughts can come from different sources, how can we discern which thoughts are from God? First, thoughts from God should always agree with the Word of God. Second, they are spontaneous and not from a logical progression of thoughts. Third, they are as if God is speaking in first person. Fourth, they are gentle, loving, and never condemning. Fifth, they cause a special reaction within our being (i.e., a sense of excitement, conviction, faith, joy). Sixth, they come with persistent, affirmative confirmation. Seventh, they are subject to our spiritual authorities.

The challenge for those engaged in prayers of communion is for them to be better listeners. We need to recognize the voice of God. Jesus said that His sheep know His voice (John 10:27). How can we become better listeners? To become a better listener, we first need to stop doing all the talking in prayer. Psalm 46:10 gives us some insight into how to know God, "Be still, and know that I am God." During our prayers of communion, we need to be still before the Lord, waiting to hear from Him. Try to keep your mind clear and listen for thoughts from the Lord. It is helpful to have a journal to write down the thoughts that you receive (Hab. 2:1–2). Remember to always make sure that whatever thoughts you receive are in line with the Word of God and the other six determining factors.

In addition to the different types of prayer, it is important to understand the various modes of prayer. There are three modes of prayer: presence praying, private praying, and public praying. All the modes of prayer should be practiced with none being neglected. Presence praying is the maintaining of a sense of God's presence within ourselves throughout the day. Throughout each day, one can keep in constant contact with God though worship and prayer. When our minds are not completely occupied with something requiring our full attention, our minds can gravitate toward talking to God. Presence praying is praying without ceasing (1 Thess. 5:17). This mode of prayer reflects a person's level of relationship with God. One will either be carnally minded or spiritually minded.

Romans 8:5 describes how the mind set on the flesh functions in contrast to the mind set on the things of the Spirit. "For those who are according to the flesh set their minds on the things of the flesh, but those who are according to the Spirit, the things of the Spirit." A person who is carnally minded will be dwelling on the things of the flesh and will not be able to maintain presence praying. However, a person who is spiritually minded will be thinking about spiritual things and will be able to maintain a sense of God's presence. The advantage of this mode of prayer is that we can pray anytime and anywhere. We should not rely entirely on this mode of prayer because there is value in practicing the other two modes of praying.

Private praying is the mode of praying when one secludes himself from distractions, activities, and people. The purpose of this mode of praying is to meet exclusively with God in prayer. Christ described this mode of prayer as praying in secret: "But you, when you pray, go into your inner room, close your door and pray to your Father who is in secret, and your Father who sees *what is done* in secret will reward you" (Matt. 6:6). Christ referred to the "inner room" as a place of seclusion for private praying. Quite often, Jesus went away into the mountains to a secluded place to pray. This mode of prayer enables one to freely pray all the different types of prayer: adoration, thanksgiving, confession, petition, intercession, and communion.

This mode of prayer requires effort and discipline; it requires a special time and place. The advantages of this mode of praying are its great impact in changing our personal lives and relationship with God. Since private praying is so important, Satan will try to disrupt this mode of prayer because it is the easiest to stop. Our times of seclusion are prone to disruption because our minds are so easily distracted. Even with our best efforts, it will be a challenge to find a time and a place where there will be the least amount of distraction.

The last mode of praying is public praying. This mode of prayer is when believers join together with others in prayer. When we join with others, our prayer become more effective (Matt. 18:19; Lev. 26:8). There are different ways to pray in public: one person can lead in praying while others pray along, different people can lead in prayer, or one at a time while others pray along, or all can be praying together but separately and to themselves. There are some advantages to public praying. One is that it helps the new Christian learn to pray by hearing others pray. Another advantage is that public praying draws us closer to those with whom we pray, such as family, church members, and friends. This mode of praying helps us become more aware of other's needs.

Some cautions need to be heeded when it comes to praying publicly. When someone leads in public prayer, he can do so with the intention of impressing those who are listening. Jesus gave a warning about public prayer: "When you pray, you are not to be like the hypocrites; for they love to stand and pray in the synagogues and on the street corners so that they may be seen by men. Truly I say to you, they have their reward in full" (Matt. 6:5). Some individuals lead in prayer speaking in a manner other than how they normally speak. Some speak in the "King

James Version" English, thinking it is somehow more spiritual to use antiquated language. Some speak with great eloquence and booming voices. There is also a danger that those who lead in prayer at prayer meetings may dominate the whole time of prayer and not allow others to lead in prayer.

The subject matter of what is appropriate to pray for in public prayer meetings should be given consideration. Some private matters should not be openly mentioned in public prayer. There is no need to go into great detail about certain needs. This can become a form of gossip or giving of bad reports. Prayer meetings have gained the reputation of being the place to be if you want to know all the latest scoop on what is happening in the church. If cautions are taken in public prayer, it can be a source of blessing for all who participate instead of a place to hear and spread gossip.

Humility and Prayer

One of the most important means of grace that we can practice is prayer. Prayer, if practiced correctly, can open the floodgates of God's grace. Just praying in any manner does not guarantee an outpouring of God's grace.

> *Having the right attitude in prayer is more important than having the right words.*

What is the right attitude? God is turned off by any pride that we may have in our prayers but is pleased when He sees humility. The Scriptures say that God is opposed to the proud but gives His grace to the humble (James 4:6). Having a humble attitude toward God in prayer will clear the way for God's grace to flow freely.

One of the most important ways that a believer can show humility is in his dependence on God through prayer. I have noticed that the seriousness of our need often determines the amount we pray. When there is a great need for God's help, people tend to seek Him more in prayer. When a person feels that there is no great need for God's intervention, he prays less. Certainly, pride can hinder a person's prayer life because he feels that he can take care of almost anything without God's help. The less a person feels that he needs God, the less he will pray.

A humble believer will pray more because he is aware of his great need for God all the time, not just in emergencies or serious problems. The humble person begins each day by declaring his weaknesses and his dependence upon God's grace. Throughout each day, the humble believer will call on God for help. The humble believer will be in constant communication with God, "praying without ceasing," seeking His help, protection, provision, wisdom, and strength.

Not only does a humble believer pray more, but the way he prays is marked by humility. How does a person pray with humility? A humble believer approaches God in prayer with humility knowing he can only approach God through His grace. To approach God, one must humble himself by confessing his sins and weaknesses. A proud person will come to God in prayer boasting about how good he is and how God must be pleased with him. This was the point of Christ's parable about two people who went into the temple to pray (Luke 18:9–14). One was a Pharisee and the other person was a tax collector.

The Pharisee stood and was praying thus to himself, "God, I thank Thee that I am not like the other people: swindlers, unjust, adulterers, or even like this tax gatherer. "I fast twice a week; I pay tithes of all that I get." The Pharisee prayed thanking God that he was more righteous than others, and assumed God would answer his prayers because he was more deserving. The tax collector prayed a markedly different sort of prayer. When he prayed, he was not even willing to lift up his eyes to heaven, but was beating his breast, saying, "God, be merciful to me, the sinner!" Which one do you think had his prayers answered? It was the one who humbled himself. I tell you, this man went down to his house justified rather than the other; for everyone who exalts himself shall be humbled, but he who humbles himself shall be exalted.

It was not the person who thought he merited God's favor but the one who humbled himself before God in prayer who received God's grace.

An unpretentious person demonstrates humility in the way he approaches God in prayer. The humble person does not assume that God owes him anything but solely trusts in God's grace. The humble believer does not make demands on God but always makes an appeal to God. When a person humbly appeals to God, he appeals to God on basis of what would bring the most glory to God. When Moses prayed to God on behalf of the Israelites, he appealed to God's reputation not to destroy them (Exod. 32:7-11). A humble appeal can remind God of the promises that He has made in His Word. Additionally, a humble appeal in prayer does not demand God to act because Scripture is quoted; some have the audacity to think they can command God to do what they want. Some, in their distorted thinking, believe that commanding God in prayer shows deep faith. This audacious attitude does not show faith; it shows a great amount of disrespect for the sovereignty of God.

Some have been taught that to say, "If it be your will," in prayer is showing a lack of faith. I disagree with this teaching. I think surrendering the answer into God's sovereign will shows humility. In the Garden of Gethsemane, Jesus prayed these words, "Father, if thou art willing, remove this cup from Me, yet not my will, but Thine be done" (Luke 24:42). Jesus was humbling Himself to let the Father do His will. Believers are thus to follow Jesus's example of praying. If Jesus surrendered to the Father's will, should not all followers of Christ do the same? It is arrogant to assume that we know the will of God in everything by refusing to say, "If it be your will." What a person desires as he petitions God does not always agree with what God wants. Remember, God always answers prayer. The answer may be yes, or it may be no, or it may be not yet. The praying person does not always get the answer he wants, but in humility he surrenders to the Father's will.

Humility and Fasting

Fasting is something Christians need to practice at times in conjunction with prayer. As one studies Scripture, he will discover that many great men and women of God practiced fasting. Great prayer warriors have learned that fasting gives greater power to their prayers. Although fasting appears to be a dying practice among modern American Christians, it is just as important as ever for those who are serious about getting answers to prayer. It is quite possible the reason we do not see more prayers being answered today is because Christians have neglected to combine fasting with prayer.

What is it about fasting that adds more power to our prayers? I believe that there are several factors in fasting that strengthen our prayers. First, fasting demonstrates to God how serious we are about

Him answering our prayers. Second, fasting shows greater faith in God answering our prayer. Third, fasting shows God our humility. To fast requires us to humble ourselves by denying our flesh what it desires. Fasting makes us weak physically and more dependent on God.

Application

1. What is your greatest purpose in praying?

2. Do you feel that you are growing closer to God?

3. Have you ever sensed God's presence when you prayed?

4. What types of prayer do pray most often? Example: petition, adoration, confession, and so forth.

5. Check off those types of prayers that you have prayed.
   Prayers of adoration
   Prayers of thanksgiving
   Prayers of confession
   Prayers of petition/intercession
   Prayers of communion

6. Have you ever felt that God was speaking to you while you were praying?

7. How often do you think about and talk to God throughout your normal day?

8. Do you have times of private prayer?

9. Have you participated in public prayer?

10. Have you ever led in public prayer?

11. In what ways do you show humility before God when you pray?

12. Have you ever fasted and prayed?

CHAPTER 18

Regular Christian Fellowship

We will examine Christian fellowship as the third means of grace. The first two means of grace were regular study of God's Word and daily prayer. Christian fellowship is just as important as a means of grace as Bible study and prayer. Even though regular Christian fellowship is a vital means of grace, it is the most neglected. When the Bible talks about fellowship, it is referring to believers coming together regularly and developing close relationships with each other. A large portion of Christians do not see the need for fellowship with other Christians or for being connected to a local church. Many Christians may have tried to get connected with other Christians then found that it requires a lot of patience and perseverance to establish close relationships.

It is important to understand that church attendance and fellowship are not exactly the same thing. You can attend a church but not have fellowship. It is unfortunate that some Christians can attend a church but not get connected in friendships with others in the church. People are looking for more than a smile and a handshake; they are looking to develop friendships and a sense of family. Some churches are better than others when it comes to having real fellowship. Attending a church but not connecting with others in friendship does not qualify as fellowship.

Just because some churches are not conducive to developing fellowship does not mean that a person should stop going to church. By attending church, a person can find opportunities to meet others and develop friendships. Staying home from church greatly reduces the chances of finding Christian friends. Looking for fellowship is just one of many reasons for attending church. Becoming committed to a church provides an avenue for the other means of grace such as hearing God's Word, praying, worship, giving, and serving. In spite of all the means of grace that churches can provide, many believe that they do not need church. Many Christians feel that they can do just fine without being part of any church. If people can read their Bibles, pray, and watch services on TV at home, what is the need for church? Many who call themselves Christians make excuses as to why they do not need to or want to belong to any church, "They are just a bunch of hypocrites," "All they want is my money," or "I was hurt by someone in the church so now I just stay home."

No matter what excuses those who consider themselves Christians give for not becoming committed to a local church, they do not negate the fact that they are not obeying all the "one another commands" found in the New Testament. It is only in the context of close relationships with other believers that these "one another commandments" can be fulfilled. The command to love one another as fellow believers is the most mentioned of all the "one another commands." When a person claims to be a Christian but does not want to have fellowship with other believers, he is in direct disobedience to Christ's commands that believers love each other. "This is My commandment, that you love one another, just as I have loved you" (John 15:12).

If you love someone you will want to be together with him. If you love someone you will be devoted to him. If you love someone you will accept, serve, forgive, pray for, encourage, bear his burdens, and care for him. In order to be able to obey all these commands, one must become part of a group of believers who are devoted to fellowshipping with each other as a church or small group. It is helpful when church-sponsored opportunities for fellowship such as small group meetings are provided. If your church does not offer structured opportunities, you can take the initiative to reach out to some in your church and try to develop a friendship with them. These friendships can develop wonderful fellowship.

The "One Another Commandments" of the New Testament

1. "Love one another"	John 13:34, 35; 15:12, 17, Romans 13:8; 1 Thessalonians 3:12, 4:9; 1 Peter 1:22; 1 John 3:11, 23; 4:7, 11, 12
2. "Be devoted to one another"	Romans 12:10
3. "Prefer (honor) one another"	Romans 12:10
4. "Serve one another"	Galatians 5:13
5. "Bear one another's burdens"	Galatians 6:2
6. "Forgiving one another"	Ephesians 4:32; Colossians 3:13
7. Bearing with one another	Colossians 3:13; Ephesians 4:2
8. "Be kind one to another"	Ephesians 4:32
9. "Encourage one another"	1 Thessalonians 5:11; Hebrews 3:13, 10:25
10. "Build up one another"	1 Thessalonians 5:11
11. "Confess your faults one to another"	James 5:16
12. "Pray one for another"	James 5:16
14. "Accept one another"	Romans 15:7
15. "Admonish one another"	Romans 15:14; Colossians 3:16
16. "Teach one another"	Colossians 3:16
17. "Care for one another"	1 Corinthians 12:25
18. "Comfort one another"	1 Thessalonians 4:18
19. "Be subject to one another"	Ephesians 5:21
20. "Regard one another"	Philippians 2:3 21.
21. "Stimulate one another"	Hebrews 10:24 22.
22. "Humility toward one another"	1 Peter 5:5 23.
23. "Be at peace with one another"	Mark 9:50; 1 Thessalonians 5:13, 24.
24. " Do not lie to one another"	Colossians 3:9, 25.

25. "Not to judge each other"	Romans 14:3 26.
26. "Do not challenge one another"	Galatians 5:26 27.
27. "Not to envy one another"	Galatians 5:26

These "one another commandments," located in the letters written to various New Testament churches are Christ's commands to His disciples. The direct audience of these commands is the body of Christ or the Church in general. These commands are directives on how believers are to treat each other as a loving family. When these commands are obeyed, relationships will be greatly strengthened, and fellowship will flourish. These "one another" commandments, which instruct us how to treat others, are applicable in any relationship such as marriage, family, and friendships. God wants His children to love each other and have strong bonds of unity within His family.

God loves all of humanity and desires a close relationship with them. The whole plan of salvation was for the purpose of restoring humanity to a right relationship with God. Through God's plan of redemption, people are now able to become children of God. God loves us and desires for us to love Him through being part of His family. By being adopted into God's family, we can now know and experience God's love. Is everyone considered part of God's family or is there only a select group who is considered part of God's family? All are created by God, but not all are His children who belong to His family. There is a universal call for all to become part of God's family, but to become part of God's family one must believe in Christ and be born again. When a person is born again, he then becomes a child of God and is adopted into God's family.

While being part of God's family brings many blessings of grace, it also brings some responsibilities. One of the important responsibilities of being a member of God's family is that God commands us to love Him and to sincerely love the other members of His family. God wants His family members to love each other just as He has loved them. "A new commandment I give to you, that you love one another, even as I have loved you, that you also love one another" (John 13:34). God wants His love shown in His family by those family members loving each other and getting along with each other. When Christians show love to each other, there is a great witness to the world that we are Christ's disciples: "By this all men will know that you are My disciples, if you have love for one another" (John 13:35).

My wife and I have a family of three children who are now adults. As our children were growing up, they did not always get along with each other. At times there was division and strife among our children. When I saw this strife among the siblings, I was grieved and tried to help my children love and forgive each other. I feared that the division between them would become a permanent division throughout their adult lives. I am happy to report that now, as adults, my children love each other and get along well with each other. When I see them enjoying doing things together, it brings great joy to my heart. One of the most joyful times in my life is when our family gathers for special occasions such as getting together for a family vacation every year.

This is how it is with our heavenly Father. Our heavenly Father is grieved when He sees division and strife among His children. It brings great joy to the Father when He sees His family loving each other and being close to one another. God desires for His family to gather frequently and to grow in love and unity with each other, "that they may all be one; even as You, Father, *are* in Me and I in You, that they also may be in Us, so that the world may believe that You sent Me" (John 17:21).

When a person becomes a child of God, he is made part of the Body of Christ. The Body of Christ is made up of all those who are children of God all over the world. This body of Christ is also referred to as the Church. This Church is a universal church that includes all believers in Christ all over the world. This universal church is not any organization of man but a spiritual group comprised of all who are God's family on earth. The universal church is an abstract concept that believers understand by faith. God knows those who are part of His family. Believers do not know all who make up the Church nor can they relate to all of them. Yet, the practical aspects of being in God's family are not realized in the universal church but in the local expression of the Body of Christ in churches. Being part of the universal church is not enough; every believer must become part of a local church to fully benefit from being part of the family of God. Believers must get connected to real people not just to an abstract concept of being part of the body of Christ.

Many people think that going to church means going to a building called a church. The local church is not the building called a church but a group of people who come together as believers in Christ. A local church can meet in a building considered a church building or any other meeting place. The local church can meet in theaters, rented office space, schools, homes or any place considered appropriate for meeting. The local church is not a place but is a group of closely connected believers who are committed to love each other, serve each other, and work together to fulfill God's purposes.

In order to have regular fellowship as a means of grace, every believer must get connected to a group of other believers who are a local church. Belonging to a local church is of utmost importance for every believer. There are many excuses that people use to avoid going to church. None of these excuses are valid reasons to disobey God's command that we come together and love each other as Christians. Getting connected with other Christians is not easy because churches are groups of imperfect people and imperfect people have problems getting along with each other. We cannot abandon belonging to a church just because there are people in churches who do not live up to the standard of perfection. The whole point of coming together is to be committed to loving each other in spite of shortcomings.

In the book of Acts, we observe that the early church was devoted to fellowship (Acts 2:42). Commitment to attend church services is just a part of what is involved in the concept of fellowship. The Greek word for "fellowship" used in Acts 2:42 is *koinōnia* (2842) denotes much more than just meeting together. People can regularly meet with a large group each Sunday and not experience *koinōnia*. *Koinōnia* means "communion, fellowship, sharing in common."[95] Another form of this word is *koinōnos* (2844) which denotes "a partaker" or partner."[96] Put in modern terms, it means to become the closest of friends, to share common interests, projects, possessions, and lives. To be devoted to fellowship means more than a commitment to attend church. A person can be devoted to attending church services but still not have fellowship or communion. Fellowship requires not only a commitment to attending church services but a commitment to developing close personal relationships with others in one's church.

Koinōnia fellowship requires not only commitment to develop close personal relationships but also the giving of time to get to know and develop friendships with others in the church. This type of fellowship involves serving each other and serving together in ministry. Getting involved in ministry together helps build strong bonds of fellowship.

Faithful attendance to church services provides involvement in several means of grace: listening to God's Word, praying together, worshiping God, and, hopefully, a chance to develop *koinōnia* fellowship. *Koinōnia* fellowship develops best in small group settings rather than in large church services. *Koinōnia* fellowship is a means of grace in small group settings or in personal fellowship.

How does fellowship provide a means of receiving God's grace? God uses believers as conductors of His grace both to the unsaved and the saved. In the next Part Six: Horizontal Grace, of this book, I will explain in more detail how God uses believers in showing horizonal grace. Vertical grace is what God freely gives to humanity; horizontal grace is the grace of God believers are to freely give to others. There is a great emphasis in Scripture on how believers are to show an abundance of love, grace, and mercy to other believers. Certainly, grace cannot flow through believers if there is not a close connection between them. By becoming part of a church and experiencing close fellowship, all the grace gifts (Rom. 12:6–8) that God has given to individual believers can be expressed. If the grace gifts are fully functioning in church, they will benefit believers by anointed proclamation of God's Word, practical help in service, words of encouragement, instruction in God's Word, financial assistance if needed, guidance by leadership, and being shown compassion and mercy in times of suffering.

Thus, the stronger the bonds of fellowship, the stronger the grace gifts will flow. If a believer chooses to avoid attending church and fellowship, he will miss out in this vast amount of horizontal grace. God never intended for believers to try to make it on their own. He designed for each believer to be part of a body of believers who would strengthen and serve each other. Parts of a body can only function if they are connected to each other. The parts of a body that are cut off will not survive on their own; neither will a believer survive spiritually if separated from the body of Christ.

In addition to the benefits of the grace gifts, fellowship can also provide fertile ground for spiritual growth. Fellowship enables us to mature spiritually through personal care and nurturing. Being part of God's family in a local church should provide mature spiritual mothers and fathers to help nurture and mentor younger believers. Churches should be like a family that takes care of each other. When a person becomes a new Christian, he is like a newborn baby that is completely dependent on his family. The only way for us to effectively care for each other is to be closely connected to each other through fellowship. It is through the development of close relationships that mentoring and discipleship are most effective.

One of the things that happens when people grow closer to each other is that they discover each other's strengths and weaknesses. One of the reasons people resist fellowship is their fear of others discovering who they really are. They fear that when people find out their imperfections, they will be rejected. For fellowship to flourish there needs to be an atmosphere of grace where people are not judged for their weaknesses and failures.

> *For fellowship to flourish in relationships, there needs to be freedom to be honest and authentic.*

This freedom to be open and honest comes when a person feels that he will receive compassion and mercy no matter what weaknesses are exposed. Rather than being judged, one will have confidence that he will be helped and lifted up rather than being put down and cast out.

As people get to know each other through fellowship, personal weaknesses will be exposed. This exposure of weaknesses should not be seen as a threat but welcomed as an opportunity for growth in character. Close relationships are like mirrors that reflect back the character of each person. Some of what is seen will be good and some will not be so good. When we look into a mirror we are looking to see if there is something that we need to improve. We may need to wash our face, comb our hair, brush our teeth, straighten our clothes, and many other things that need correcting. When people get close to each other, they will reflect back what they see in the other person. Fellowship can flourish as we take advantage of opportunities to praise other's good character qualities and lovingly help each other fortify weak areas.

Another benefit of fellowship is that it bonds believers together to help protect one another. Every believer has weaknesses that can defeat him if he does not have the support of others. Fellowship gives us strength through unity. If one person is weak, the others will provide the strength that is needed. Fellowship is like the rope that connects mountain climbers. If one slips, the others hold on until that person regains his position. Without fellowship, a person who slips spiritually has no one to help catch him. Without fellowship, a person who is missing from church has no one who notices.

If a person is joined in fellowship with other believers, all will come to his defense when he is under attack. Fellowship helps believers cover each other's backs. When I was going through school, I never had any problem with anyone bullying me at school. How did I accomplish that? I had a twin brother who was my closest friend. No one dared attack either of us. If anyone attacked one of us, he attacked both of us. Only one person that I can remember ever took that challenge; he regretted it and never did it again. Likewise, believers joined in fellowship can protect each other just like my twin brother and I protected each other.

Humility and Fellowship

Humility is imperative for true fellowship. Humility is required to even possess the motivation for fellowship. A prideful person sees no need for fellowship because he believes that he is self-sufficient. The humble person knows he needs the help of others, so he pursues fellowship. There is a new dynamic of humility in fellowship. In humility, we are to surrender to God and be dependent on Him. Additionally, we are to be both independent and dependent upon others. We are dependent on others in fellowship to help us in our weaknesses; we are also independent so we can offer help to those in need. In fellowship there is to be a flow of giving and receiving. Humility is essential when conflicts occur in relationships. We need to go in humility to a person who has been offended by us or with whom we are offended.

> *The humble person initiates the steps that lead to a restored relationship.*

It is the humble person who will ask forgiveness to restore a relationship.

Application

1. Do you believe that you need other Christians to be strong spiritually?

2. Are you attending church and making efforts to develop friendships?

3. If you are attending church, are you connecting with people and developing fellowship?

4. If you are attending a church, are you practicing some of the "one another commandments"?

5. Do you have close friends on whom you can call in times of spiritual need?

6. How well have you dealt with conflicts with others?

7. What character qualities do you possess that help develop fellowship?

8. What characteristics do you have that hinder the development of fellowship?

CHAPTER 19

Heart-felt Worship

The fourth means of grace that we will examine is regular, heartfelt worship. Believers can worship the Lord in various ways: partaking in communion, singing songs, praising Him, giving, and serving. I define the type of worship that is a means of grace as being heartfelt worship. The reason I make this qualification is because people can participate in the various forms of worship with a casual indifference. For some, worship is no more than a mechanical motion of the body. Participation in worship can just be empty ritual without any inner change in a person's heart or spirit. This type of worship is powerless, religious activity that will provide very little grace. Only heartfelt worship is acceptable to God and blessed by Him as a means of grace. Such worship is done with sincerity from one's heart and spirit.

Jesus spoke of a time when worshippers would worship in spirit and truth: "But an hour is coming, and now is, when the true worshipers will worship the Father in spirit and truth; for such people the Father seeks to be His worshipers. God is spirit, and those who worship Him must worship in spirit and truth" (John 4:23–24). Jesus was referring to the time, soon after His ascension, when His followers received the Holy Spirit. Once the Holy Spirit indwells a person, he is born again or comes alive spiritually. A person who has come alive spiritually through receiving Christ as his Savior is capable of worshipping from his spirit. However, just because a person is born again does not mean that he will automatically know how to sincerely worship from his spirit.

What exactly is worship? By examining the original words used to describe worship, we can get a better idea of what worship of God actually is. The Hebrew word used most often in the Old Testament for worship is *šāhăh* (7812). The word means "to worship, to prostrate oneself, bow down."[97] This word "is found more than 170 times in the Hebrew Bible."[98] This outward physical expression of becoming prostrate or bowing down is an expression of submission and respect. The Greek word used in the New Testament that is most frequently rendered "to worship" is *proskuneō* (4352), "to make obeisance, do reverence to." This Greek word is made of two parts, "pros" means "toward" and *kuneŏ* means "to kiss." Combining the two parts means to "to kiss toward."[99] This Greek word describes an expression of love and adoration. When used in reference to the worship of God, it means to "to kiss toward God," or to express one's love and adoration to God.

The English word that we have for worship comes from an Anglo-Saxon word meaning "worth-ship."[100] This Anglo-Saxon word "connotes action motivated by an attitude that reveres, honors, or describes the worth of another person of object."[101] This word means a recognition of the worth of someone. When someone worships God, he is recognizing God's worth. God is eminently worthy of our worship. God alone is worthy of our wholehearted worship. We can see from the meanings of these words that worship involves both an outward physical expression and an inner expression from the heart.

We are to worship God because He is worthy. Why is God worthy of our wholehearted worship? First, God is worthy of our worship because of who He is. We can worship God for the qualities of His divine essence such as: He is the source of all life (Ps. 36:9), He is self-existent (Exod. 3:14), and He is eternal (Gen. 21:33). God is worthy of our worship as the one true God who is omnipresent (Ps. 139:7–12), omniscient (all knowing; Jer. 23:23–25), omnipotent (all powerful; Gen. 17:1), and immutable (never changes; Malachi 3:6). God is the almighty Creator of all that exists, "Worthy art Thou, our Lord and our God, to receive glory and honor and power; for Thou didst create all things, and because of Thy will they existed, and were created" (Rev. 4:11).

God is to be worshipped eternally because He is perfect in holiness. "And the four living creatures, each one of them having six wings, are full of eyes around and within; and day and night they do not cease to say, HOLY, HOLY, HOLY, is the Lord God, the Almighty, who was and is and who is to come" (Rev. 4:8). He is to be praised for His righteousness (Ps. 7:17), for His lovingkindness (Ps. 117:1–2), for His excellent greatness (Ps. 150:2), His splendor and majesty (Ps. 104:1), and for His excellencies (1 Pet. 2:9). We could go through all the attributes of God and yet would not even begin to exhaust all the reasons why God is worthy of worship. There is an immeasurable number of reasons why we should praise the infinite magnificence of God.

The second reason why God is worthy of our praise is because of what He has done. There seems to be a small distinction between worship and praise; pure worship is worship of God for who He is, while praise focuses more on praising Him for what He has done. We are to praise God for His mighty deeds (Ps. 150:2), for the prayers He has answered (Ps. 28:6), for being our strength and shield (Ps. 28:7), for His great faithfulness, for providing for us (Matt. 6:33), for His love and mercy, for our salvation, for His forgiveness, and for the gift of eternal life. Our praise to God should be continuous because of His countless blessings and all the wonderful works He has done.

Worship of God should never be just an outward act; it should always be an expression of adoration from the heart. Worship is our way of expressing our love and adoration of God. Just as we are pleased when someone we love expresses his love for us, so it also brings great delight to God when we express our love for Him. There are many ways we can express our love to God. There are numerous physical expressions of worship mentioned in Scripture. We have already seen from the meaning of the Hebrew word for worship that it involves bowing down or being prostrate before God. Physical expressions of worship seen in Scripture include: bowing (1 Chron. 29:20), clapping of hands (Ps. 47:1), lifting of hands (Ps. 134:2; 1 Kings 8:54), dancing (Ps. 149:3), and kneeling (1 Kings 8:54; Dan. 6:10; Luke 22:41). Additionally, there are various verbal expressions of worship that are mentioned in Scripture: singing (Ps. 147:1; Eph. 5:19), making a joyful noise (Ps. 98:4), declarations to God (Isa. 6:3; Rev. 4:8), testimonies (Ps. 105:1), joyful shouting (Ps. 5:11; 47:1), giving thanks (Eph. 5:20; Heb. 13:15), and rejoicing (Ps. 5:11). Musical instruments are also used to express and enhance worship (Ps. 150:3–5).

It is unfortunate that for many Christians, worship has lost its true purpose. There is a wide spectrum of different forms of worship from liturgical forms of worship on one end to charismatic worship on the other end. Sadly, there has been a loss of the true purpose of worship for many on both ends of the worship spectrum. Some who practice a liturgical form of worship become focused on following a certain liturgy and devotion to their traditions. The focus of worship can be on the precise practice of a traditional form of worship. People can worship the form more than they worship God.

On the other end of the spectrum, there are those who worship the feelings they get when worshiping. Worship, for some, has become something about themselves rather than being about God. Worship is too often evaluated on how much the worshiper gets out of it rather than what God receives from it. Worship is for God's sake, not ours. Worship is to get us focused on God and on becoming God-centered. When people focus on what they are feeling in worship, they are being self-centered and not God-centered. Praise and worship are indeed joyful and pleasant (Ps. 147: 1) to the worshipper, but that should never be the goal of worship. The sole purpose of worship is to please God.

Corporate Worship

Just as prayer has three modes: public prayer, private prayer, and presence prayers, so there are three modes of worship. The three modes of worship are public (corporate) worship, private worship, and lifestyle worship. Public or corporate worship is what most people think of when they think of worship. Corporate worship is a very important mode of worship and is in fact one of the main purposes of Christians coming together as a church. An important advantage that corporate worship has over private worship is the inspiration from others joining together in worship. Worshiping with others can be quite inspiring. I have found this is especially true when I am with a large group of people who are praising God. It is almost like you are in heaven with the multitudes of angels and saints worshiping God. Corporate worship gives us a little taste of the corporate worship in heaven.

Another benefit of corporate worship is that it can assist in teaching new worshipers how to worship. People learn best through having an example to follow. Corporate worship helps new worshipers learn songs that they can use in their private worship times. Some new worshipers may be just spectators at first, but as they watch, they can learn how to enter into worship. At some point in time, after attending a number of services, a person should begin to participate in worship. Times of worship in a gathering should not have a nonparticipating group perpetually watching others worship. The primary goal of corporate worship is to glorify God by having everyone join together in worshiping God. It is not pleasing to God if only a few are worshiping Him in a service.

Partaking of Communion

One of the most common ways to worship God corporately is through partaking of holy communion. Partaking in communion or the Lord's Supper is one of the most sacred and important forms of regular worship. Churches offer communion during worship services in different ways and times. Some offer communion every service, some once a month, some less than once a month. Some churches have what is called closed communion. That means only certain people are allowed to join in the communion service. Some limit participation to members only while other churches have open communion allowing participation by all those who believe in Christ. Those who participate in communion must always remember that it should never be an empty ritual. Partaking of communion must always be a sincere act of worship.

The apostle Paul instructed the Corinthian church that those who take communion should examine themselves before partaking, "But let a man examine himself, and let him eat of the bread and drink of the cup" (1 Cor. 11:28). This verse is addressing the need to soberly examine oneself and ask the Holy Spirit bring to light anything that is displeasing to God. As things come to light, a person needs to confess and repent of any sins. Preparation for partaking of communion should be a time of spiritual cleansing as sins are confessed to God. When a person partakes of communion, it should also be as an act of faith in Christ and His atoning sacrificial death on the cross. By a person's participation in communion, he is applying the atoning blood of Christ to his sins. When a person takes communion with a sincere heart, he will experience a flow of God's grace by being reassured of God's love and forgiveness. With the assurance of forgiveness of sins, a believer should experience a sense of great joy.

The early Christians were devoted to the "breaking of bread" (Acts 2:42, 46). Most commentators believe this is a reference to partaking of the Lord's Supper. The early practice of communion was part of a shared meal, just as the twelve disciples shared their last Passover meal with the Lord. Until recently, partaking of communion has always been a corporate expression of worship. The Lord's Supper was always something done together with others rather than as a private expression of worship. Unfortunately, some churches have begun the practice of having a communion table at the back of the sanctuary for self-service. Rather than offering communion corporately, it is only provided for private worship.

A very important aspect of communion being taken together with other believers is that it is a unifying factor in the body of Christ. The apostle Paul gave instructions on how to partake of communion in the context of division in the Corinthian church. Some began eating their own food before others could partake instead of waiting to share. This behavior originated from an impatient and selfish attitude. Those who came later had no food to eat. Paul addressed this issue by telling them if they were so hungry that they could not wait for others, they should eat at home first (1 Cor. 11:20–22):

Therefore, when you meet together, it is not to eat the Lord's Supper, for in your eating each one takes his own supper first; and one is hungry and another is drunk. What! Do you not have houses in which to eat and drink? Or do you despise the church of God and shame those who have nothing? What shall I say to you? Shall I praise you? In this I will not praise you.

If believers in the Corinthian church did come to the communion meal, they were to wait for the others to come so that they could partake together. When communion is taken together with other believers, it helps build unity. Taking communion privately can be personally edifying, but it does nothing for building unity among believers. Whether communion is taken publicly or privately, it should always be personal and earnest.

Participating in Singing Praises to God

Another very common form of corporate worship is singing praises to God. Most churches do not offer communion every Sunday but almost all churches sing songs of praise as part of their main weekly service. There is a wide variety of musical styles all the way from traditional to contemporary and everything in between. Some churches do not use musical instruments to accompany worship. Some churches just sing hymns; others just sing contemporary choruses. Some churches have choirs, some have worship teams, some just have one song leader, and some sing along with DVDs or YouTube.

It is commonplace for people to prefer a certain style of worship; however, some go further to believing that their style of worship is the only correct style. It is perfectly acceptable for a person to prefer a certain style of worship, but others should not be judged simply because they prefer a different style. The important thing in all this variety is that people are worshiping God the way He desires in spirit and truth.

Some equate music to worship. Worship is more than music. Christian music is not the same as worship because one can have music without worship and worship without music. For example, a Christian concert can be just entertainment without worship. A good indicator that music is entertainment and not worship is if there is more emphasis on the sounds of instruments rather than the words being sung. If you cannot hear the words to a song and are unable to sing along, how can that be worship? In some "worship" services, there is more entertainment than worship. When the congregation just watches a musical performance, it can be entertaining and inspiring but it is not worship because worship requires participation. Music may be helpful in worship but worship does not require musical accompaniment. People can worship without music. Many Christians have become so dependent on music for worship that they cannot worship without it; as soon as the music stops, the worship stops.

For some, the style of music dictates whether or not they will worship. Everyone has his own favorite style of music: traditional, contemporary, country, Hillsong, classical, or hip pop, and so on. Many churches have been divided over the issue of what musical style will be used during worship. Some churches have tried to solve this conflict by having a different style of worship during separate services. Worship should not be dependent on a certain style of music. Remember, worship is for God's sake and not ours. God does not care what style of music is used for worship. What God cares about is that He is worshiped in spirit and truth, that He is praised and exulted, adored, honored, and reverenced with or without musical accompaniment.

Corporate singing is the most common type of corporate worship where everyone is welcome to participate. Some may feel uncomfortable because they are not used to singing. Some will not sing because they think they cannot sing. There are some who do not sing because they are unfamiliar with the songs. No one should ever feel forced into singing because genuine worship must always be voluntarily. True worship should flow sincerely from the willing heart. Once a person learns the songs, he should begin to participate in corporate singing. If a person is to worship in corporate singing, he must become a participant and not remain a spectator. Singing should never be done to impress others around us. We are to sing unto the Lord to bless Him alone.

Worship is more than singing Christian songs. People can just mouth words without worshiping God. In order to become a worshiper, a person must learn to sing from his heart and not just with his mind. Talking can often be just an expression from the mind whereas singing more often rises from the heart. There is something about singing that causes a person to express himself from his soul. Songs can move the soul and heart of a person more than mere spoken words. Listening to a song can move a person's heart while singing that song can magnify its impact on the heart. When we are singing from our hearts, the Holy Spirit can assist our worship to the point where we are worshiping from our spirit. Worshiping from our spirit is the highest form of worship. God desires for us to worship Him in spirit because He is spirit (John 4:24).

Participating in Praising God

There is more to praising God than singing praises to God. I have previously listed the different expressions of corporate worship seen in Scripture. God can be worshipped with physical expressions of our body such as raising one's hands, kneeling, bowing, standing, dancing, and clapping of hands. The Bible also mentions different verbal expressions of worship: singing, shouts of joy, making a joyful noise, and making loud declarations. There are churches that will not allow any of these types of physical or verbal expressions of worship during corporate worship. Some churches allow physical and verbal expressions to be done together when directed by a worship leader. Some churches do not permit the raising of the hands while others encourage it. Some churches encourage self-directed physical and verbal expressions of worship if they are done in an orderly manner.

It is important to remember that we are talking about corporate worship. In corporate worship, we are to worship in the same manner as the other worshipers in the service. It is out of order for someone to make a spectacle of himself and draw attention away from God. The focus should always be on God and not on an individual worshiper. Corporate worship is to be done in a spirit of unity. The individual should always show deference to what is practiced and allowed in a particular setting. If a person desires to physically and verbally express himself in ways that are not allowed in a church, he should find another church where they are practiced and encouraged. If a person desires to stay in a church that restricts his public display of worship, he should confine those physical and verbal expressions of worship to times of private worship.

Participating in Giving as an Expression of Worship

The secular world questions the validity of churches receiving monetary donations as a means of worshipping God. They tend to think churches are more motivated by donations or "offerings" than anything else. This perception of the public is somewhat warranted because of the manner in which funds are sometimes collected. I have personally seen questionable methods of offering collection in churches where I have been a guest preacher. One church took as many as five offerings during the service. Each time an offering was taken, the deacons counted the offering at the front of the church. Then they reported the amount of the offering to the pastor. If the offering was not sufficient, the pastor would tell the congregation that the offering was not enough, so they would take another offering. Sometimes it took five offerings before the pastor was satisfied with the total amount. This multi-offering approach may get the needed funds, but it does not leave a good impression of the priorities of the church leadership. If someone were a visitor that day, I have little doubt that this method of collecting money would reinforce his thinking that churches are just after money.

Some churches have even done away with taking corporate offerings to fight against the prevailing impression that the churches are primarily motivated by money. Due to the fear of offending someone who does not want to or is not able to give an offering, an offering box is placed somewhere in the sanctuary for those who want to give. Churches should not allow the world to dictate how they worship God in giving. The church should be more concerned with pleasing God than with pleasing visitors. I believe that if visitors see the church honoring God in their giving, it will be a powerful witness of their love and devotion to God. Giving that honors God is pleasing to Him and should not be removed as an expression of corporate worship. The time for giving in a church service should be a time of celebration when people who love God boldly and without apology joyfully worship God by giving.

The primary objective of worship is to honor or glorify God. Giving to God can be a way that we honor God, "Honor the LORD from your wealth, And from the first of all your produce" (Prov. 3:9). When it comes to giving to God, it is important to understand that not all gifts to God are honorable and acceptable to Him (Gen. 4:4–5). If we are to honor God in our giving, whether in a corporate collection or in a private donation, there are certain requirements that must be met. First, in order for giving to be considered worship, it must be done as unto the Lord. If offerings are given to anything other than to the Lord, they are not worship. A person can give an offering in a church service as unto the Lord, or he can be just giving to the church. If a person thinks he is only giving to a church and not unto the Lord, he is doing a good thing—but not worshiping God.

Unfortunately, many who give offerings during a church service see it as an obligation to fulfill as a duty to their church rather than an act of worship. In churches that require their members to tithe, it is understandable that some members may look at giving their tithe as a duty to be fulfilled to their church rather than an act of worship to honor God. In some churches, funds are raised through pledges to meet the yearly budget. Some of those who make pledges may feel like they are paying their pledged amounts like a bill to be paid off by the end of the year. If offerings are taken for a particular person such as a guest missionary, givers should not consider their offerings to be for the person but as unto the Lord. Even though giving an offering directed to an individual is an act of charity and appreciation, it is not an act of worship unless it is done "as unto the Lord." An offering can be given as worship even if it is given for the benefit of a specific person or ministry.

In certain churches, there is great emphasis on giving to receive a blessing. Those who attend this type of church perceive giving as an investment in their financial security. For example, these "prosperity gospel" churches will claim before taking an offering that whatever people give will be multiplied back to them ten-fold. People are motivated to give on the basis of what they will receive in return for their offering. The idea of giving to honor God is not in their thinking; instead, they are giving to be blessed; they are giving to get. The focus of such giving is not God but themselves. People who are motivated by selfishness in their giving may give more; however, that is not worship, and it does not bless God. Of course, God does bless those who give, but that should never be the primary purpose for giving to God.

The second requirement for giving to honor God is that it must be heartfelt. As with all forms of worship, giving to God must be an expression from the heart. Giving to God should be an expression of our love for Him. Giving is the very essence of love. When we love someone dearly, we will want to give generously of whatever we have to that person. When we love someone, we will freely and joyfully give to them. If we love God, we will freely and joyfully give to Him. God delights in our giving when we give cheerfully as an expression of our love for Him, "Each one *must do* just as he has purposed in his heart, not grudgingly or under compulsion, for God loves a cheerful giver" (2 Cor. 9:7). It is honoring to God when we give willingly, wholeheartedly, and gladly. "Then the people rejoiced because they had offered so willingly, for they made their offering to the LORD with a whole heart, and King David also rejoiced greatly" (1 Chron. 29:9). If we are to honor God in our giving, we must give with the right attitude. We do not honor God if we give to Him with a reluctant or unwilling attitude.

The third requirement for giving to honor God is that it must demonstrate that God is first in our lives. God desires for us to love Him with all our heart, with all our soul, and with all our mind (Matt. 22:37). We demonstrate our love for God by loving Him above everything else. When we love God above all else, we will put Him before anything else. We can demonstrate this love in the way we give to Him. Giving in a way that honors God is an exercise of the heart. Jesus declared, "where your treasure is there will your heart be also" (Matt. 6:21). If God is the greatest treasure of our heart, we will be fully devoted in our love for Him. If we treasure anything more than God, our heart will not be fully devoted to Him. Jesus told us that we cannot serve two masters; we will either love money or we will love God, "No one can serve two masters; for either he will hate the one and love the other, or he will be devoted to one and despise the other. You cannot serve God and wealth" (Matt. 6:24). If we love God, we will freely and happily give to Him. If we love money more than we love God, then any giving to God will be done reluctantly.

We demonstrate God is first in our lives by what we give in offerings to Him. In the Old Testament, the Lord required the Israelites to set aside the first tenth of the harvest and the firstborn from their animals (Deut. 18:4; Neh. 10:35). The first fruits were considered the best of the harvest and the firstborn were considered the best of the flock. Giving the first fruits demonstrated to God that He was first in the life of the giver. Giving first fruits likewise was a reminder to the giver that God was the owner of all that he possessed. We honor God by bringing Him the first fruits; if we bring God what is left over and what is of inferior quality, we are dishonoring Him. When the Israelites brought animals to sacrifice, they had to be without any blemish. "When a man offers a sacrifice of peace offerings to the Lord to fulfill a special vow or for a freewill offering, of the herd or of the flock, it must be perfect to be accepted; there shall be no defect in it" (Lev. 22:21).

We demonstrate that God is first in our lives when we give something that is of value to us. When King David wanted to offer a sacrifice to God, he wanted to buy an animal from Ornan, but Ornan offered to give it to David for free. David refused to make an offering of something that cost him nothing and insisted that he pay the full price. "But King David said to Ornan, "No, but I will surely buy *it* for the full price; for I will not take what is yours for the Lord, or offer a burnt offering which costs me nothing" (1 Chron. 21:24–25). When a woman came to Jesus and anointed Him with oil, she used an alabaster vial of very costly perfume (Matt. 26:7–9). The disciples complained that she was wasting something of great value that could have been sold to help the poor. Jesus corrected them by saying that what the woman did was right because the anointing of perfume was done for the preparation of His body for burial. Jesus added that because of her sacrificial gift, she would be remembered every time the gospel was preached.

Another example of giving something of great value was the gift given by the poor widow. One day Jesus was watching what people gave into the temple treasury. Some gave great sums of money out of their wealth, but one poor widow came and gave something that impressed Jesus. Jesus commended how the poor widow gave two copper coins into the temple treasury. The two coins were not of much value to others, but they were extremely valuable to this impoverished woman because she gave all she had (Luke 21:4). The greater our sacrifice, the more God is honored. Learning to give sacrificially to God is a wonderful way that we can worship God. As we give sacrificially to honor Him, God will bless us with an abundance of grace. What Jesus said about it being more blessed to give than to receive is true (Acts 20:35).

Practicing Private Worship

Our times of worship can be so much more than what we experience during a church service. If we limit our times of worship to the times of corporate worship at church, we are missing the tremendous blessing that comes from private worship. The time that we have to worship in corporate worship is only a small portion of the time we have the rest of the week. If believers engage in private worship during the week, they will greatly enhance worship as a means of grace in their lives, and the results will be truly transformative. The Psalmist declared his desire to praise God all day long: "And my tongue shall declare Your righteousness *And* Your praise all day long" (Ps. 35:28).

Just as I wrote about prayer having three modes (public, private, and presence prayer) there is private worship that can become presence worship. As we sense God's presence with us throughout the day, we can sustain our communication with God by continually praying and praising Him: "I will bless the Lord at all times; His praise shall continually be in my mouth" (Ps. 34:1). Christians should make it a practice to have an attitude of worship each day. Listening to Christian songs during our day can encourage us to worship. Even if we are not able to listen to worship songs, we can have songs of worship on our mind throughout the day as we make melody in our hearts unto the Lord. We can worship from our spirit throughout the day as we acknowledge that God is ever present with us. Imagine how much better our days would go if we were glorifying God all day!

In addition to maintaining an attitude of worship during each day, we need to have special times when we give God our undivided attention in worship. There should be a time and a place set aside to get alone with God to communicate with Him in private prayer. These times of being alone with God in prayer can also be wonderful times of worship. I have experienced great blessing from both public and private worship. Yet, the greatest times of worship that I have experienced have been in my private time with God. The times that I have felt the closest to God were in moments of private worship. It has been my experience that the more time I spend in God's presence in prayer and worship, the more peace and joy I have. "Praise the LORD! For it is good to sing praises to our God; For it is pleasant *and* praise is becoming" (Ps. 147:1).

When I get weighed down with things that concern me, I begin to feel anxious. When fearful thoughts begin to creep into my mind and spirit, I start to feel a spirit of heaviness. There have been times when I gave in to this spirit of heaviness and became depressed. I have learned that when I start to experience this spirit of heaviness, I should immediately begin to worship God in my spirit. As I worship and praise God, the heaviness goes away. The more I sense God's presence, the more my worries and fears melt away. As we spend more time with God in prayer and private worship, the greater God becomes in our perception and the smaller our problems become. The more we focus on our problems, the greater they become. With God's help, we can learn to keep our focus on God to have His peace. "The steadfast of mind You will keep in perfect peace, because he trusts in You" (Isa. 26:3).

Practicing Lifestyle Worship

So far, I have covered the first two modes of worship: public (corporate) worship and private worship. The last mode of worship is lifestyle worship. Lifestyle worship is a different type of worship but every bit as important as corporate and private worship. Lifestyle worship is living our lives in a way that brings glory and honor to God. Worship is not just something we do at church, but how we live all week long to honor God. We are to glorify God daily by our actions. Our whole life should be lived as an expression of worship to please God. In some aspects, lifestyle worship is much more important than corporate and private worship. If the first two modes of worship are not backed up with lifestyle worship, they become meaningless and a sham. For many professing Christians, there is a dichotomy between who they are at church and who they are during the week. Many church attenders are not bothered by the inconsistency of worshiping God on Sunday and living a life that is indistinguishable from nonbelievers during the week. Let us not be that type of inconsistent Christian.

Living a Life of Obedience

> *Living a life of obedience to God is our greatest expression of worship.*

God desires our obedience more than our participation in worship, "Samuel said, "Has the LORD as much delight in burnt offerings and sacrifices as in obeying the voice of the LORD? Behold, to obey is better than sacrifice, *and* to heed than the fat of rams" (1 Sam. 15:22). Worship that is not backed up by a life of obedience is unacceptable to God. If it comes down to a choice between participating in worship or living a life that honors God, He prefers a life of obedience. This is not to say that living a lifestyle that honors God is all that God desires in worship. Since all three modes of worship are essential to fully worship God, we need to practice all three to maximize worship as a means of grace.

In order to live a life of obedience, we must first humble ourselves by recognizing that we are totally dependent on God's grace to enable us to live that life. Additionally, we need to humble ourselves by recognizing God's sovereignty over every aspect of our lives. We must be totally dependent on God by submitting to His authority. A humble person bows his knees and heart before his Lord in submission. Early in a believer's life, he must humble himself by fully surrendering to the Lordship of Christ. When a person humbles himself before God, he removes self from the throne of his heart and puts Christ on that throne. It is not easy to remain submitted to God. There will be an internal struggle with the old self which wants to keep putting itself back on the throne. Pride wants to keep self on the throne of our heart. The prideful self wants to be the one who rules—not God. There cannot be two masters who sit on the throne of the heart. In order to keep Christ enthroned on a believer's heart, he must humble himself in submission on a daily basis.

To walk humbly before God means to daily surrender to His will in every area of life. There will be times when a believer will allow his sinful self to succeed in reasserting itself. When self regains control in a believer's life, he will fall back into yielding to what the sinful nature desires. When this happens, a believer must not despair but must humble himself by asking God's forgiveness. Whenever a believer fails, he must humbly reaffirm his total dependence on God's grace to overcome sin and submit to His authority. Grace is poured out in our lives when we humble ourselves and submit to God.

For many Christians, submitting to God's authority is an abstract idea that does not have much relevance in how they live their lives. They confess Christ as Lord but, in reality, they live a lifestyle that is identical to unbelievers. Just how does a person demonstrate that he is submitting to God's authority in his life? In what ways does a person show humility in submitting to God's authority?

Submitting to God's Word

Lifestyle worship is living our lives in obedience to God's Word. One of the most important ways to submit to God's authority is to submit to His will as revealed in the Word. The Bible is much more that a unique book; it is God's Word to humanity. It is essential that every Christian has the conviction that the Bible is God's infallible Word. Once a person accepts the Bible as God's Word, it should become the most powerful influence in his life. When someone submits to the authority of God's Word, it means that the individual believes the Word of God is the truth. God's Word is not just a truth among many truths, but is the *truth* for all of humanity and for all time. The truth of the Bible lays out the boundaries and sets the standards. The Word of God distinguishes truth from falsehood, what is good from what is evil, and what is right from what is wrong. The Word of God must be the standard of belief and conduct for all Christians. God's Word is to have complete and final authority in every area of a Christian's life. Unfortunately, a person can read, study, and memorize the Bible but yet not submit to its authority in obedience. A person must not be just a hearer of the Word but also a doer of the Word (James 1:22).

A doer of the Word of God must first hear, read, study, and come to have a good understanding of Scripture. As followers of Christ, we need to understand the basic doctrines and principles of Scripture. We must have an accurate interpretation of a passage of Scripture before we can make personal application because a faulty interpretation can lead to a faulty application. Submission to God's Word requires making personal application of the truth of the Word. Every time a believer hears, reads, and studies God's Word, he should look for more than gaining information; he must carefully look for personal application. When a believer is reading the Bible for personal devotions, he should watch for ways that God is speaking to him directly. A person should humbly ask God to show him personal applications from the Word. When a believer listens to a sermon or a Bible lesson, he should listen with humility. A person should have the attitude that he does not know it all and that there is much more that he can learn. Even if a person thinks he already knows and understands what is being taught, he should still humbly listen for something he did not know or has not applied to his life. Even if it is not something new, a person should listen intently for God to show him a fresh application. Humbling oneself in obedient submission to God's Word will provide a means to receive an abundance of God's grace.

Surrendering to the Control of the Holy Spirit

Lifestyle worship is living a life surrendered to the control of the Holy Spirit. Along with submitting to God's Word, believers need to learn to submit to the authority of God by living under the control of the Holy Spirit. In order to live a life controlled by the Holy Spirit, one must first experience the indwelling of the Holy Spirit. When a person invites Christ to come into his life, he receives the indwelling of the Holy Spirit. It is by the indwelling of the Spirit of Christ that a person becomes born again. Without the indwelling of the Holy Spirit, one is not a child of God (Rom. 8:9). Once a person has spiritual birth, he has the Holy Spirit indwelling him and working in his life. How fully one cooperates with the Spirit of God determines how much the Holy Spirit can do the works of grace in his life. The Spirit can only work with a cooperative individual. If a person resists God, He will not be able to help him. It is when we fully cooperate with the Spirit's control that God can do the most for us. Remember that because the Holy Spirit is the agent of grace; the more we cooperate with the Holy Spirit, the more we will have God's grace released into our lives.

Living a Life of Service

Lifestyle worship is living a life of service to God. Serving God in ministry is a hands-on way of glorifying God. When we use the talents and gifts that God has given us to serve Him, this brings great pleasure to Him. We are to use what God has given us to serve Him in ways that will glorify Him:

As each one has received a *special* gift, employ it in serving one another as good stewards of the manifold grace of God. Whoever speaks, *is to do so* as one who is speaking the utterances of God; whoever serves *is to do so* as one who is serving by the strength which God supplies; so that in all things God may be glorified through Jesus Christ, to whom belongs the glory and dominion forever and ever. Amen. (1 Pet. 4:10–11)

God is glorified when sinners are brought to faith in Christ. The more we impact people's lives for Christ, the more it glorifies God, "My Father is glorified by this, that you bear much fruit, and *so* prove to be My disciples" (John 15:8). We honor God when we sacrifice something of great value to us. One of the most precious things that we possess is our time. When we serve God in ministry, it requires a sacrifice of our time. When we die to serving self and live to serve God in ministry, we become a living and holy sacrifice for God's glory. "Therefore, I urge you, brethren, by the mercies of God, to present your bodies a living and holy sacrifice, acceptable to God, *which is* your spiritual service of worship" (Rom. 12:1). Becoming a living and holy sacrifice in service to God is our spiritual service of lifestyle worship.

Glorify God by Doing Good Works

Along with serving in ministry, lifestyle worship involves doing good works for others. When we do good works for others it is a powerful witness to the world.

> *The world may turn a deaf ear to preaching, but they will certainly take notice of good works.*

We can be a witness both with our words and our actions. Quite often, our actions will speak louder than our words. Jesus instructed us to let our light shine before men by our good deeds: "Let your light shine before men in such a way that they may see your good works, and glorify your Father who is in heaven" (Matt. 5:16). When people see our good works, it can bring glory to God. The apostle Paul thanked the Philippian church for the generous gift they sent to supply his needs. Paul described their gift as "a fragrant aroma, an acceptable sacrifice, well-pleasing to God" (Phil. 4:18). When God's people do good works by sharing with those in need it is a fragrant aroma to God. He accepts good works done for others as a sacrifice of worship that greatly pleases Him, "And do not neglect doing good and sharing, for with such sacrifices God is pleased" (Heb. 13:16).

Glorifying God in Our Work

Most people who work view their job as just something they need to do to make a living. Some enjoy their job while others detest their job. For many, their work has become a drudge to endure without any sense of purpose or real achievement. Some Christians believe that work is part of the curse put on humanity because of Adam and Eve's sin. This interpretation of the Genesis account concerning the results of the fall of mankind is incorrect. Adam worked in cultivating the garden before the fall (Gen. 2:15), but now, as a result of the fall, his work became more difficult (Gen. 3:17–19). This greater difficulty of work causes many to have a negative view of work. A large percentage of believers in Christ and nonbelievers do not have a favorable attitude toward work.

Many Christians think that the only meaningful work is that done for the Lord in ministry. For many Christians, there is a clear distinction between work done in ministry and work done at their secular jobs. Work done in ministry has purpose and meaning to them while their secular work is not perceived as having any spiritual or eternal purpose. This view of work is unfortunate because everything done for the Lord has eternal significance. If we do our work for the Lord and not for men, it becomes an act of worship. If we do our work to the best of our ability as an act of worship to glorify God, it will take on greater spiritual meaning. Our work can become a sacrifice to please God. Every kind of work can become spiritually significant if it is done to glorify God. Even menial work can be done in a way that will give purpose and bring great joy.

I was thirteen years old when I received Christ as my Savior. It was not long after I was born again that I discovered Colossians 3:23, "And whatsoever you do, do it heartily, as to the Lord and not unto men." This verse became the theme verse of my life. I grew up in a home where the children were all expected to do their assigned chores. Up to that time in my life, I hated doing chores and put minimal effort into doing a good job. One day, as I was sweeping the kitchen floor as one of my chores, I had a great revelation. I had just read Colossians 3:23 a few days before, but now it came alive to me. Instead of doing my chores poorly, I decided to do my very best as a sacrifice for the Lord. Suddenly, work became something meaningful and enjoyable to me because I was not doing the chores for my parents but for the Lord. From that point on in my life, I purposed to do my best with all my heart in whatever work I did. My life became exciting with new challenges to do my best for God. My study and school work drastically changed for the better. I did not get all A's but I did my best in every class I took. I do not profess to be the smartest person, but I believe I certainly was one of the hardest-working students throughout my years of academic training.

I kept this hardworking attitude in all the different jobs I worked over the years. As a pastor for about forty-eight years, I have always done my best to be the finest pastor I could be by the grace of God. It is my greatest desire to glorify God in all that I do and accomplish. Even when I use the artistic talent that God gave me, I do it to bring glory to God. Whenever I paint a portrait of a person, I sign the bottom of the painting with my name and the letters TGBTG (To God Be The Glory). Every day can be exciting when we do everything to the best of our ability to glorify God.

Humility and Worship

In order for all the means of grace to be effective in providing God's grace, they all must be performed with an attitude of humility. Participation in any of the means of grace will not provide grace if humility is not shown toward God. "God resists the proud but gives grace to the humble" (James 4:6). The means of grace are ways that we can show humility toward God. We show humility when we learn and obey God's Word, when we put our trust in God through praying, and when demonstrate our need for others through commitment to regular fellowship. Of all the means of grace, heartfelt worship is the clearest expression of humility. The very act of worship is humbling oneself before God. Worship is exalting God while humbling ourselves. We cannot both exalt ourselves and worship God at the same time. We cannot truly worship God if we do not humble ourselves before we express any worship. We must realize our own sinfulness before we worship God as a holy God. We must realize our finiteness before we can worship God as almighty. The various physical expressions of worship, such as kneeling or raising our hands, are outward demonstrations of humbling ourselves before God. Learning to worship regularly in spirit and truth during corporate and private worship will truly open the flow of God's grace into our lives.

Application

1. Do you participate in corporate worship on a regular basis?

2. If you do worship God, would you describe your worship as heartfelt?

3. If you participate in communion, do you first have a time of confessing your sins before God?

4. Do you participate in singing during corporate worship?

5. Do you cheerfully participate in giving generously in the offering?

6. Do you have times of private worship?

7. Does your lifestyle glorify God?

8. Have you surrendered yourself fully to Christ as a living sacrifice?

9. Have you surrendered to the authority of God's Word in your life?

10. Do you glorify God by living a life of service?

11. Do you glorify God by doing good works?

12. Do you purpose to glorify God in all that you do?

PART SIX
HORIZONAL GRACE

CHAPTER 20

Speaking Words of Grace

Up to this point, I have shown how God's grace can have a miraculous effect on one's life. God's saving grace has restored people's relationship with God, and His enabling grace has given them the power to live transformed lives. There is even more to God's work of grace in our lives. God's grace can also have the power to substantially affect relationships. What does God's grace have to do with one's relationships with others? The more a believer learns how blessed he is by God's grace, the more he will learn to show that grace toward others. When a person believes that God loves and accepts him through his faith in Christ even though he does not deserve it, he should, in turn, be more accepting and gracious to others. There is vertical grace that God extends toward believers, and there is horizontal grace that God wants His people to extend to others.

The Ripple Effect

A few years ago, I was in a Dollar General store checking out with a few items. There was a person ahead of me having his items scanned and a man behind me in line. As I waited in line, I noticed the man behind me looked concerned over whether or not he had enough cash to pay for his groceries. I felt God tell me in that moment to pay for his groceries. When I got to the register, I asked the lady who was checking me out if she would add the amount of the next person to my bill. I told the person behind me that I would pay for his groceries. You should have seen the look of surprise and relief on his face. He expressed gratitude and thought I did this because, at that time, it was a fad in our area to pay for the next person in line "to pay it forward." I responded to him by saying that God wanted to bless him and that at some time he should do the same for someone else. Our gracious God has blessed multitudes of people in so many ways. Consequently, God does not want those He has blessed to hoard His blessings. Christians are to treat others with the same kindness that God has treated them. Those who have been blessed by God's grace need to learn to pass His grace along to others. God's grace should have a ripple effect on all relationships. As God shows His abundant grace, one is to show that grace to others. The ripple effect happens when those who have received God's grace pass it on to others and they, in turn, continue to pass it to others.

When an object is dropped into a body of water, the kinetic energy from the falling object dissipates into concentric ripples from the point of impact. Similarly, when God's grace impacts a person's life, it should have a ripple effect. The ripple effect should be seen in multiple ways in the life of a Christian. God's Word instructs Christians to forgive others as God has forgiven them. "Be kind to one another, tender-hearted, forgiving each other, just as God in Christ also has forgiven you" (Eph. 4:32). Scriptures tell believers to comfort others just as they have been comforted: "Blessed *be* the God and Father of our Lord Jesus Christ, the Father of mercies and God of all comfort, who comforts us in all our affliction so that we will be able to comfort those who are in any affliction with the comfort with which we ourselves are comforted by God" (2 Cor. 1:3–4). As God has shown His grace to an individual, that person is to show that grace to others. It is God's design that His grace would have a ripple effect to touch all those who are in the believer's circle of influence. How does a person show God's grace to others? A very important way to show God's grace is through our speech, "I thank my God always concerning you for the grace of God which was given you in Christ Jesus, that in everything you were enriched in Him, in all speech and all knowledge" (1 Cor. 1:4–5).

> *How well one communicates with those around him will determine the quality and strength of his relationships.*

God's grace can help a person to greatly improve the way he communicates with others and thus improve those relationships. The grace of God enriches the believer's life in every way. The grace of God enriches one's speech by changing the manner in which he talks to others.

Believers in Christ are empowered by God's grace to speak words of grace to others. Our words have a powerful impact on others. They even have the power of life and death, "Death and life are in the power of the tongue, And, those who love it will eat its fruit" (Prov. 18:21). Words are so powerful that they can impact life or death in relationships. When I was an adolescent, there was a phrase that we would use when someone said something meanspirited to us, "Sticks and stones may break my bones, but words will never hurt me." This response seemed right at the time, but now that I am older and wiser, I realize that words actually can hurt even more than "sticks and stones." A person can recover from bodily harm, but words can hurt for a lifetime. Everyone can remember hurtful words that were said to him during childhood. It is a wise person who understands the power of his words and uses them appropriately. The Proverbs teach that a wise man speaks gracious words. "Words from the mouth of a wise man are gracious, while the lips of a fool consume him" (Eccles. 10:12).

What are the characteristics of gracious words? First, words of grace give life. Gracious words can restore relationships by bringing new life into relationships. Using gracious words can help start a new relationship and also help maintain existing relationships. My wife and I have been married for forty-seven years and have a wonderful marriage. We both purpose to speak graciously to each other. Whenever we fail to speak graciously to each other, we ask for forgiveness. When a person does not use gracious words toward others, a person's spirit can be wounded and a relationship destroyed. Proverbs 16:28 reveals just how destructive words can be to relationships: "A perverse man spreads strife, And, a slanderer separates intimate friends."

Second, words of grace edify. To edify means to build up, to encourage, to renew hope, and to strengthen. A believer in Christ is to pursue what brings peace and what builds others up in all his relationships. "So then we pursue the things which make for peace and the building up of one another" (Rom. 14:19). If one truly loves others, he will show it by edifying them, "Now concerning things sacrificed to idols, we know that we all have knowledge. Knowledge makes arrogant, but love edifies" (1 Cor. 8:1). The apostle Paul admonished believers to guard what they say to others. The words one speaks should always edify by giving grace to those who hear. "Let no unwholesome word proceed from your mouth, but only such *a word* as is good for edification according to the need *of the moment,* so that it will give grace to those who hear" (Eph. 4:29).

In all your conversations with people, you need to be sensitive to the spirit of the other person. If you sense that a person is down in spirit, you need to say words of encouragement to edify that person. The Bible speaks of two men in the Old Testament whose words gave strength to those who were weak in spirit. Job was praised for his words that helped the weak, "Your words have helped the tottering to stand, And, you have strengthened feeble knees" (Job 4:4). Isaiah spoke about how the Lord God gave him the power of words to sustain the weary, "The Lord GOD has given Me the tongue of disciples, That I may know how to sustain the weary one with a word" (Isaiah 50:4). Words can lift a person's spirit from being weighed down, "Anxiety in a man's heart weighs it down, But, a good word makes it glad" (Prov. 12:25). Your words can either be discouraging or encouraging to others. If you discern that a person is discouraged, give him words from Scripture that offer hope and build faith and then pray with that individual.

A third characteristic of words of grace is that they are kind. The word *kind* is defined as being sympathetic, helpful, or forbearing in nature. Words of kindness demonstrate sympathy and patience. One can show kindness both in his actions and words. In one's conversations with others, he needs to understand how important it is to show an interest in what the other person is saying. Showing interest by listening to what a person is saying conveys a sense of worth. If all one does is talk about himself and his problems, he will not build many friendships and certainly not build others up. When one takes an interest in what problems others may be experiencing, he shows kindness by asking questions and sharing gentle words to bring comfort.

Proverbs 31 gives a lengthy description of the characteristics of a virtuous woman. One of the characteristics of a virtuous woman is that she speaks with kindness: "She opens her mouth in wisdom, And the teaching of kindness is on her tongue" (Prov. 31:26). Opening one's mouth in wisdom means to guard what is said by always being guided by wisdom. Everyone needs to take a moment to consider what he is about to speak. Before saying something, a person needs to consider how he would feel if someone said those same words to him.

A fourth characteristic of words of grace is that they are spoken in a gentle way. It is not just what we say to a person but how it is said that can make all the difference. It can alter how the words are received. One can say the exact words to a person but say them in an ungraceful manner or attitude. One's attitude can be reflected in his tone of voice. For example, I could say to a person, "What is your problem?" I can say those words in gentleness or with harshness. It all depends on what words I emphasize. I can say, "What *is* your problem?" and a person would take offense to how it was said. So often, words are spoken out of irritation or impatience. A person can be very sharp and even nasty with his tongue. Tender words can calm a person who is angry but responding with harsh words will only cause an escalation of anger. "A gentle answer turns away wrath, But, a harsh word stirs up anger" (Prov. 15:1). Speaking gently to someone is making one's words soothing to hear: "A soothing tongue is a tree of life, but perversion in it crushes the spirit" (Prov. 15:4).

Speaking gently to others is important in maintaining a good marriage. Being gentle in speech is especially important for how a husband speaks to his wife, "Husbands, love your wives, and do not be harsh with them" (Col. 3:19, ESV). Husbands are not to be harsh with their wives in the way they speak. Husbands have to be especially careful to speak to their wives in a gentle manner. First Peter 3:7 instructs husbands to dwell with their wives with understanding, "You husbands in the same way, live with *your wives* in an understanding way, as with someone weaker, since she is a woman; and show her honor as a fellow heir of the grace of life, so that your prayers will not be hindered." Every husband must try to understand his wife's weaknesses and do all he can to protect her. I discovered over many years of marriage that my wife is especially sensitive to how I speak to her. When I have spoken harshly to her, I wounded her spirit. There have been times when I was not in the best of moods. When I am having a lot of pain in my back or being frustrated about something, I can be unpleasant in my tone of voice. Even though my wife had nothing to do with how I was feeling, my tone of voice was not full of grace. I was not being very pleasant with my wife. I was taking out my frustration on her. After being treated poorly, my wife would come to me in tears, asking if I had something against her for the way I was talking to her. I quickly explained it was not her but some other things that were bothering me. I asked her forgiveness and then purposed to be gentle in the way I speak to her.

Wives also need to be careful about how they speak to their husbands. Wives can show disrespect in the way that they speak to their husbands. Once again, it is not just what is said but how it is said. Peter instructs wives to show respectful behavior toward their husbands even if they are disobedient to the Word, "In the same way, you wives, be submissive to your own husbands so that even if any *of them* are disobedient to the word, they may be won without a word by the behavior of their wives, as they observe your chaste and respectful behavior" (1 Pet. 3:1–2). Peter goes on to instruct wives not to put an inordinate focus on physical appearance, but rather to develop a beauty of inner character such as gentleness and a quiet spirit, "But *let it be* the hidden person of the heart, with the imperishable quality of a gentle and quiet spirit, which is precious in the sight of God" (1 Pet. 3:4).

The fifth characteristic of words of grace is that they are timely. Words are most powerful when they are spoken at just the right moment. Words of grace need to be spoken according to the need of the moment, "Let no unwholesome word proceed from your mouth, but only such *a word* as is good for edification according to the need *of the moment,* so that it will give grace to those who hear" (Eph. 4:29). When words of grace are spoken according to the need of the moment, they will give grace to those who hear. When a person is at a point in his life that he is about to give up or do something destructive to himself or others, that is the precise time to offer words of grace. Do not wait for a later time to say something; say what is needed at the moment. When a person discerns that someone is discouraged, that is the time to speak words of encouragement. God has placed that person there at that moment of need to speak words of grace. Proverbs 25:11 shares how beautiful words are that are spoken in the right circumstance, "*Like* apples of gold in settings of silver is a word spoken in right circumstances."

Application

1. How would you describe the manner with which you speak to others?

2. Have your words been full of grace?

3. Are your words kind and helpful, or are your words unsympathetic and insensitive?

4. Have you asked God's forgiveness and His help in speaking words of grace to others?

5. If you have offended others with your speech, have you gone to them to ask their forgiveness?

CHAPTER 21

Showing Acts of Grace

The words we speak to others can be quite influential in themselves, but when they are backed up with our actions, they will have an enormous impact. If our words are not backed up by our actions, our words will soon lose credibility. When it comes to building relationships, there must be an establishment of trust. When a person demonstrates God's grace by his words and actions, he can build a foundation of trust upon which relationships can flourish. Showing grace in one's words and actions can help in building new relationships and in rebuilding broken relationships.

Most relationships are broken because at least one person in the relationship perpetrates an offense, willingly or unwillingly, against the other party. Offenses will occur no matter how strong the relationship. It is not a question of if offenses will occur but how they are dealt with when they do occur. What usually happens when offenses occur is that the offended person withdraws from the relationship emotionally or physically leaves the relationship. The offended person raises a relational wall to protect against any further offenses. Most relationships never recover from this emotional severing. This is where God's grace can intervene and bring restoration.

One of the wonderful works of God's grace is His restoration of humanity's relationship with Himself through faith in Jesus Christ. Every person is alienated from God because of his offenses against God. Man's relationship with God was severely broken with no hope of reconciliation, but by the grace of God, He made a way for that relationship to be fully restored. As God's grace worked to restore the broken relationship with humanity, it can enable us to restore our relationships with others.

Showing Acts of Grace through Forgiving Others

One of the most important acts of grace that a person can show relationally is forgiving the people who have offended him. As God has shown grace toward His children, He wants that same type of grace shown to others. In his letter to the church of Ephesus, Paul admonished them to be gracious to each other: "Be kind to one another, tender-hearted, forgiving each other, just as God in Christ also has forgiven you" (Eph. 4:32). According to this verse, a Christian is to forgive others in the same way that God has forgiven him.

In what manner does God forgive? God completely forgives those who have faith in Christ. God forgives the repentant believer one hundred percent of his sins. The only sin that God will not forgive is the rejection of Jesus Christ. If a person rejects God's only means of salvation, then there is no forgiveness of sin for him. As a follower of Christ, one is to completely forgive people just as God has completely forgiven him. God does not want believers to be selective in what offenses they will forgive. God forgives the contrite sinner of all his sins no matter how many or how terrible they may have been. A believer is not to just forgive other's minor infractions, but also the major ones. How can one possibly forgive even the worst transgressions? Many people believe they could never completely "feel like" forgiving someone. Everyone needs to understand that it is not a matter of reaching a point of "feeling like" forgiving. For the follower of Christ, forgiving is a matter of obedience by choosing to act in grace toward someone. No one has the ability to forgive as God forgives; however, with God's grace working within a person, he is enabled to do things he could never do himself.

God not only forgives the repentant sinner of all his sin, He also forgets those sins. Because He is all knowing, God cannot forget in a literal sense. What is meant by God "forgetting sin" is that He will not bring judgment on sins that have been forgiven. When God forgives sins, it is if they are buried in the depths of the sea to be remembered no more. This is how followers of Christ are to forgive others by forgetting offenses. How can a person remove the memory of a transgression? Even though one cannot delete those memories, he can choose to not bring them up anymore against the offender. What everyone needs to do is to choose not to focus on past resentment. If one is keeping a mental "black book" of the offenses of others, he must surrender that book to God. God is the only Supreme Judge. Judgment must be surrendered to God, "Never take your own revenge, beloved, but leave room for the wrath *of God,* for it is written, "Vengeance is Mine, I will repay," says the Lord" (Rom. 12:19). How can one possibly forgive and forget? It is only by the grace of God that one is able to fully forgive.

Many people struggle to forgive because they feel the offender does not deserve to be forgiven. Some have established certain standards that an offender must reach before he can be forgiven. One requirement that many insist upon is that the offender must apologize. Furthermore, that apology must meet certain standards; the apology must be sincere. The offender must practically beg for forgiveness and plead for mercy. Another standard required by some is for offenders is to make full restitution. Many feel that those who have caused suffering most pay for their transgressions as in "an eye for an eye" (Exod. 21:24). Is that how God's grace treats people? Remember, God's grace is His unmerited favor. No one earns forgiveness from God but only receives it through faith in Christ. Thus, recipients of God's unmerited favor must likewise show grace by forgiving offenders who do not deserve it. That is what grace is all about—receiving something totally undeserved.

Do not confuse forgiving a person with trusting that person. Believers should immediately forgive offenders as an act of obedience to God; however, that does not mean that one can immediately trust the wrongdoer. One can quickly forgive out of God's grace but, as far as the relationship with the offender is concerned, that person has to restore trust. Forgiveness should be immediate while rebuilding trust may take some time. The offending party must earn the right to be trusted again. Grace and trust are different in this respect; trust is earned and grace is unearned.

Application

1. Do you have people in your life, who have hurt you?

2. Do you hold on to offenses and let them embitter you?

3. Are you demonstrating God's grace by forgiving those who have offended you?

4. Have you taken yourself off the throne of judgment and allowed God to sit in His rightful place as the Supreme Judge?

Showing Acts of Grace to Those Who Have Failed

We need to rely on God's grace when those close to us fail in some way. Even though it is not an easy response, we need to show God's grace to the one who has failed. Everyone has experienced a multitude of disappointments because of the failures of others around him. People fail in their commitments, fulfilling their responsibilities, and in keeping their promises. People constantly fail in countless ways. When a person fails, he does harm himself and to those close to him. So, what are we to do when so many fail us? We can choose to become bitter and withdraw from people, vowing never to trust anyone again, or we can choose to extend God's grace to those who have failed us. Everyone needs to remind himself about how many times he has failed God, and yet God has extended His mercy and grace to him. Just as God has shown us grace in times of failure, believers in Christ need to show that same grace to those who fail them.

When those around us fail, we need to extend a hand to help lift them up. Unfortunately, people so often choose to judge and ostracize rather than offer forgiveness and assistance to those who fail. The Bible speaks of restoring the fallen. "Brethren, even if a man is caught in any trespass, you who are spiritual, restore such a one in a spirit of gentleness, *each* one looking to yourself, lest you too be tempted" (Gal. 6:1). It is the spiritually mature who are able to show mercy and grace to those who fail. The spiritually mature realize that they, too, are subject to failure. It is only by the grace of God that there is any good in anyone. It is only by the grace of God that people are held back from a life of complete failure because, "but for the grace of God, there go I."

Everyone needs to understand the principle of "reaping what we sow" when it comes to giving and receiving mercy and grace. If a person is judgmental and condemning to those who have fallen short, he will receive that same treatment when he fails. "Do not judge lest you be judged. For in the way you judge, you will be judged; and by your standard of measure, it will be measured to you" (Matt. 7:1–2). In the Sermon on the Mount, Jesus taught the immense value of showing mercy: "Blessed are the merciful for they shall receive mercy" (Matt. 5:7). No one should be so prideful that he thinks he will never fail. Failure can happen to anyone; so, let each person be sure to show mercy to those who fail so that should he fail, he will be shown mercy.

When someone fails and seeks forgiveness, he should be shown mercy. However, all need to understand that the person who fails needs more than forgiveness. He needs to receive grace. Some people try to take advantage of the merciful and keep offending with no intention to change. A person can keep making promises to change but never fulfil those promises. Mercy without grace can create a cycle of failure like this. Showing grace means a person is offered real support to overcome his pattern of failure. Grace is demonstrated by committing oneself to work with the person to help him overcome his tendency to repeat the failure. Grace offers a plan of action to come alongside the person to assist him in each step of his recovery. If a person is willing to humble himself and be accountable, he should also be offered God's restorative grace.

Application

1. Has someone close to you failed you?

2. How have you responded to the failure?

3. Have you extended grace toward those who have failed you?

Showing Acts of Grace Through Giving

Another way one can show acts of grace is in giving graciously. One of the greatest hindrances to relationships is selfishness. Selfishness causes strife in relationships by making demands to have one's way in everything. Learning to give graciously of oneself will help one to overcome his selfishness and help dissolve strife in his relationships.

What does it mean to give graciously? Giving graciously is to give generously above what is deserved or expected. God's grace is always abundant and more than what is needed. As God has given abundantly out of His grace, so followers of Christ are to give generously to others. Christ's words need to be taken to heart, "Freely you received, freely give" (Matt. 10:8). God has freely given on the basis of His grace; therefore, His desire is for people to bless others by showing them His abundant grace. Giving graciously does not always involve giving money. One can give his time graciously to help someone in need. Instead of arguing over who is going to get his way, one could act in grace by capitulating graciously to the other. People act in grace when they give something of value to another person.

A better understanding of grace can be achieved by examining examples of grace given in Scripture. One of the best examples of grace giving is found in 2 Corinthians, chapters 8 and 9 where the apostle Paul commends the Macedonian churches for their gracious giving to fellow believers who were in great need. The background for Paul's commendation was the taking of a collection to help the believers in Jerusalem who were starving because of a famine. Paul referred to this collection as a "gracious work" (2 Cor. 8:6, 7, 19). In Paul's letter to the church of Corinth, he encouraged them to give like the Macedonian churches. Paul explained how the Macedonian churches were able to give as an act of grace. It was the grace of God that enabled them to give in the manner in which they gave, "Now, brethren, we *wish* to make known to you the grace of God which has been given in the churches of Macedonia" (2 Cor. 8:1). God's grace inspired the Macedonian churches to give graciously.

Great Generosity

1 Now, brethren, we *wish* to make known to you the grace of God which has been given in the churches of Macedonia,

2 that in a great ordeal of affliction their abundance of joy and their deep poverty overflowed in the wealth of their liberality.

3 For I testify that according to their ability, and beyond their ability, *they gave* of their own accord,

4 begging us with much urging for the favor of participation in the support of the saints,

5 and *this*, not as we had expected, but they first gave themselves to the Lord and to ⁿˢ by the will of God.

6 So we urged Titus that as he had previously made a beginning, so he would also complete in you this gracious work as well. (2 Cor. 8:1–6)

By taking a closer look at chapters 8 and 9 of 2 Corinthians we can discover notable characteristics of grace giving. The first characteristic of grace giving is that its source is the grace of God, "the grace of God which has been given in the churches of Macedonia" (8:1). The believers in the Macedonian churches were enabled by God's grace to give graciously. Grace giving is not a product of man's own doing, which comes from his own goodwill and benevolence. Grace giving comes from God's grace working through the believer.

The second characteristic of grace giving is that it is not based on circumstances. This is demonstrated by the Macedonian churches who were going through an "ordeal of affliction," and had "deep poverty" themselves (8:2), yet gave generously. Grace giving is not affected by circumstances because it is based on the grace of God, not on circumstances. To a great extent, giving *is* based on circumstances. If a person feels that he can afford it, he will give a certain amount. If he thinks he cannot afford to give, he will not give. Some adopt a budget that limits their amount of giving for a year. Even if a person is prompted by God to give to a need, he will not give if it exceeds the budget. This is not how grace gives.

> ***God does not have a budget for the amount of grace He will give to us.***

God's grace gives more than what is needed, more than expected, and it is not limited by a budget. Just as God has given to the recipients of His grace, God wants them to learn how to give through grace.

A third characteristic of grace giving is that is accompanied by joy. When the giver is motivated by God's grace, he will experience an abundance of joy. Those who have learned to give graciously understand what Jesus meant when He said, "it is more blessed to give than to receive" (Acts 20:35). The joy that comes from receiving only lasts for a short time. The gift received will most often lose its value over time. If money is received, it will soon be spent. If an item is received, it will eventually be put away somewhere and forgotten. In contrast, the joyful memory of giving will not be forgotten.

The fourth characteristic of grace giving is that there is a "wealth of liberality" (8:2). The Macedonians Christians who gave did not give out of their abundance; instead, they gave out of their "deep poverty." When one gives out of his abundance, little grace is required. When a person gives out of insufficiency, that requires God's grace. Grace giving is never stingy; it always gives generously.

The fifth characteristic of grace giving is that it is sacrificial, "they gave beyond their ability" (8:3). Paul used Christ's example of self-sacrifice to encourage the Corinthians to also be sacrificial in their giving. "For you know the grace of our Lord Jesus Christ, that though He was rich, yet for your sake He became poor, so that you through His poverty might become rich" (2 Cor. 8:9). The greater the sacrifice in giving, the greater the grace required.

Sixth, grace giving is always done with the right motives. The grace of God enabled the Macedonians to give with the right motives. There are right and wrong reasons for giving. In the ninth chapter of 2 Corinthians, Paul mentions several wrong reasons to give:

> [5] So I thought it necessary to urge the brethren that they would go on ahead to you and arrange beforehand your previously promised bountiful gift, so that the same would be ready as a bountiful gift and not affected by covetousness.
>
> [6] Now this I say, he who sows sparingly will also reap sparingly, and he who sows bountifully will also reap bountifully.
>
> [7] Each one must do just as he has purposed in his heart, not grudgingly or under compulsion, for God loves a cheerful giver. (2 Cor. 9:5–7)

In verse 5, Paul instructed that giving should not be affected "by covetousness." How could covetousness affect our giving? One would think that covetousness would prevent someone from giving. How can a person be motivated by covetousness to give? Paul reminded the Corinthians of the principle of sowing and reaping, "Now this *I say*, he who sows sparingly will also reap sparingly, and he who sows bountifully will also reap bountifully." Knowing that there are benefits to giving does encourage people to give, but that should never be the primary motivation for giving. If receiving is the main reason for giving, then covetousness could be the motivation. Giving should not be motivated by selfishness. It should flow from a desire to demonstrate the wonderful grace of God.

There are some who manipulate people into giving more through appealing to their greed. There are some who preach a false gospel that through giving the giver will become rich. These false prophets appeal to people's covetousness to motivate them to give more. The motivation for giving is to get more to feed their covetousness. Some of these prosperity preachers even tell people to believe God for certain status symbols such as expensive cars, fancy clothes, or a big home in the suburbs. This is not true of grace giving; it is not influenced by greed or covetousness.

Another wrong attitude when giving is to give "grudgingly," or "unwillingly," or "under compulsion." I have been in church meetings where fundraising for a project occurred. The method I encountered was a real turn-off for me. Leaders would call out people and ask them to state what they would give. After people responded with a certain amount, the spokesperson would call the person forward and embarrass him by telling him to do better and increase the donation. The spokesperson would increase the amount of the person's pledge and get him to agree to the larger amount in front of others. I could see that these people resented being pressured into giving more than they were willing or able to give. These pressure tactics certainly put people under compulsion to give. Churches should not resort to worldly methods to raise funds, no matter how worthy the cause.

Another incorrect reason to give is the expectation of receiving something in return. Jesus spoke about giving without expectation of receiving anything in return. If Christians only give with an expectation of return, they are no different from sinners who lend with the expectation of receiving something back. Giving to help others should not be done out of any selfish motives, "If you only give for what you hope to get out of it, do you think that's charity? The stingiest of pawnbrokers does that. I tell you, love your enemies. Help and give without expecting a return. I promise you'll never regret it. Live out this God-created identity the way our Father lives toward us, generously and graciously, even when we're at our worst" (Luke 6:34–35, MSG).

A number of years ago when I was just starting as a pastor, I got a call from an elderly man who said he would give a donation to the church. I thanked him, and a few days later a check for $25 came in the mail. He called me a few days later and asked if I would help him do some work around his house. Wanting to meet the man, I agreed to go over and help him. Several weeks later, the man sent another check in the mail. What do you think happened next? You guessed it. He called me again to do more work around his house. In my mind I was just being kind and giving a practical demonstration of the love of Christ. So, I helped him again. Then it occurred to me what was really happening with this man. He was giving donations to the church, expecting me to do work for him in return. The next time he called, I had to inform him that I had a full-time job as a pastor, and I was not going to assist him anymore because of all the demands of pastoring. What do you think happened to the man's donations? You guessed right again. The donations stopped. That was not the last time that people expected me to do things for them because they gave to the church. When we help someone, it should not be done as a loan or with the expectation of receiving something in return. To give graciously means to give as a gift. Remember, God's grace is free.

Learning to give without any expectation of return was not an easy truth for me to acquire in my pastoral ministry. For years, I worked hard at helping people who had need. I helped people move, gave rides, provided food and clothing, and loaned money. I even helped paint several people's houses for free. I did not expect these people to give me money in return; however, I did expect those to whom I loaned money to repay me. What percentage of people I loaned money to would you guess paid me back? You might guess 50 percent or 75 percent, but you would be way off. Zero percent paid me back!

In addition to expecting loans to be repaid, I have to confess I did also expect something else in return from the people I helped. I expected them to show their gratitude for my help by coming to church. Having that expectation caused me a great amount of frustration with people. People would promise to come to church but never came. I figured that after all I did for people at least they could come to my church. Loaning people money had the opposite effect on people than I expected. Instead of coming to church, people to whom I loaned money would avoid me like the plague. My frustration with people began to turn into bitterness. I was becoming angry with people because I was getting almost nothing in return for all the help I gave. I was tempted to just stop doing anything for people. I sought the Lord concerning this inner struggle. It took me a while to understand grace giving. The Lord spoke to me numerous times about the type of giving that has no expectation of return. I was to show God's love and grace without any expectation of people coming to church. God wanted me to just show His love and leave the results to Him.

Since I learned to give without any expectation in return, I never loan money. If someone comes to me for financial help, I will pray about what God wants me to give. If God wants me to give, I will give the most generous grace gift that I can. I make it very clear that it is a gift from God and not a loan. All I ask from those who receive a grace gift is that they will likewise bless someone else in the future. God wants to start a ripple effect of grace giving in every person's life.

Learning the importance of grace giving in my personal life has been a valuable lesson. I have made it the motivation for the ministries of the church as well. The church I serve is in the inner-city of Buffalo, New York. There are many poor people in the surrounding community. As a means of demonstrating the love of God, our church has developed several outreach ministries to the poor. For many months, our church provided a free community meal to about thirty to seventy-five people. We also provided food and clothing for those people to take home. During the meal, we sat with the visitors to welcome them and get to know them. We shared a short devotional and had a prayer room for those who wanted prayer or counseling. For a number of years, our church has reached out to the homeless during the winter months to provide warm clothing and food. Our sole purpose is to show God's love and grace. Guess what? God is working in people's lives. We are experiencing results with some receiving Christ and even some coming to church.

Probably the worst reason to give is to receive honor from men. Jesus condemned this kind of giving. "So when you give to the poor, do not sound a trumpet before you, as the hypocrites do in the synagogues and in the streets, so that they may be honored by men. Truly I say to you, they have their reward in full" (Matt. 6:2). Jesus was addressing the Pharisee's way of giving to the poor. The Pharisees would bring attention to themselves by having someone blow a trumpet or ring a bell before they would give to a poor beggar on the streets. Jesus said that those who do this do it to get glory and honor from people. God's desire is for giving to the poor to be done in secret. One day, the giver will be rewarded openly by God.

God's grace motivates people to give for the right reasons. The Macedonian churches were motivated by God's grace to give "of their own accord" (2 Cor. 8:3). The grace of God moves people to give willingly and cheerfully. God's grace also motivates people to give out of a heart of compassion. When the need of the Jerusalem believers was made known to the churches of Macedonia, they "begged" to be able to participate in the collection (2 Cor. 8:4). Verse 5 of 2 Corinthians 8, reveals the fundamental principal of motivation for grace giving, they "first gave themselves to the Lord." This is the key to a person's giving.

> *The priorities of a person's heart will determine his giving.*

If a person has wholeheartedly given himself to the Lord, he will not have a problem giving generously. However, if a person has not given himself wholeheartedly to the Lord, he will not be generous but will be motivated by self-interest. In that case, self sits on the throne of his heart. The person who has surrendered everything to the Lord recognizes that all he has belongs to God. Another true indicator of the Macedonian Christians' motivation for giving was that they first gave themselves to "the will of God" (2 Cor. 8:5). When a person has surrendered to the lordship of Christ, he has purposed to do the will of God in his life. The Macedonian Christians gave graciously as they believed God had directed them. Grace giving is directed by the Lord. Grace giving flows from a life that is obedient and surrendered to God's will.

In order to understand grace giving, we need to realize that there are various degrees of grace involved in giving. Some types of giving do not require much grace. If there is not much sacrifice in giving, it requires only a small amount of grace. Giving out of an abundance does not require much grace. Giving to a family member does not usually require much grace because it is one's responsibility to care for his family. When a friend helps his friends that does not usually require much grace because even sinners practice that type of giving. What requires more grace is giving to a stranger. When the apostle Paul collected donations from churches to help the starving Christians in Jerusalem, he asked them to give to people they had never met. Even though these were fellow believers, they were still strangers. It requires more grace to give generously to strangers. Giving liberally to strangers who are not fellow believers requires even more grace.

Jesus's Parable of the Good Samaritan addresses showing mercy and grace to strangers (Luke 10:30–35). This parable is a story about a man who traveled by foot on a dangerous path between Jerusalem and Jericho. The path was notorious for thieves who hid behind large rocks and then jumped out on defenseless people to rob them. In Christ's parable, a traveler was robbed and beaten almost to death. The first people to come down the path after this brutal incident were a priest and a Levite. Surprisingly, they did nothing and "passed by on the other side" (Luke 10:32). The parable does not tell us why these religious people did nothing. For some reason, they avoided getting involved with the man in great need. Everyone can make excuses for why he is not helping the needy. Maybe the issue is busyness or maybe the person simply does not care about others because he is so wrapped up in his own problems. It has been my observation that those who get involved in helping others receive a greater portion of grace from God to help them with their own personal problems.

After the priest and the Levite passed by the wounded man, another person, who was a Samaritan, came down the path and came upon the beaten man lying on the side of the path. This man did not just "pass by" like those before him but instead, went over to get a closer look at the situation. He was not afraid to get close to the person in need. It was only by getting close that he saw the need and began to do all he could to help out. This Good Samaritan was moved by compassion (Luke 10:33) to do something about the man's desperate need. The Samaritan showed mercy by pouring oil on the wounds to cleanse them and wine on the wounds to disinfect them. He bandaged the wounds, put the man on his beast, and brought him to an inn where he could rest and have time to recover from his injuries.

What the good Samaritan did next was to go beyond showing mercy to showing grace. He showed grace by doing far more than expected. He paid the innkeeper two days wages to cover the immediate costs, and then asked the innkeeper to keep track of the extra expenses involved with the wounded stranger's recovery. The good Samaritan promised to pay the full amount when he returned. This is pure grace giving. The grace giving that the Samaritan demonstrated exceeded everyone's expectations.

There is another type of grace giving that requires more grace than all others. Remember, God's grace is His unmerited favor; it is giving to someone who is undeserving. The more undeserving a person is and unmerited the help, the more of God's grace is required to offer assistance. What kind of giving am I speaking of? It is giving to help one's enemies. When the Scriptures teach doing good to one's enemies, they refer to enemies on a personal level. Those people who oppose, speak evil of, slander, insult, hate, or tell lies about us are enemies on a personal level. Everything within our fleshly nature wants to get even with our enemies and to return evil for evil.

The Scriptures tell us not to return evil for evil, "Never pay back evil for evil to anyone" (Rom. 12:17). Instead of returning evil for evil we are to return good for evil, "Do not be overcome by evil, but overcome evil with good" (Rom. 12:21). Jesus told us to love our enemies and do good to them: "But I say to you who hear, love your enemies, do good to those who hate you" (Luke 6:27). Jesus told us to pray for our enemies, "But I say to you, love your enemies and pray for those who persecute you" (Matthew 5:44). The apostle Paul, when writing to the church in Rome, quoted from the Proverbs about how we are to treat our enemies. "BUT IF YOUR ENEMY IS HUNGRY, FEED HIM, AND IF HE IS THIRSTY, GIVE HIM A DRINK; FOR IN SO DOING YOU WILL HEAP BURNING COALS ON HIS HEAD" (Prov. 25:21; Rom. 12:20).

Peter instructed believers not to return evil for evil but to give a blessing instead, "not returning evil for evil or insult for insult, but giving a blessing instead; for you were called for the very purpose that you might inherit a blessing" (1 Pet. 3:9). Instead of trying to hurt our enemies, God wants us to help them by giving them what they need. This is the greatest form of grace giving. It is only by the grace of God that a person is able to give his enemies a blessing instead of retaliation.

I believe two important things happen when a person gives a blessing to his enemies. First, grace giving to one's enemies brings the giver joy and more love toward his enemy. My wife and I have experienced this many times during our ministry with people who have opposed us and who spoke evil about us behind our backs. We discovered that by giving grace to these people along with forgiving them, our ill feelings toward them were significantly diminished. Consequently, we were able to love those people and continue to minister to them without any resentment. The second transformational part can occur in the recipient's life, but there are no guarantees. The recipient may react to grace giving with great suspicion and question the motivation. In some cases, I have seen my grace giving really turn things around in my relationships with people. Some of the people to whom we have grace given are now close friends. When we learn to model God's grace through speaking words of grace, showing acts of grace through forgiving others, and giving graciously, our relationships will be enhanced.

Application

1. Are you willing to start practicing grace giving in your life?

2. Have you fully surrendered to God?

3. Do you recognize God as the owner of all that you possess?

4. Are you willing to surrender your money and possessions to God to be used as He directs?

5. Do you enjoy giving?

6. When you give to help others, do you give without any expectation of return?

CHAPTER 22

Showing Grace in Our Attitudes

Showing Grace in Our Attitudes Toward Those with Differing Opinions

In addition to showing God's grace through our words and actions, we need to show God's grace through our attitudes. Attitudes have a tremendous impact on relationships. There are certain attitudes, such as pride, that are very detrimental to maintaining relationships. The Bible teaches that pride stirs up strife: "An arrogant man stirs up strife, but he who trusts in the LORD will prosper" (Prov. 28:25). There are a number of reasons why people become prideful. A person can become arrogant because of his level of education. The Bible tells us that knowledge can make a person arrogant: "Now concerning things sacrificed to idols, we know that we all have knowledge. Knowledge makes arrogant, but love edifies" (1 Cor. 8:1). When a person accumulates knowledge through learning, he can become prideful by thinking that he knows it all. In reality, when a person thinks he knows it all, he is showing how little he truly knows. "If anyone supposes that he knows anything, he has not yet known as he ought to know" (1 Cor. 8:2). Quite often when children reach their late teens, they believe that they know more than their parents. The same kind of thing happens with some new Christians. When a new believer begins gaining Bible knowledge in his first years of study, he may, unfortunately, become prideful and begin to think that he knows more than his spiritual elders.

In addition to having pride about one's knowledge, one can become prideful and believe he is wiser than others. If a person has much knowledge, he can wrongfully conclude that he also has much wisdom. Wisdom requires knowledge, but many have knowledge without wisdom. Wisdom is the skill to make right decisions. The Bible warns us not to become "wise in our own eyes"—"Do not be wise in your own eyes; Fear the LORD and turn away from evil" (Prov. 3:7). "Be of the same mind toward one another; do not be haughty in mind, but associate with the lowly. Do not be wise in your own estimation" (Rom. 12:16).

When a person is arrogant in his opinions, it will bring strife. An arrogant person believes he has nothing to learn from others. Arrogance can stir up animosity if opinions are expressed in offensive ways. Nearly everyone believes that his opinions are the only right opinions and that everyone else is wrong. I noticed a new bumper sticker that reads, "Everyone is entitled to my opinion." Strong differences of opinion on politics and religion have caused a great amount of division and strife in relationships. These differences have divided marriages, families, churches, and even our nation. Differences of opinion in themselves do not have to be detrimental to relationships. It is how one deals with differences of opinion that will damage or restore his relationships.

Some are so arrogantly opinionated that they cannot tolerate being around anyone with a different opinion. For some, opposing views are considered hate speech, which should be shut down, thereby limiting free speech. Thus, anyone who does not agree with them is cut off and excluded from any further association. This is what some describe as the "cancel culture." The "cancel culture" can go to extremes in some cases by violently attacking those who do not agree with them. It is becoming all too common to view scenes of people verbally attacking others. We see scenes of mobs on college campuses and in many cities destroying property because they do not agree with a guest speaker's views, a fatal police action, or a court decision. The animosity between opposing views keeps building to a fevered pitch until some resort to violence. Mobs show up at homes to threaten the families of politicians and TV commentators who have views with whom they disagree. We even saw a vehicle run down protesters in Charlottesville, Virginia, and a gunman shooting down scores of people from a hotel window in Las Vegas. We saw a gunman shooting and wounding several congressmen at a Republican baseball practice and bombs being sent to political leaders. We have seen how gunmen have entered churches to kill Christians and into synagogues to kill Jews. We have recently witnessed the attack on our Capitol building by rioters. There is far too much hatred and vitriol manifested all across our country.

What are Christians to do in the midst of such heated rhetoric? If Christians are not careful, they can get caught up in the spirit of hatred pervading our nation.

> ***This spirit of hatred that pervades our nation should never be allowed in the heart and mind of a follower of Christ.***

Christians should not be participating in personal attacks on social media against those of opposing views. Christians should not be engaged in name calling and the use of profanity to express their views. This spirit of animosity toward those with opposing views should never be brought into the church.

How is a Christian to act toward those who have different views from him? The Bible does have something to say about how a Christian is to deal with differences of opinion. Besides speaking words of grace to others (including those who have differing views), a Christian is to display humility in his attitude rather than prideful arrogance.

> ***Humility is the attitude of grace.***

Humility is the attitude of grace because humility is necessary to receive God's grace (1 Pet. 5:5). Everyone must humble himself before God by repenting of pride and self-reliance. To humble ourselves before God means to submit to His rule in our lives and to trust in Him. What does it mean when the Bible declares, "God opposes the proud"? The idea of the word *oppose* is that of an army arrayed against us ready to attack at any time. If God opposes someone that means He will not assist that person in any way. God lovingly allows failure and defeat in a believer's life to bring him to the point of humbling himself and confessing his need for God. A person humbles himself by realizing his need of God and by surrendering to Him.

Many do not understand that humbling oneself before God also includes humbling oneself before others. There is vertical humility that a Christian must have before God and, likewise, horizontal humility that he needs to show toward others, "You younger men, likewise, be subject to *your* elders; and all of you, clothe yourselves with humility toward one another, for GOD IS OPPOSED TO THE PROUD, BUT GIVES GRACE TO THE HUMBLE" (1 Pet. 5:5).

> *If a person truly is humble before God,*
> *he will also be humble before others.*

If a person has an attitude of humility before God, that same attitude should carry over into his relationships with others. Followers of Christ are to clothe themselves with humility. Everyone should have the attitude of humility toward God, himself, and others. A person with humility has a balanced view of himself; he knows his strengths and his weaknesses. It does not mean that a person puts himself down or possesses a poor self-image. Humility toward others means that a person regards others as more important than himself. "Do nothing from selfishness or empty conceit, but with humility of mind regard one another as more important than yourselves" (Phil. 2:3).

A prideful person is wise in his own eyes, but the humble are the ones who are truly wise. Humility brings wisdom, "When pride comes, then comes dishonor, but with the humble is wisdom" (Prov. 11:2). A humble person is wise because he has learned to put his trust in God and not in himself. The humble person is wise because he knows that he has much more to learn. A humble person knows that he does not know it all and can always learn from others. The humble are wise because they know that they need the help of others. Out of a humble attitude comes wisdom that is from above: "But the wisdom from above is first pure, then peaceable, gentle, open to reason, full of mercy and good fruits, impartial and sincere" (James 3:17, ESV).

Being humble does not mean that we cannot possess strong opinions. What it does mean is that we are to express those opinions in a peaceful manner. The wisdom from above is peaceable and gentle. Rather than having pride and arrogance toward others, the humble will show humility when dealing with differing opinions. Being humble does not mean that someone has to agree with other's views. It does mean that he is open to reason (James 3:17). Being open to reason means that respect is shown by listening to what a person has to say. Being open to reason does not mean a Christian is to be open to unscriptural concepts but that he cares enough about the person who disagrees with him to understand his point of view. Through understanding a person's differing views, one will be better equipped to ask questions that will expose weaknesses of opinion.

> ***Rather than trying to win debates with people, we need to cultivate relationships.***

The objective of a humble, non-combative, grace-filled approach is to permit a person to let down his defenses and to open up to what each party has to say.

The humility of grace does not allow for any judgmental attitude or attitude of contempt for others. This should be true especially between those who are followers of Christ. Unfortunately, it has been my experience over my many years of ministry that there is not much humility of grace shown between different church groups. Rather than showing grace to each other, there is an enormous amount of judgment and contempt displayed among Christian denominations. I found this to be especially true whenever I participated in directing city-wide evangelistic outreaches. I experienced pastors who refused to work with any other pastors who were not from their particular religious group. It is understandable that because there are divisions on matters of doctrine, it is unrealistic to expect churches to agree on everything. Having a humble, graceful attitude toward other Christian groups happens when people look for areas of common ground on major doctrines. This is especially crucial when there is a need for cooperation for greater impact in ministry and evangelism. Rather than looking for common beliefs on the major doctrines, many pastors focus on trivial differences and are unwilling to participate in any cooperative effort. There are some pastors who have contempt for other churches who do not have the same standards for holiness. If church leaders would humble themselves before each other and show the attitude of grace, there would be much greater unity and peace between those who name the name of Christ.

Showing an Attitude of Grace toward Fellow Believers with Differing Convictions

Division between believers is certainly not a new thing. The apostle Paul addressed the problem of division within the church in Rome (Rom. 14). There were divisions among the Roman Christians caused by differing convictions. Some believers strongly believed that Christians should eat only certain foods while others believed that they were free to eat anything. Paul instructed those who believed they were able to eat anything not to look down on those who had a restricted diet: "Let not him who eats regard with contempt him who does not eat" (Rom. 14:3). Those who had certain convictions concerning food should not judge those who did not have a restricted diet: "And let not him who does not eat judge who him who eats" (Rom. 14:3). This issue of what food should be permissible was not the only controversy in the early church. There was division over which days were considered more important than others. Some had a conviction that one day a week (the Sabbath) was more sacred than the other days, while others regarded every day the same (Rom. 14:5).

How can Christians have peace and harmony with so many differing convictions? Is compromising one's personal convictions the solution to division? Although the world tries to solve division through compromising on beliefs, this is not God's way. Personal convictions are strong beliefs that a person holds as true for himself. Personal convictions have great value and should not be compromised or discarded: "One man regards one day above another, another regards everyday *alike*. Let each man be fully convinced in his own mind" (Rom. 14:5). Paul instructed Christians to be strong in their convictions by being fully convinced that their convictions were right *for them* to hold and practice.

There are convictions that are based on a person's interpretation of Scripture and convictions that are a matter of a person's conscience.

For a person's doctrinal beliefs to be valid, they must have a strong biblical foundation.

> *Doctrinal beliefs cannot be based on circumstances or feelings, but on a comprehensive understanding of the Word of God.*

In addition to convictions concerning doctrinal beliefs, one should possess convictions about his personal behavior. Convictions concerning one's own personal behavior determine what practices he prohibits and what practices he allows or promotes. Personal convictions regarding behavior can come from both Scripture and a person's conscience.

On matters dealing with a person's conscience, there will be a broad array of differing convictions. There is a wide range of convictions because everyone has different strengths and weaknesses. Each person will have different convictions about what he can or cannot permit in his life. Personal convictions are important because they help one defend himself against his areas of weakness. If a believer does not have a clear conscience about practicing something, then he should not practice it. "The faith which you have, have as your own conviction before God. Happy is he who does not condemn himself in what he approves" (Rom. 14:22). Every Christian should maintain his own convictions about what is right and wrong for himself. If a person participates in something that he doubts is right and feels guilt about it, then he should establish his own conviction against it, "But he who doubts is condemned if the eats, because his eating is not from faith; and whatever is not from faith is sin" (Rom. 14:23).

I experienced an example of someone having an unusual personal conviction of conscience during my years at Bible college. While residing in a dormitory, I had a roommate who was a recent convert to Christ. He had come out of a culture of drugs and hard rock music. He had been an accomplished guitarist in a rock band for many years. When he came to know Christ, he quit the band and decided to come to Bible college. I asked him once if he was still playing the guitar. He told me that he had sold his guitar. When I asked him why he sold his guitar, his answer surprised me. He said that he could not play the guitar for some time because it reminded him of his past. For him, being reminded of his past was a temptation to return to that former way of life. My roommate realized that he had a weakness and needed to be protected by a strong conviction not to play the guitar for a while. This personal conviction was unusual, but it was necessary for him until he felt strong enough to play again. He could not, in good conscience, play a guitar at that point in his life. It would be wrong to make fun of this person's conviction or to look down on him in distain. As long as a person is sincerely following what he believes pleases the Lord in regard to personal behavior, we should gracefully respect that conviction.

The discord of differing convictions does not come just because people have strong personal convictions. Conflict comes because people try to apply their personal convictions to everyone else. Personal convictions are just that—personal and not meant for others. Some make the mistake of believing that if they have a certain conviction, then everyone else should share it. Some believers are guilty of judging others who do not have the same convictions. My college roommate would be wrong to judge others who did not have the same personal conviction about playing a guitar.

The apostle Paul explained that personal convictions should be practiced for the purpose of pleasing the Lord: "He who observes the day observes it for the Lord, and he who eats, does it for the Lord, for he gives thanks to God; and he who eats not, for the Lord he does not eat, and gives thanks to God" (Rom.14:6). Each person must do his very best to live a life that is pleasing to God because he knows that everyone will give an account to God for the way he conducted himself (Rom. 14:12). It is not anyone's position to judge others who have distinct convictions. "But you, why do you judge your brother? Or you again, why do you regard your brother with contempt? For we shall all stand before the judgment seat of God" (Rom. 14:10). Christians need to show grace to each other by respecting each other's personal convictions. Respect is shown by not looking down on or judging those who hold to different convictions. Grace is demonstrated by showing deference to those who are weak in conscience.

No one is to become a "stumbling block" by causing others to fall by his example (Rom. 14:21).

Showing an Attitude of Grace Toward Those in Authority

Showing the humility of grace must also involve one's attitudes toward those in authority. Showing horizonal grace to God's delegated, earthly authorities is especially important. In addition to submitting to the authority of God's Word, believers must humble themselves by submitting to God's delegated authorities. God has established levels of authority in everyone's life to help protect him. God established the family structure, the church, employers, and government to be His delegated authorities on earth. For these God-given structures of order to function well, people must submit to them as to God's authority (Rom. 13:1).

The Bible is very clear that Christians are to be submissive to those in authority in their lives. In the family structure, husbands are to love their wives as Christ loved the church, and wives are to be subject to and show respect for their husbands. Children are to be obedient to their parents (Eph. 5:22–6:1). In the church setting, believers are to cooperate with spiritual leaders (Heb. 13:17; 1 Cor. 16:16). In the employment structure, employees are to cooperate with their employers, and employers are to be considerate of their employees (Eph. 6:5–9). Regarding government structure, Christians are to be subject to their governing authorities (Rom. 13:1–7; 1 Pet. 2:13–14). If a person is not willing to cooperate with his God-given authorities, he is not really surrendered to God. If a person is not showing a humble attitude toward his earthly authorities, he is not truly submitted to God. Some will pridefully proclaim that they are only under God's authority and not under man's authority. They claim that they only answer to God but, in reality, they are only ruled by their prideful rebellious hearts.

Having humility is the key to receiving God's grace. The more we learn to walk in humility, the more grace will be supplied. Being humble toward those who are in authority in our lives is a vital part of exhibiting humility and receiving God's grace. One of the verses most referred to concerning God giving grace to the humble is found in the context of being subject to elders in the church. "You younger men, likewise, be subject to *your* elders; and all of you, clothe yourselves with humility toward one another, for God is opposed to the proud, but gives grace to the humble" (1 Pet. 2:13–14). If a person clothes himself with humility toward others, God will supply His grace. It is important to recognize that showing humility to others, especially those who are our authorities, can be an expression of humility toward God.

Application

1. Do you think you can learn from those with less education than you have?

2. Are you tolerant of others with differing opinions from yours?

3. Do you have a balanced view of yourself?

4. Do you judge those with differing opinions?

5. Do you show respect for those who have different convictions of conscience?

6. Are you showing a humble attitude toward those who are in authority in your life?

Trophy of Grace: Pastor Kenneth H. Wilson

When Jesus walked this earth, preaching and teaching the heart and mind of God, preaching and teaching the truths of God, He often told stories to illustrate these things. He used stories because He knew people are better able to understand the truths of God when hearing a story. With this in mind, I want to share a real-life, true story of the grace of God. This is a story intended to show how the grace of God actually works in real life.

When God creates us, we are each fearfully and wonderfully made. Listen to the words of Psalm 139:14, "I will give thanks unto you; for I am fearfully and wonderfully made: Wonderful are your works." Often, the devil whispers in our ears that we are no good, that we are worthless, and that we have no purpose for living. Sadly, the world around us often repeats these same lies from the pit of hell until we begin to believe them. Even sadder is how often parents repeat these lies to their children. The child in this story of grace heard these lies all of his life. In fact, he often tells this story that took place around the age of seven. His mother and father had been fighting for days. They were talking of separating and arguing about with whom the three boys should live. This little seven-year-old boy's mother took him aside and told him, "You are no good, just like your rotten father! And since you are no good, I should send you to go live with him, but I won't." This little boy grew up believing the words of his mother, that he was no good.

Many children, such as the boy in this story, grow up being told by their parents that they were never wanted, that they were never planned, that they were a mistake, and that they were an accident. The mother of the little boy in this story always told him that he was not wanted and that he was a mistake. His mother always told him that she wanted a daughter, not a son. She always told him that on the day he was born, she screamed at the doctor to take him back because she didn't want him. Yet none of us are born into this world by accident. We are born because God chooses to form us after His own image and likeness. We are born by God's choice. We are born by God's plan.

The young boy in this story of grace was born into a nightmare. His parents were never married; in fact, they could not be married. They could not be married because his mother was legally married to another man. This young boy's father was a heavy drinker; he was a very jealous man and a very angry and violent man. From a young age, this little boy would cower in a corner as he watched his father beat his two older brothers with his fists. And although this little boy avoided the beatings, he was unable to avoid the molestation by his father, and later by his oldest brother. This little boy grew up believing that fathers were very violent, evil people. He grew up believing that fathers are cold and distant and that fathers should be avoided whenever possible.

Every morning this boy's mother would leave for work with the children clinging to her legs, begging not to be left with their father. Every morning after his mother left for work, if school was not in session, the father tied the three children onto their beds until just before their mother returned home from work so that he did not have to be bothered by them.

When this child was five, the family lived in an upstairs apartment on Hudson Street in Buffalo, New York. There was a very large storage room across the hall from this second-floor apartment. Every evening around 7 or 8 o'clock, the three brothers were marched to this storage room that had been converted to a bedroom. They were given a pitcher of water to share during the night and given a metal mop bucket to use as a toilet. Every night, the door was closed behind them, and they would hear the snap of the padlock and hasp on the outside of the door. And they knew that they were locked in that room until the following morning. Each night, as they went to sleep in that little storage room, they hoped that there would be no fire as they were trapped with no way of escape. Each night, they hoped someone would come back the next morning to let them out again.

Growing up, these three little boys were not allowed to leave their home unless necessary. They were not allowed to have friends with whom they could play or hang out. The parents could not chance anyone finding out about what went on in their home. They were not allowed to visit with relatives unless the parents were with them to be sure they told no one of their nightmarish existence.

As these three boys grew up in this dysfunctional and troubled family, life took a toll on them. The oldest brother started running away from home at the age of ten, yet was always brought back into this nightmare home. As a teenager, he started abusing alcohol and drugs to deal with the pain and frustration of life. And sadly, by the time he was twenty-four, he was dead from an overdose of drugs and alcohol, leaving behind a three-year-old daughter and a wife pregnant with a son who would never know his father.

As the middle brother came into his teenage years, he took after his father and became a very angry and violent young man. This young man always felt rejected by his father and thought that if he became like his father, maybe his father would finally accept him. During his late teenage years, he started getting into trouble with the law. As he got into his twenties, looking for acceptance, he began to ride with various motorcycle gangs and adopted their lifestyle of lawlessness. Throughout a large part of his adult life, he was always in trouble with the law and always in and out of jail.

Knowing the family dynamics of this home and the upbringing of these three boys, the fate of the two older brothers should come as no surprise to anyone. The only surprise in this story is that the youngest brother did not end up the same way. The youngest brother was born into and raised in the same dysfunctional family. The youngest brother witnessed and endured the same years of neglect, violence, and abuse. He was raised in the same environment of fear and hopelessness. There was no one in this family who was a Christian or serving the Lord. There was no one in this family teaching these children to love, trust, and serve the Lord or to live according to the Word of God. There was no one in this family praying for the salvation of any of these children. Yet, at the age of thirteen, the youngest of these three brothers prayed to accept Jesus Christ as his Lord and Savior. At the age of thirteen, this young man asked God to be his father and to accept him as His son. At the age of fourteen this young man from a non-Christian home, experienced the baptism of the Holy Spirit, with the evidence of speaking in other tongues as the Spirit gave utterance. At the age of sixteen, this young man was called into the ministry through a word of prophecy spoken at a prayer meeting.

The question is, "Why?" Why did he, the youngest of these brothers, turn out differently? Why did the youngest of these brothers take a different path during his teenage years? It wasn't because he was better than his brothers. It wasn't because he was somehow more worthy or deserving than his brothers. It wasn't because someone was praying for him. There was no earthly reason for him to take a different path and no earthly reason for him to turn out differently. So, what was the reason? The answer is the grace of God.

No one comes to God by accident. No one comes to God and is saved because he is better or more worthy than others. No one just happens to find God. No one just happens to recognize that he is a sinner cut off from God by sin. No one just happens to discover that God is a holy and righteous God who is highly offended by sin. No one just happens to discover his need of a savior. No one just happens to discover his need to repent and submit his life to the Lordship of Jesus Christ. We discover these things because in His grace, in His love, in His mercy, God chooses to reveal these things to us.

From the time he was a young child, God shined His light into the nightmare world in which the boy in our story of grace lived. Around the age of five or six, this child used to buy little figurines of the baby Jesus, of Mary, and of Joseph during the school Christmas bazaar. And the Spirit of God that was pursuing him always made him understand that there was something special about the baby Jesus. This was around the time in his life that his family moved to the upstairs apartment on Hudson Street. And, almost directly across from their apartment, there was an Italian Pentecostal church.

The folks from this church introduced themselves to this new family in the neighborhood. They started helping the family with food and clothing. And, they provided this poor family with little things to decorate their home. They gave the family black velvet posters with words written on them in gold glitter. Two of these posters were the Ten Commandments. Another was the Lord's prayer. They also gave this family a clock that had twelve little pictures of different Bible scenes attached. Although this family was not Christian, they had these things on their walls as decorations for many years. And every day for years, the little boy in this story of grace used to read those posters and look at the pictures on that clock. Every time he looked at these things, the Spirit of God who was drawing him to Christ would make him know that there was something special about these pictures and the words on these posters.

Because the people of this church were doing so much to help and bless this non-Christian family, when the people asked this young boy's parents allowed him to go across the street every Sunday to attend Sunday school and children's church, they allowed him to go. This went on for two years until and during his last Christmas at this church, his Sunday School teacher gave him a King James Bible with the words of Jesus printed in red. The Spirit of God pursuing this young boy made him understand that the words in red were the most important because they were the actual words spoken by God. This little boy from a non-Christian home treasured that Bible and kept it until well into his twenties.

At the time he received this Bible, he was too young to read, let alone understand the words of a King James Bible. Yet, as he got older, around the age of ten, God's Spirit led this young boy to read that Bible cover to cover. He did not really understand what he was reading and, for the most part, thought of the Bible like a history book. He did not understand that it was really a love story—a story of God's love for each and every one of us. He did not understand that it was God's instruction manual for living. He did not understand that it was God's roadmap to salvation. He did not understand it was God's grace that was making him aware of God's existence, God's commandments, and God's Word. And, make no mistake, it was God's grace that put the desire in this young boy's heart to read the Word of God and to pay special attention to the words of God, written in red.

But the boy still did not understand that sin separated him from the God that had created him. This boy still did not understand about his personal accountability to God or that he was created to have a personal relationship with God. The boy did not understand his need of repentance, his need of a savior or of God's provision of the savior that was needed. But God's grace had not stopped; God's grace was sufficient to continue what He had started in the life of this child. God's Spirit continued to pursue him and draw him unto God for no reason other than the fact that God chose to do so.

At Thanksgiving time of his thirteenth year, this boy's uncle Bob showed up at the family home for Thanksgiving dinner. It was the first time this boy had ever met his uncle. However, in the week leading up to this visit, he heard a lot about him from his father. The boy's father bragged about how he had at one point slept with his brother Bob's wife. He joked about how Bob's wife had left him, had taken the kids, and took him for every penny she could get from him. To hear the stories his father had shared about his uncle Bob, the boy expected to meet a very angry and bitter man. But when his uncle Bob showed up for dinner, he was all smiles and good natured. Instead of an angry and bitter man, he was filled with joy.

Over dinner, he told the family that at one time he was very angry and bitter but he was no longer the same. He excitedly told them how his landlady had introduced him to Jesus Christ and how he had accepted Jesus as his Lord and Savior. He excitedly told the family that Jesus was not just some historical figure but that He was alive and still in the business of changing lives. He told them that the Bible was not just an old history book but a roadmap to finding a relationship with God and a blueprint for living. Before his uncle left that day, he invited the family to attend church with him that Sunday. Although his mom and dad and his two older brothers were not interested, the Spirit of God led this young man to accept his uncle's invitation to attend church that Sunday.

As Sunday morning rolled around, he was excited as he waited for his uncle Bob to pick him up for church. He had not really been to church since he was a young boy and much too young to remember anything about it. But something inside of him told him that there would be something special about that day. His uncle picked him up for church and drove him to a little church on Indian Church Road in South Buffalo. It was called the Church of God, an old-fashioned Pentecostal-holiness church.

On that first Sunday in church with his uncle, he listened as the people sang songs, such as "Power in the Blood" and "Amazing Grace." And, as he heard these songs for the first time, the Spirit of God within him began to stir within his heart causing him to know that the words of these songs were important and had meaning for his life. He listened as they sang, "Would you be free from your burden of sin; there is power in the blood, power in the blood?" And the Spirit of God within led him to understand that he, too, could be set free from the burden of sin. He listened as they sang, "Amazing Grace, how sweet the sound that saved a wretch like me." And the Spirit of God within him led him to understand that the amazing grace of God was available to save him. As the worship service ended, this young man knew that something was happening but did not yet understand what it was. Then he began to listen as the pastor began preaching the Word of God.

That day as he heard the words of Romans 3:23 which says, "For all have sinned, and fall short of the glory of God," the Holy Spirit of God led him to understand that this applied to him and that he had failed to live up to God's standards. That day, the Spirit of the Lord helped him to understand that he was not the good and decent person he always imagined himself to be as he heard the words of Romans 3:10, "As it is written, there is none righteous, no, not one." For the first time that day, he finally understood the words of Romans 5:12, "Therefore, as through one man sin entered into the world, and death through sin; and so, death passed unto all men, for that all sinned." That day, the Spirit of God led him to realize that he too was a sinner separated from God and under a death sentence.

And that day, when the pastor gave the altar call, this young boy responded to the amazing grace of God that had been working in him and drawing him unto God for so many years. That day, because of the grace of God, this young man began his new life as a child of God. And I know this story of grace to be true because this story of grace is my own personal story.

God is no respecter of persons. What he has done for me, he is ready, willing, and able to do for anyone. If you are reading these words today, it is because God is drawing you and reassuring you of his grace, His love, and his mercy. It is because God wants you to understand your need of a savior and his provision of the savior that is needed.

As I shared the beginning of my grace story, I spoke of the dysfunctional family I was born into and the nightmare world in which I was raised. I spoke of the violent and abusive father that raised me and how it caused me to distrust fathers. I shared the fact that there was no earthly reason for me to come to Christ and become a Christian. I was not raised in a Christian home, not taught the ways of God while growing up, and there was no one praying for me. I shared the truth that, like anyone that comes to Christ, it was only because God the

Father chose to send the Holy Spirit to me to draw me to Christ, to teach me my need of a savior, and to offer God's provision of that savior (John 6:44).

Earlier, I shared the actual means God used to draw me unto Christ and unto salvation. I shared how the Father sent the Spirit to me at a young age to teach me of His existence and to make the Ten Commandments and the Lord's Prayer known to me. I shared how God put a Bible into my hands at a young age and gave me the desire to read it. I shared how God sent my uncle to bring me to church as a teenager so that I could respond to the grace of God and accept Christ as my Lord and Savior. I shared how God used my uncle to bring me to church so that I could begin to understand all of the truths of God that I had either never understood or had misunderstood. I shared how God led me to salvation at the age of thirteen, gave me the baptism of the Holy Spirit at fourteen, and called me into the ministry at sixteen.

Now I want to continue my story of grace in the hope that it will help us to better understand the breadth, and length, and height, and depth of the love of Christ. I continue to hope that, as we better understand the wonderful grace of God and the wonderful love of God, we will be strengthened in our love and trust of Christ and in our commitment to serving Christ and living as children of God. As I began my new life as a child of God, I would have to not only learn that it was only by the grace of God that I could be saved. I would have to learn that it was also only by the grace of God that I could live out the Christian life.

Because I was not raised in a Christian home and was not taught the Word of God growing up, when I came to Christ as a teenager, there were so many things that I did not understand and even more things that I misunderstood. And, from the moment I accepted Christ, the devil came after me with every trick at his disposal to turn me back if possible or at least to prevent me from growing in Christ and becoming who God wanted me to be.

I was taught that God was my heavenly Father but, sadly, the only thing I knew about fathers, I learned from my earthly father. As I shared previously, my father was very cold and distant, and so I thought of God as being cold and distant. My father was very demanding and hard to please, and so I naturally thought of God as being very demanding and hard to please. My father was very quick-tempered and often angry and violent, and sadly, that was how I thought of my heavenly Father.

In my mind, God was a cold and distant father who really did not like me very much but felt compelled to give me a second chance since He created me to begin with. As these thoughts went through my mind, I could hear the words of my mother telling me that I was an accident, that I was unwanted but that she would keep me anyway. In my mind, God was saying to me, "I know you. I know that you are a miserable, no-good sinner but I am giving you one more chance anyway." As these thoughts went through my mind, I could hear my mother telling me as a child that I was no good just like my rotten, no-good father.

In my mind, God was saying, "Make no mistake, I have given you a second chance and you better not mess it up. I have given you the gift of salvation, but I can take it back just as quickly." In my mind, God was saying, "You are saved, you are my son, but I will be watching you every moment. The first time you mess up and sin, I will take back my salvation and you will no longer be my son." And the devil was there every moment of every day, screaming these lies into my heart and mind over and over and over again. And, based on my experience with my own mother and father growing up, these lies concerning the nature of God were very easy to believe.

In those early days, every time I read the Bible, I seemed to come across all of the verses talking about God's holiness, God's righteousness, God's hatred of sin, and God's promised punishment of sin. And night and day, the devil made sure that I did not forget any of them. Yet, at the same time, the devil made sure that I would always just read right past those verses talking of God's great compassion, His great love, His great mercy, and His wonderful grace without ever really giving them a second thought. Because of my childhood, it was very difficult for me to think of my heavenly Father as being loving, compassionate, and merciful.

Needless to say, in those early days I seldom ever experienced the joy and peace of the Lord. I was always afraid that this would be the day that, somehow, I would mess up and forget to do something God required or in a moment of weakness do something God told me not to do. I feared that this could be the day that God would take back His gift of salvation.

Because of my life experience growing up it took many, many years for God to help me understand the words of 1 John 2:1, "My little children, these things write I unto you that you may not sin. And if any man sin, we have an Advocate with the Father, Jesus Christ the righteous." It took many years for God to help me understand that these words were written to and for the church. It took time for me to understand that the forgiveness Christ secured for me did not just cover my sins before coming to Christ but, rather, covered all of my sins, past, present, and future. It took many years for me to understand that Christians are not perfect, that Christians cannot earn their salvation, and that Christians don't get to keep their salvation by being perfect.

Sadly, the church where I accepted the Lord did not have a discipleship course to teach people about salvation and about living out the Christian life. Sadly, like the Pharisees in the days of Christ, this was a church that was all caught up in living holier than anyone else. They prided themselves on how holy they were and how perfect they were. When I accepted Christ, they told me I needed to become a member of the church and then gave me a multiple page list of dos and don'ts that God and the church required of me. They taught me that, as a Christian, I was required to live a life completely free of sin. They taught me that, if I sinned in any way and that if I were not holy enough, the church would reject me and God would take back His gift of salvation.

When I was sixteen, a young man who attended the church was asked to leave because he was not holy enough. He refused. The next Sunday, the church had him beaten down to the ground on the front lawn of the church and told him to never return. All of this reinforced the negative image I had of God and stole even more of my peace and joy.

It took many years for me to understand that God does not change His mind about giving us the gift of salvation. It took many years for me to understand that God does not give us salvation one day and decides to take it back the next day. It also took many years for me to understand that if God loved me enough to send Christ to pay for my sins before I became a child of God, He would continue to extend this grace to me now that I had become His child.

As I began my new life as a child of God in this church, that in many ways had lost its way, I began to think like them, to see God as they saw God, and I began to act like them. As I began my new life in Christ, I began to read the Word of God constantly to ensure that I knew and understood every law and commandment of God and did not break any of them. As I began my new life in Christ, I would spend hours upon hours each and every week seeking God in prayer. As I began my new life in Christ, I prided myself on not only avoiding any manner of sin but also avoiding even the appearance of sin.

And it was not very long before I became arrogant and proud in my heart. It was not very long before I became judgmental and critical of others. And it was not long before, in my pride and arrogance, I convinced myself that, somehow, I had found God and that, somehow, I deserved God's salvation. It was not very long before I forgot that there was only one reason that I was saved, and that one reason was the grace of God. For as it says in Ephesians 2:8-9, "For by grace you are saved through faith; and that not of yourselves: it is the gift of God: Not of works, lest any man should boast."

By this point in my relationship with God there was so much that I did not understand. By this point, there was so much arrogance and pride in my life that it was not possible for me to do what God had called me to do. There was so much pride and arrogance in my life that I could not possibly be a minister of His gospel as He had called me to be through a word of prophecy. There was too much pride and arrogance in my life to be a servant to others and to be a servant of His church or to lead others to Christ. Fortunately, God did not abandon me because of my pride but, instead, He continued His work of transformation through His loving discipline.

Sometimes, it is easy to forget that when God disciplines us it is not to punish or hurt us. Rather, He does it out of love to teach us, to help us, to develop character within us, and to perfect us as His sons and daughters. In His wonderful grace, God began to discipline me, yet I found His discipline to be most grievous and frustrating. It was grievous and frustrating because, at the time, I did not realize what God was doing or why. But years later, looking back, I see that what He did to discipline me was necessary, and I was glad that He did.

Up until that time, the Holy Spirit had done a fast and great job of sanctifying me. The Holy Spirit had done a deep work of transformation within me, which helped me to live a life of righteousness and avoiding sin. But, because I had become proud and arrogant, I failed to acknowledge that any holiness or righteousness in my life was because of God's grace and Spirit.

God withdrew the help of His Spirit and allowed me to see just how sinful and wretched I was apart from Him. For a long time, no matter how hard I tried to do what was right in the eyes of God, I would fail over and over and over again. For a long time, no matter how determined I was to not sin in any way, instead of doing the good things I wanted to do, I found myself doing the bad things I did not want to do. I became extremely frustrated.

In my frustration and failure, after three years, I gave up trying. After three years, I became convinced that no matter how hard I tried, I was never going to be able to live a life that was pleasing and acceptable unto God. I can still remember coming to God in prayer and saying, "Father, I don't get it. I don't understand why I can't just live free of sin and do all of the things You ask of me."

I went on to say, "Father You know that in my heart, I want to be Your son, want to love and trust You, want to honor and please You, but I can't seem to get it right. So, I give up; I am going back to the world and hope that someday You will come and rescue me." And with that prayer, I walked away from God for many, many years. And as I walked away from God, my life became a living nightmare in many ways.

As I walked away from God there was a deep sadness and emptiness inside of me. There was a great void that I could not seem to fill. I quickly became involved in alcohol and drugs just like my oldest brother who had died from an overdose. But no matter how much alcohol and drugs I consumed, I could not get rid of the deep sadness and emptiness inside of me. During those years of abusing alcohol and drugs, I nearly overdosed numerous times, but God, in His grace, had not given up on me. God, in His grace, was still looking over me, protecting me, and keeping me alive.

Like my middle brother, I quickly became violent and started getting into trouble with the law. I started selling drugs to support my alcohol and drug habits. I can even remember roaming the streets at night with a knife, looking for people to rob. I can remember getting into barroom brawls just like my father used to do. And I can remember the day I got arrested for throwing a young man through an upstairs window over a drug deal that went bad. But, God had not given up on me. In His grace, He continued to watch over me, to protect me, and to keep me out of jail.

God was extremely patient with me and extremely kind toward me. God spent decades watching over me by always sending people to me to ensure that I never forgot about Him. In His grace, God spent decades using every means possible to draw me back to Him and to help me understand everything I had been confused about. In His grace, God sent me a wonderful wife and gave me a family to help me break free of the alcohol and drug abuse. In His grace, God used my friend and co-worker, Tina Sawyer, to get me going back to church. In His grace, God eventually led me to Victory International Assembly of God and to the ministry of Pastor Ronald Thorington and his wife, Susan. In His grace, God used Victory and the Thoringtons to lead me to recommit my life to Christ. In His grace, God used the Discipleship Course developed by Pastor Thorington to help me understand so many things I had been so confused about over the years.

I came to realize that all of those past years were not really wasted years. During all those years, God's grace was working to take the pride and arrogance out of me. All of those years, God's grace was working to break that critical and judgmental spirit that I once had. All of those years, God was working to teach me that every aspect of our salvation is all about His grace.

It is God's grace that teaches us of God's existence, His holiness and righteous nature, our need of a savior, and His provision of that savior. It is God's grace that leads us to repentance and to call upon the name of the Lord for salvation. And it is only by the grace of God that we can live a life that is pleasing and honoring unto God. None of us has anything to boast about. We did not find God; God in his grace made Himself known unto us and drew us to Christ by His Holy Spirit. None of us have anything to boast about. Anything holy, good, or decent within us is because of Christ and the Holy Spirit who lives and works within us.

In His grace, God eventually brought me to the place where, with Paul, I could truthfully speak the words of Galatians 2:20 which says, "I am crucified with Christ: never-the-less I live; yet not I, but Christ lives in me: and the life which I now live in the flesh I live by the faith of the Son of God, who loved me, and gave himself for me."

Today, I want to thank God for His grace and mercy. I thank God for sending His Holy Spirit to me at a young age to draw me to Him. I thank God for using a little neighborhood church and its people to make me aware of God's laws and commandments and put His Word into my hands. I thank God for the seeds the people of that church sowed into my life. I want to thank God for His grace that led me to salvation, even when there was no earthly reason for Him to do so. I thank God for

His grace that led me to call upon Christ for salvation. I want to thank God for His love that was willing to discipline me when I needed it. I thank God for a love that was willing to do what was necessary to rid my heart and mind of arrogance and pride. I want to thank God for never giving up on me during those years when I walked away from Him. I thank Him for watching over me and protecting me all of those years. I thank Him for doing everything in His power to bring me back to Him. I thank Him for such wonderful grace. And I want to thank God for allowing me the privilege of being a pastor in His church even though I am so unworthy of this privilege.

In Memory of Pastor Ken Wilson

Since the time Pastor Ken wrote his testimony, he has gone to be with the Lord. Pastor Ken was loved by everyone who knew him. Ken was a true servant of God. The last twenty years of his life were lived as a living sacrifice to Christ. Ken never sought to have titles or recognition; he simply wanted to serve in any way that he could. Ken was an active member of Victory International Assembly of God, Buffalo, New York, for over two decades. In Ken's last five years of ministry, he was recognized as an executive pastor at the church by lead pastor, Rev. Dr. Ronald Thorington. Ken was dedicated to ministry to the needy in Buffalo. In his position at the church, he oversaw monthly outreaches to the homeless in downtown Buffalo by providing warm clothing, blankets, breakfast, and hot coffee. Under Pastor Ken's leadership, the church began a free community dinner once a month. It would be difficult to list all the things that he did in service for Christ, but we know God was keeping record and will greatly reward him for his faithful service. Pastor Ken was a wonderful example of a person whose life was transformed by the grace of God. Pastor Ken was truly a genuine trophy of God's grace.

Conclusion

God's grace is so infinite and beyond our understanding that no library of books could ever completely describe it. To fully comprehend God's grace would be equivalent to fully knowing God; this is impossible. Consider this passage, "Can you discover the depths of God? Can you discover the limits of the Almighty?" (Job 11:7). The human mind is incapable of completely understanding the deep things of God. Even though our human intellect is limited when it comes to totally understanding grace, we are capable of understanding what God has revealed in His Word. By studying the Scriptures, we can learn what God has revealed about His grace. Even this act of learning about His grace is an act of grace on His part. Grace is the foundation for our understanding of the Bible and our knowledge of God Himself. Without His gracious act of revealing Himself to us in the Bible, we would not know His character and be exposed to the full range of His attributes.

Through an in-depth study of Scripture, I have uncovered much of what the Bible says about grace. My study consisted of much more than just looking up Scriptures that deal with grace; I dug deeper into the meaning of the words used in each verse. From these word studies, I gained many new insights into God's grace. I presented my research in a format that clearly shows the different aspects of God's grace. I started with the source of God's grace and then expressed how grace is the ultimate expression of His love. I explained how God's grace saves us and enables us. I explained how the Holy Spirit is the agent of grace working to bring all the benefits of God's grace to the believer. I described several ways that we can tap into grace through study of Scripture, prayer, Christian fellowship, and worship. The book finishes with why and how we are to demonstrate God's grace to others.

There is an emphasis on the importance of humility toward God throughout this work. Why is there this emphasis? Humility toward God is crucial for a believer to understand and experience God's grace. The key factor in determining who receives grace is humility. This determinative factor has nothing to do with merit, but only with a person's receptivity. Before I go any further, it is important to clarify what is meant by humility toward God. Humility toward God is not some form of self-abasement. Self-abasement is a false form of humility. God is not fooled because He sees the heart of the person. God seeks true humility from the heart. True humility shows God that we are receptive to what He wants to do in our lives. True humility is not something that we can manufacture within ourselves, but must be a result of the working of the Holy Spirit.

A person with true humility does not look at humility as a means to manipulate God. True humility toward God recognizes His sovereignty and never demands anything from Him. God will show grace to whom He chooses. Humility toward God is a response of faith in His existence and a recognition of, and submission to, His sovereignty. Humility is a way of thinking about oneself in his relationship with God and others. This character trait comes from recognizing one's dependence on God as well as one's interdependent relationship with others.

The Bible clearly states that God gives grace to the humble (James 4:6; 1 Pet. 5:5). Another Scripture declares, "Humble yourselves in the presence of the Lord, and He will lift you up" (James 4:10). First Peter 5:6 says something very similar to James 4:10: "Humble yourselves, therefore, under the mighty hand of God, that He may exalt you at the proper time." I view these Scriptures as a guide to understanding how to receive God's grace. By researching this topic, I realized that humility is the vital character trait that is necessary in order to experience the blessing of God that comes through the different forms of grace. These components include all the different ways grace saves us, all the ways grace enables us, all the ways that the Holy Spirit assists us as the agent of grace, all the various spiritual practices that are a means of receiving grace, and being able to show grace to others. Having true humility before God is the difference between those who receive grace and those who do not.

If we are to really understand grace, we first must humble ourselves by acknowledging that we desperately need God's help. As you read through this book, ask God to open up the eyes of your understanding to clearly see what the Bible says about grace. Relying solely on human intellect will inhibit your perception of God's grace. If we humble ourselves and ask for assistance, He will give us divine insight into His grace.

Our understanding of grace must begin with the biblical conception of God. If our conception of God is inaccurate, we will never be able to comprehend grace. A biblical understanding of who God is forms the foundation upon which a person must build in comprehending grace. The first part of the foundation is understanding God's essence. God's essence is a description of what kind of a being He is; He is a personal, spiritual being. As a personal, spiritual being, He exhibits divine qualities that He alone possesses, such as being the source of life, being self-existent, being eternal, omnipresent (everywhere), omniscient (all knowing), omnipotent (all powerful), and immutable (never changing).

In addition to God's essence, we need to recognize His moral nature. God's moral nature is the source of His grace. His moral nature includes attributes such as: holiness, righteousness, justice, truthfulness, and love. However, the foundation of God's moral nature is the holiness, which is central to all He is and does. God demonstrates His love by His goodness, benevolence, mercy, and grace. The ultimate expression of His love is through grace.

All the other attributes of God's nature, His righteousness, justice, mercy, and love can never conflict with His holiness. Some have the mistaken idea that God's love overrules His holiness; that could never happen. Others believe that God's love overlooks sin to offer forgiveness; that would violate His holiness and justice. How does God's attribute of love work harmoniously with His holiness? How can God offer forgiveness to humanity without disregarding His holiness? On the other hand, would it not also be a violation of God's love to provide humanity no way to escape eternal punishment?

This perceived dilemma between God's holiness and His love stems from a lack of understanding grace. By grace, He is able to offer forgiveness and at the same time satisfy the demands of His holiness. Grace is particularly demonstrated in His plan of salvation for humanity. In God's infinite wisdom, He created a plan that would fully express love but not in any way violate holiness and justice. The price of sin, which is death, must be satisfied before any forgiveness and restoration by

God could be offered. Out of love for humanity, God Himself paid the penalty for sin. The Son of God took the form of a human in Jesus Christ to die on a cross as a substitute for us. Because of Christ's death, salvation is offered to all humanity as an expression of grace. All God requires of us is that we humble ourselves by accepting His plan of salvation through believing in Christ as our savior. Through faith in Christ, God is able to offer a person all the benefits of grace. God offers forgiveness of sins, the impartation of Christ's righteousness, the restoration of man's relationship with God, and being made a new person through the indwelling of the Holy Spirit.

It is at this point in our understanding of God's plan of salvation that we must move from just comprehending to experiencing God's grace. It is in experiencing grace that a person can understand it in a much fuller way. It is when a person moves from a mere mental comprehension to experiencing God's grace that he begins to grasp the sheer magnitude of this grace. How does a person move from mental comprehension to experiencing this reality? In order for a person to be saved, he must humble himself before God by acknowledging that he is a sinner without any hope of saving himself. A person must humbly confess his total dependence on God for salvation through faith in Jesus Christ as his Savior.

It would be a great shame for a person to read *Miracles of Grace* and possess only a mental understanding of God's plan of salvation but never experience it. The transformation of a person cannot happen without experiencing salvation. Remember, salvation is not just forgiveness of sins; it is being indwelt by the Holy Spirit. It is through being born again with the indwelling of the Holy Spirit that our lives can truly change. If you have not done so already, look back over the applications at the end of chapter 3 and make sure you have put those into practice.

It is through the indwelling of the Holy Spirit that we have the power of God within us to deal with life's trials, tribulations and temptations. With the Holy Spirit in us, we have the power of God's grace. Remember grace does so much more for us than just save us. God's grace is also the power and favor of God to help us throughout our Christian lives. Our weaknesses do not have to destroy us but can actually become a blessing if we learn to humble ourselves to receive grace. Understanding grace will strengthen our relationship with God because we will experience the welcome to His throne of grace. This is in contrast to that of fearing His throne of judgment. God's enabling grace will help sustain believers through times of trials, discouragement, personal failure, and times of grief. Contrary to what some may believe, trusting in grace does not cause a person to sin more freely; instead, it will help him to live a godly life. When a believer understands that he is saved and continues to be saved only by the grace of God, he finds a greater sense of security in his salvation.

If a person desires God's enabling grace to fully function in his life, he will need to have God's Spirit working within him. The way to have God's enabling grace fully functioning within us is by humbling ourselves and calling on God for His support. Rather than trying to live for God in our own strength, we need to learn how to walk humbly before Him by continually depending on His assistance. Gods' enabling grace will empower us to face all of life's challenges.

The indwelling of God's Spirit does more than aid us with our struggles in life; it also works wonderful changes in us. With the indwelling of God's Spirit, the power of grace is released to perform an amazing transformation. While a person was incapable of changing himself, grace can transform even the most desperate person. How well the Holy Spirit works change within us is dependent on our cooperation. If we resist what the Spirit of God wants to do in our lives, there will be little change in us. The more we humble ourselves and cooperate with the Holy Spirit, the more change we will experience. Some of the testimonies in this book are from people who were incapable of changing themselves. These hopeless people were able to become trophies of God's grace through the help of God and others.

There is genuine hope for all those who humble themselves by turning to God. Are you struggling with making changes in your life? It is not a matter of trying harder or making resolutions. You need to look outside yourself for support; call on God to intervene. If you humble yourself before God and confess your inability to change yourself, God will pour out His grace upon you and revolutionize your life. Look back at the applications in chapter 4 and make sure you are applying them in your life.

In Part Four: The Agent of Grace, I went into great detail regarding the many ways the Holy Spirit aids us. If a person humbles himself by cooperating with the Holy Spirit, God's grace will help him from the time of his salvation until the time he is ushered into God's presence in heaven. There are three major ways that the Holy Spirit is our agent of grace: first, our salvation; then, our sanctification; and then, our service for God.

The Holy Spirit's work of grace in our salvation begins even before we experience salvation. The Holy Spirit first works to call us. Before a person comes to God, the Holy Spirit is working to get his attention in different ways. This calling may begin with a sense of emptiness or dissatisfaction within a person's life. The Holy Spirit can create a longing for something more than what he has already experienced. A spiritual hunger can be stirred deep within a person's being to begin searching for something beyond the material realm. Once a person begins to search for meaning and purpose in life, the Holy Spirit works to convince the person that there is a real, personal God who loves him. Once a person is convinced that God really exists, he begins to understand that God is holy and becomes convicted of sin. No one comes to God without the working of the Spirit.

At the moment of salvation, the Holy Spirit works as the agent of grace in our conversion, confession, spiritual conception, and confirmation. After a person becomes convinced of God's existence and is convicted of sin, he comes to the point of deciding to turn to, or reject Him. If a person decides to turn to God, he will need to confess his faith in God and in Jesus Christ, God's Son. After confessing faith in God, a person will need to humble himself by confessing his sins to God and by inviting Christ into his life. It is at this point that the Holy Spirit comes into the person and conceives a new spiritual life. When a person experiences this new spiritual life, he will sense that there is something very different happening deep within.

With new spiritual life, a person will have a fresh sense of God's presence within himself, accompanied by deep inner joy. The Holy Spirit's confirmation of spiritual birth is more than just changes in feelings; there will be changes in his heart. True transformation can only happen when there is a change in the heart. One of the changes of the heart will be a change in desires. Where he once loved to sin and hated God, he now hates sin and loves God. Where once there was no hunger for the things of God, now there is a deep longing to know and experience God.

Once a person is saved, the Spirit of God will work as the agent of grace in his sanctification. Basically, sanctification is what the Spirit of

God does in the believer's life after salvation. The Holy Spirit will help believers in every imaginable way. I explained eight ways that the Holy Spirit can help in the believer's sanctification. The Holy Spirit will act as a counselor who gives personal guidance and a teacher who opens up a fuller understanding of Scripture. Because prayer is such an important way for us to communicate with God, the Holy Spirit will give believers assistance in knowing how to pray and what to pray for.

God understands how believers struggle with constant attempts of their old sinful nature to regain control. To counteract this tendency, God's Spirit works in believers to encourage growth in commitment. There are many challenges to growing in Christ. God never intended believers to face their problems alone. God desires that Christians work together so they can strengthen each other. The Holy Spirit draws Christians together so He can use them to support one another. The Holy Spirit strives to bring unity among believers because there is strength in unity. The Holy Spirit will be with us to bring comfort in our times of sorrow and grief.

Sanctification is the process of transformation that the Spirit of God accomplishes in a believer's life. Once a person receives a new, spiritual nature at salvation, the Holy Spirit will work with that new nature to facilitate its growth. A major objective of the Holy Spirit's work of sanctification is to conform every believer into the image of Christ. This process of conforming believers into the image of Christ involves times of correcting, cleansing, and then transforming. The Spirit of God brings our attention to areas where we need to make improvements. As we humbly cooperate with God, He makes those needed modifications. Is it important to understand that it is not us personally that is making the changes, but the change is a result of the working of God's grace. As long as we believe that we are responsible to alter our nature, we will continue to fail.

> ***Our part is not to transform who we are, but to surrender to God so that He can transform us.***

With the indwelling of the Holy Spirit, the stranglehold of the old sinful nature is broken, but not totally removed. Remnants of the old sinful nature linger, wanting to regain control. There is an internal struggle between the old nature and the new nature in every Christian. Believers experience many failures in this internal struggle. Many feel like giving up at some point. This is where humility comes into play again. Instead of trying to win this battle on our own, we must humble ourselves and become dependent on God's grace.

In order for a person to win this inner battle, he must come to a point where he totally surrenders his life to the lordship of Christ. Areas that are not surrendered to Christ's lordship are dangerous because they are open doors for sin to enter and gain control. With our humble cooperation, the Holy Spirit will work to remove the harmful elements of the old nature and replace them with things that will strengthen the new, Christlike nature. The Holy Spirit helps a person to "put off" the old ways and to "put on" the new ways of living. This "put off" and "put on" process must continue throughout the believer's life. A believer is a lifelong work in progress.

The Holy Spirit is the agent of grace first in our salvation and then in our sanctification. The time period for sanctification is from the point of salvation until glorification. Sometime during this lifelong, transformation process, the Holy Spirit will urge the believer to become involved in ministry. Even though the Holy Spirit's work of sanctification is a major work that continues throughout life, there is much more that the Spirit does in a believer's life. The process of transformation does not have to be complete before a person can be involved in ministry. If complete transformation were required, then no one would qualify. There are many opportunities for service in which a recent believer can get involved. There are, however, some ministries that require a higher level of maturity.

One reason God is making changes in believers is so that they will desire to serve Him by helping others. The Holy Spirit enables believers to serve God in ministry. The transformation of God's grace moves a person from being self-centered to being Christ-centered. Being Christ-centered means that a person puts Christ first and is willing to serve Christ by ministering to the needs of others.

Every follower of Christ needs to understand that he is called into ministry. No, not every believer is called to become a pastor, minister, or missionary, but he is called to serve God in some unique way. Through the grace of God, every believer is given individual abilities for service.

God wants those grace-given abilities to be used for the maximum benefit. The Holy Spirit, as the agent of grace for service, will call believers into ministry. Each believer will come to the realization that that God has created him for a purpose. That higher purpose is to serve God in some distinct way.

Each believer will be faced with a choice; will he live his life in pursuit of selfish desires, or will he surrender to the Holy Spirit's call to live a life of service? We can either resist the call to ministry now or eventually come to a place where we are humbled and surrender to God's will. By surrendering your life in service to God you are saying, "I will say what God wants me to say, do what He wants me to do, and go where He wants me to go." Once a person surrenders to the call to minister, the Holy Spirit will stir up a passion to serve and love people. This love for people will compel him to serve in whatever ways the Spirit leads.

Just as humility was required in our salvation and sanctification, it will likewise be required in our service for God. When a person gets involved in serving in some form of ministry, he will experience many surprises. Ministry will not be what he expected. Many start out in ministry with the expectation that things will run smoothly without any difficulties or challenges. Ministry will seldom go as planned. You will not always have success in your efforts. People will not always cooperate and will sometimes oppose you. Instead of people being thankful for what you are doing, they will criticize and complain. Ministering to people will test the limits of your strength. At some point in ministry, you will conclude that you do not have what is needed for ministry. You can give up involvement in ministry or turn to God and ask for His support. Receiving God's grace in service requires us to learn to serve with humility as we depend on grace.

If you are involved in ministry and feel like giving up, let me encourage you not to give up ministry but to give up trying to serve in your own strength. In my fifty-plus years of ministry, I have reached my limits more times than I can remember. When I reached the limits of what I could do, I learned to turn to God for His strength. When I ran out of my love, I sought God to refill me with His love. When my patience ran out, I sought God to give me the strength to endure. When my spiritual strength was depleted, I cried out to God to refill me with His Spirit. The longer I ministered, the more I realized how much I must trust in God's enabling grace. Every time that I turned to God for His help, He abundantly supplied His grace. By learning to trust in God's grace, I experienced that His grace is indeed more than sufficient.

If you have experienced salvation and see that God is making changes in you, begin praying for God to give you direction regarding where to serve. You need to understand that for your transformation to fully progress, you will need to become involved in ministry. Where can you go to serve? The road to ministry begins with finding a church to attend. If, after attending for a while, you believe that this is the church where God wants to plant you, begin to look for ways to get involved. It is God's design that those who serve Him will serve primarily within the context of a local church.

Part Five: the Means of Grace, explains several means of grace. The study of Scripture, prayer, Christian fellowship, and worship are four major ways that we can gain access to God's grace. These means of grace are often referred to as spiritual practices or spiritual disciplines. Practicing or participating in these spiritual disciplines can promote growth in grace. If a believer does not practice these means of grace, he will not mature spiritually. It is when practicing these disciplines that God pours His Spirit and grace into a person's life. We must realize that participating in these means of grace will not guarantee an abundance of God's grace. There are certain conditions that must be met in order for us to benefit from observing them. An attitude of humility is necessary as we approach Scripture, prayer, Christian fellowship, and worship.

When practicing these means of grace, we should always demonstrate humility before God. Unfortunately, if we are not careful, we can develop religious pride in performing spiritual disciplines. The more faithful a person becomes in the spiritual disciplines, the more he will be tempted to compare himself to other Christians who are not as faithful. This comparison can lead a person to begin thinking of himself as being spiritually superior to those less faithful. The person who prays thirty minutes a day should not think he has more status than one who only prays five minutes, nor should the person who prays thirty minutes a day feel inferior to the one who prays an hour a day. It is not so much the amount of time we spend participating in spiritual practices but the quality of our humility that determines how much of God's grace we receive.

We should not think that by following these spiritual disciplines we will gain greater spiritual status before God and other Christians. When we begin to believe that we have more status before God, we can also begin to believe that we are more deserving of God's favor and blessing. Having religious pride because of our participation in spiritual disciplines is detrimental to receiving God's grace, "God is opposed to the proud, but gives grace to the humble" (James 4:6). A person can be devout in the spiritual disciplines, nevertheless, because of religious pride, he will not receive much of God's grace. When a person's heart is filled with pride, there will be little room for God's grace.

Our participation in the means of grace should not be viewed as a way to earn God's favor or blessing. We must remember that grace can never be merited. Many believe God rewards them because they have faithfully practiced the spiritual disciplines. Thinking that God is obligated to reward us with His favor, blessing, and answered prayer in response to practicing spiritual disciplines is an indication that we are trying to earn God's grace.

We should not think that merely performing the spiritual disciplines is all that is required to receive God's grace. Yes, Christians need to faithfully participate in all the means of grace, but this needs to be done for the right reasons. Christians are to humbly participate in the means of grace with the desire to receive more grace. For some, it does not matter whether or not they get anything out their practice of spiritual disciplines; they are satisfied that they have just done their duty. Many Christians do their duty to have devotional time or go to church with the expectation that God will reward them for being good Christians. Some people can go to church regularly but do not get anything out of the service. So, why do people continue the practice? They believe that they are gaining God's favor by just attending church.

Some make a goal of reading through the Bible in a year with a commitment to read X numbers of chapters per day. Reading through the Bible certainly is a worthy goal to which every Christian should aspire; however, the problem with this is that a person can go through the motions of reading the assigned chapters for the day without getting anything out of the verses. We should not look at merely participating in spiritual practices as our final objective; these practices are a means to an end. It is not the practice of these means that is the objective; it is through participation in these means that we can gain access to God's grace. Our goal in participating in the four spiritual disciplines is to receive more grace, not to achieve a superior spiritual status to impress God and others.

How can we receive the maximum amount of grace when we participate in the spiritual disciplines? It is through approaching these practices with humility. We need to see our participation in the four spiritual disciplines as ways to approach God. We must always approach God with humility, whether it is when we are learning God's Word, praying, fellowshipping with other believers, or worshiping God. How do we approach God with genuine humility? When we approach God, we must think of ourselves as being spiritually empty and, therefore, remove from our hearts all pride, self-righteousness, or self-centeredness. When we come before God, we must see ourselves as empty of any self-righteousness, any worthiness, any knowledge, any wisdom or understanding. We must see ourselves as having nothing to offer God and therefore totally dependent on His grace.

When we study the Bible by reading, memorizing, or meditating, we must think of ourselves as knowing nothing compared to what we have yet to learn. When we listen to a sermon, we should listen like we have never heard what is being preached. When we read a passage of the Bible, we need to read it like we have never read it before. When we pray, we must pray like we are empty of God's power and presence, and desperately need to receive from Him. When it comes to fellowshipping with other believers, we need to empty ourselves of the pride of spiritual self-sufficiency. Even though self-sufficiency is good in some areas of life, it is not good when it comes to our spiritual well-being. Our spiritual well-being is dependent not only on help from God, but also the help of other believers. It is only when we empty ourselves of spiritual self-sufficiency that we realize just how much we need others. A humble person knows that he cannot survive spiritually on his own.

I encourage you to review Part Five: The Means of Grace again. It is not enough for you to merely know the spiritual disciplines; you must put them into practice in your life. If you are not accustomed to participating in these spiritual disciplines, I suggest that you start with small steps. Some make the mistake of trying to do too much at the start. If you have a lot of spare time to devote to the spiritual disciplines, then, by all means, do as much as you are able. However, most people do not have a lot of spare time available. Most people have a busy schedule full of demands. If you are to develop new spiritual habits, you will need to make a commitment to create time for them in your schedule. Do not make the mistake of committing yourself to unattainable goals; start with attainable goals. Instead of committing yourself to reading the Bible for several hours each day, start with a chapter or two. The idea is to develop new habits through repetition. It is better to consistently read two chapters a day than to start with too large a goal and last only a couple days. Make sure that you are reviewing the applications for Part Five and are continuously asking for God's help in making these spiritual practices a central part of your life.

The concluding Part Six: Horizontal Grace explains how to demonstrate horizontal grace. The grace we receive from God is vertical grace. Horizontal grace is when we show God's grace to others. The first five parts of *Miracles of Grace* deal with God's vertical grace; the last part focuses on horizontal grace. Even though five parts are devoted to explaining God's vertical grace toward humanity and only one part on horizontal grace, this in no way implies that horizontal grace is less important. Many books that deal with grace say very little, if anything at all, about showing God's grace toward others. In my opinion, this is a great oversight. Any work that claims to fully cover the topic of grace should include a discussion of how grace can be demonstrated in concrete ways. Horizontal grace is the demonstration of God's grace on a practical, person-to-person level.

Understanding and practicing horizontal grace is important for a number of reasons. First, demonstrating grace toward each other is an indispensable part of how grace impacts our lives. As God has freely bestowed His grace on us, so we are to freely show His grace toward others. God never intended for those who have received His grace to keep it to themselves. God desires His grace to be shown to the whole world through those who have received it. As those who have experienced God's grace demonstrate His grace through their words, actions, and attitudes, there will be a tremendous impact on others. Those who have received God's grace and demonstrate it will shine like lights in the darkness. Before the unbelieving world can ever comprehend God's grace, they will need to see it demonstrated in our lives. Demonstrating God's grace is a very persuasive witness to the world.

The second reason that horizontal grace is essential is that it benefits the individual believer. When someone shows grace to others, it opens the door for more grace to flow through him. When someone who has experienced grace holds back demonstrating grace to others, the flow of grace is obstructed. For example, if someone who has been forgiven does not forgive others, he will impede the flow of grace into his own life. Jesus stated in the Sermon on the Mount: "For if you forgive men for their transgressions, your heavenly Father will also forgive you. But if you do not forgive men, then your Father will not forgive your transgressions" (Matt. 6:14–15). In other words, how we speak to others, act toward others, and what attitudes we display toward others can affect the flow of grace into and through our lives. Our demonstration of grace acts as a faucet on the flow of grace. When we are being gracious toward others, God's grace flows freely. If we are not gracious toward others, the flow of grace into our lives will be restricted.

The third reason why showing God's grace is imperative is its remarkable impact on personal relationships. Just as God forgave us and restored our relationship with Him, showing grace can restore and sustain our relationships with others. How well we communicate with others will determine the quality of our relationships. Learning to speak words of grace to others can help build enduring relationships. Learning to show grace by forgiving others can restore relationships. Showing grace in our giving to others can reinforce our bonds of love for each other. Showing grace toward those with differing opinions and convictions can help us maintain peace in our relationships. If we maintain an attitude of humility in our relationships, we will enjoy quality relationships.

Understanding the importance of demonstrating grace is only the first step in horizontal grace. The next step is to develop new ways of showing grace to those around us. I encourage you to review the applications on the various ways to show God's grace in Part Six. Demonstrating grace will not come easily. Remember, it is not your grace but God's grace. Acting in grace will not come naturally; you will need to meekly depend on God's help. Learning to demonstrate grace in your speech, actions, and attitudes will be a lifelong process.

I included the testimonies of six individuals in this book. I selected these out of the many people I know who have been impacted by the grace of God. Why do I share these testimonies with you? I believe I need to show how the grace of God actually works in people's lives. Some of the testimonies show how God's grace can transform lives, while others illustrate how God's grace can sustain a person through the most difficult circumstances imaginable. I wanted to go beyond abstract concepts to the reality that people experience in life. I pray that these testimonies have inspired you to believe that God's grace can work wonders in your life.

About the Author

Starting in his young adult years, Ron Thorington has accumulated over fifty years of ministry experience. In 1976, upon graduating from the Assemblies of God Theological Seminary, he accepted the challenge to start a church in Buffalo's inner city where he felt the need was greatest. Ron has faithfully served as the lead pastor of Victory International Assembly of God in Buffalo for 46 years.

During this time, the church has been a beacon of light in the city. Through a strong emphasis on evangelism and discipleship, many have come to know Jesus Christ as their savior and have become dedicated disciples. Many of these disciples have gone on to minister in other locations.

Ron and his wife, Susan, have lovingly reached out to the Burmese and African immigrants in Buffalo. As a result of their ministry, three African and five Burmese churches were birthed. Ron and Susan have spoken at leadership conferences in the United States, England, and Africa.

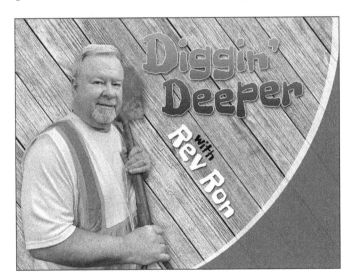

Digging Deeper

You can find his ministry resources at: "Digging Deeper with RevRon" on Facebook, YouTube, and www.diggingdeeperwithrevron.com

End Notes

1. "Miracle, *N*. def. (1)." *Merriam-Webster's Collegiate Dictionary*, 10th ed., (Merriam-Webster Incorporated, 1998), p. 742.

2. David A. Nobel, *Understanding the Times, A Survey of Competing Worldviews*, (Manitou Springs, CO: Summit Press, 2015), p. 183.

3. Ibid, p. 60.

4. Stephen Charnock, *The Existence and Attributes of God*, (Grand Rapids, MI: 49516, Baker Books, 2000), Vol.2, p. 110.

5. Henry Clarence Thiessen, *Introductory Lectures in Systematic Theology*, (Grand Rapids, MI: WM. B. Eerdmans' Publishing Company, 1969), p. 128.

6. W.E. Vine, Merrill F. Unger, William White, Jr., "Righteousness, *N*. (1)" *Vine's Complete Expository Dictionary of Old and New Testament Words*, (Thomas Nelson Publishers, 1985), Greek section, p. 535.

7. W.E. Vine, Merrill F. Unger, William White, Jr., "Righteous, *Adj.*" *Vine's Complete Expository Dictionary of Old and New Testament Words*, Greek section, pp. 534–535.

8. ("Truth," def. I. A). *The International Standard Bible Encyclopedia*, (Grand Rapids, Michigan, Volume 4: Q-Z, William B. Eerdmans Publishing Company,1988), Vol. 4, p. 926.

9. ("Truth," def. I. B). *The International Standard Bible Encyclopedia*, Vol. 4, p. 926.

10. ("Truth," def. I. C). *The International Standard Bible Encyclopedia,* Vol. 4, p. 926.

11. Ibid, p. 926.

12. W.E. Vine, Merrill F. Unger, William White, Jr., "True, *Adj.* (2)." *Vine's Complete Expository Dictionary of Old and New Testament Words,* Greek section, p. 645.

13. W.E Vine, Merrill F. Unger William White, Jr., "Truth, N. (a)." *Vine's Complete Expository Dictionary of Old and New Testament Words.* Greek section, p. 645.

14. Ibid, p. 645.

15. Ibid, p. 645.

16. W.E Vine, Merrill F. Unger, William White, Jr., "Loving-Kindness, N." *Vine's Complete Expository Dictionary of Old and New Testament Words.* Hebrew section, p. 142..

17. Ibid, p. 142.

18. ("Love," def. III. A). *The International Standard Bible Encyclopedia,* Vol. 3, p. 175.

19. W.E. Vine, Merrill F. Unger, William White, Jr., "Love, V. (1)." *Vine's Complete Expository Dictionary of Old and New Testament Words,* Greek section, p. 381.

20. "Love, N." *The Zondervan Pictorial Encyclopedia of the Bible,* (Grand Rapids, Michigan, Volume 3: H-L, Zondervan Publishing House, 1975), p. 989.

21. W.E. Vine, Merrill F. Unger, William White, Jr., "Love, V. (1)." *Vine's Complete Expository Dictionary of Old and New Testament Words,* Greek section, pp. 381-382.

22. "Mercy, N. (I)." *The International Standard Bible Encyclopedia,* Vol. 3, p. 322.

23 W.E. Vine, Merrill F. Unger, William White, Jr., "Mercy, *N*. (1)." *Vine's Complete Expository Dictionary of Old and New Testament Words,* Greek section, p. 403.

24 W.E. Vine, Merrill F. Unger, William White, Jr., "Abound, *V.* (2)." *Vine's Complete Expository Dictionary of Old and New Testament Words,* Greek section, p. 6.

25 ("Pardon," *V.* def. 1.a). *Merriam-Webster's Collegiate Dictionary,* 10th ed. p. 844.

26 ("Redeem," *V.* def. 1.d). *Merriam-Webster's Collegiate Dictionary,* 10th ed., p. 979.

27 "Redemption, *N.*" *Merriam-Webster's Collegiate Dictionary,* 10th ed., p. 979.

28 W.E. Vine, Merrill F. Unger, William White, Jr., "Redeem, *V.*" *Vine's Complete Expository Dictionary of Old and New Testament Words,* Hebrew section, p. 194.

29 Ibid, p. 194.

30 W.E. Vine, Merrill F. Unger, William White, Jr., "Redeem, *V.* (1)." *Vine's Complete Expository Dictionary of Old and New Testament Words,* Greek section, p. 515.

31 W.E. Vine, Merrill F. Unger, William White, Jr., "Redeem, *V.* (2)." *Vine's Complete Expository Dictionary of Old and New Testament Words,* Greek section, p. 515.

32 Ibid, p. 515.

33 W.E. Vine, Merrill F. Unger, William White, Jr., "Redemption, *N.* (1)." *Vine's Complete Expository Dictionary of Old and New Testament Words,* Greek section, p. 516.

34 "Propitiate, *V.*" *Merriam-Webster's Collegiate Dictionary,* 10th ed., p. 935.

35 W.E. Vine, Merrill F. Unger, William White, Jr., "Propitiate, V." *Vine's Complete Expository Dictionary of Old and New Testament Words*, Greek section, p. 493.

36 W.E. Vine, Merrill F. Unger, William White, Jr., "Atone, V." *Vine's Complete Expository Dictionary of Old and New Testament Words*, Hebrew section, p.10.

37 Ibid, Hebrew section, p.10.

38 "Atone, V. (2)." *Merriam-Webster's Collegiate Dictionary*, 10th ed., p. 73.

39 "Atonement, N. (1–3)." *Merriam-Webster's Collegiate Dictionary*, 10th ed., p. 73.

40 "Impute, V. (2)." *Merriam-Webster's Collegiate Dictionary*, 10th ed., p. 585.

41 "Impute, V." *Zondervan NASB Exhaustive Concordance*, (Grand Rapids, MI: Zondervan, A Division of Harper Collins Publisher, 1998) p. 1544.

42 ("Justify," V. def. 1.a, 2.c), *Merriam-Webster's Collegiate Dictionary*, 10th ed., p. 636.

43 W.E. Vine, Merrill F. Unger, William White, Jr., "Justification, N. (1)." *Vine's Complete Expository Dictionary of Old and New Testament Words*, Greek section, p. 338.

44 W.E. Vine, Merrill F. Unger, William White, Jr., ("Justification," N. def. 2 b). *Vine's Completed Expository Dictionary of Old and New Testament Words*, Greek section, p. 339

45 "Justification, N." *The International Standard Bible Encyclopedia*, Volume 2, E-J, p. 1170.

46 Henry Clarence Thiessen, *Introductory Lectures in Systematic Theology*, p. 366.

47 ("Reconcile," V. 1.a, b). *Merriam-Webster's Collegiate Dictionary*, 10th ed., p. 977.

End Notes

48 W.E. Vine, Merrill F. Unger, William White, Jr., "Reconcile, V. (1)." *Vine's Complete Expository Dictionary of Old and New Testament Words*, Greek section, pp. 513–514.

49 W.E. Vine, Merrill F. Unger, William White, Jr., "Reconciliation, N." *Vine's Complete Expository Dictionary of Old and New Testament Words*, Greek section, p. 514.

50 "Adoption, (II)." *The International Standard Bible Encyclopedia*, Volume 1, A-D, p. 54.

51 W.E. Vine, Merrill F. Unger, William White, Jr., "Abba." *Vine's Complete Expository Dictionary of Old and New Testament Words*, Greek section, p. 1.

52 "Sustain, V. (1–5)." *Merriam-Webster's Collegiate Dictionary*, 10th Edition, p. 1188.

53 "Persevere, V." *Merriam-Webster's Collegiate Dictionary*, 10th Edition, p. 867.

54 "Endure, V. (1–2)." *Merriam-Webster's Collegiate Dictionary*, 10th Edition, p. 383.

55 "Paideuō (Instructing)." (3811) *Zondervan NASB Exhaustive Concordance*, (Grand Rapids, MI: Zondervan, A Division of Harper Collins Publisher, 1998) p.1553.

56 W.E. Vine, Merrill F. Unger, William White, Jr., "Instruct, V. (2)." *Vine's Complete Expository Dictionary of Old and New Testament Words*, Greek section, p. 328.

57 W.E. Vine, Merrill F. Unger, William White, Jr., "Gift, V. (6)." *Vine's Complete Expository Dictionary of Old and New Testament Words*, Greek section, p. 264.

58 W.E. Vine, Merrill F. Unger, William White, Jr., ("Gift," V. def. 6.a, b). *Vine's Complete Expository Dictionary of Old and New Testament Words*, Greek section, p. 264.

59 "Charisma, N. (1)." *Merriam-Webster's Collegiate Dictionary*, 10th Edition, p.193

60 ("Prophecy," N. def. 6.b). *Full Life Study Bible, New International Version*, (Grand Rapids, MI: Zondervan Publishing House, 1992), p. 1771.

61 "Serving, V. 12:7, (1)." *Full Life Study Bible, New International Version*, (Grand Rapids, MI: Zondervan Publishing House, 1992), p. 1736.

62 "Teaching, V. 12:7, (2)." *Full Life Study Bible, New International Version*, (Grand Rapids, MI: Zondervan Publishing House, 1992), p. 1736.

63 "Encouraging, N. 12:8, (1)." *Full Life Study Bible, New International Version*, (Grand Rapids, MI: Zondervan Publishing House, 1992), p. 1736.

64 "Contributing, V. 12:8, (2)." *Full Life Study Bible, New International Version*, (Grand Rapids, MI: Zondervan Publishing House, 1992), p. 1736.

65 "Leadership, V. 12:8, (3)." *Full Life Study Bible, New International Version*, (Grand Rapids, MI: Zondervan Publishing House, 1992), p. 1736.

66 "Implement," V. (1). *Merriam-Webster's Collegiate Dictionary*, 10th Edition, p. 583.

67 ("Call," V. def. 2.c). *Merriam-Webster's Collegiate Dictionary*, 10th Edition, p. 162.

68 ("Call," N. def. 2.e). *Merriam-Webster's Collegiate Dictionary*, 10th Edition, p. 162.

69 W.E Vine, Merrill F. Unger William White, Jr., ("Call," V. def. 1.a) *Vine's Complete Expository Dictionary of Old Testament and New Testament Words*, Greek section, p. 86.

70 W.E Vine, Merrill F. Unger William White, Jr., "Calling," N. *Vine's Complete Expository Dictionary of Old Testament and New Testament Words*, Greek section, p. 87.

End Notes

71 Henry Clarence Thiessen, *Introductory Lectures in Systematic Theology*, p. 350.

72 "Convince, V. (3)." *Merriam-Webster's Collegiate Dictionary*, 10th Edition, p. 254.

73 W.E Vine, Merrill F. Unger William White, Jr., ("Turn," V. def. 4. a, b), *Vine's Complete Expository Dictionary of Old Testament and New Testament Words*, Greek section, p. 647.

74 Ibid, p. 647.

75 W.E Vine, Merrill F. Unger William White, Jr., "Confirm, V. (1)." *Vine's Complete Expository Dictionary of Old Testament and New Testament Words*, Greek section, p. 121.

76 W.E Vine, Merrill F. Unger William White, Jr., "Establish, V. (1)." *Vine's Complete Expository Dictionary of Old Testament and New Testament Words*, Greek section, p. 206.

77 "Confirm, V. (4)." *Merriam-Webster's Collegiate Dictionary*, 10th Edition, p. 242.

78 ("Consecrate," V. def. 2. a). *Merriam-Webster's Collegiate Dictionary*, 10th Edition, p. 246.

79 "Consecrate, V. (1, 2)." *Random House Webster's College Dictionary*, (Random House, Inc., 201 E. 50th St., New York, NY 10022), p. 289.

80 ("Consecrate," V. def. 2.c). *Merriam-Webster's Collegiate Dictionary*, 10th Edition, p. 246.

81 ("Correction," N. def, 1.c). *Merriam-Webster's Collegiate Dictionary*, 10th Edition, p. 260.

82 "Cleanse, V." *Merriam-Webster's Collegiate Dictionary*, 10th Edition, p. 212.

83 W.E Vine, Merrill F. Unger William White, Jr., ("Cleanse," V. def. 1.b). *Vine's Complete Expository Dictionary of Old Testament and New Testament Words*, Greek section, p. 104.

84. W.E Vine, Merrill F. Unger William White, Jr., "Comforter, N. (5)." *Vine's Complete Expository Dictionary of Old Testament and New Testament Words*, Greek section, p. 111.

85. "Conform, V. (1)." *Merriam-Webster's Collegiate Dictionary*, 10th Edition, p. 242.

86. W.E Vine, Merrill F. Unger William White, Jr., ("Conformed," Adj. def. 1. a) *Vine's Complete Expository Dictionary of Old Testament and New Testament Words*, Greek section, p. 122.

87. W.E Vine, Merrill F. Unger William White, Jr., "Conformed, V." *Vine's Complete Expository Dictionary of Old Testament and New Testament Words*, Greek section, p. 121.

88. ("Ambassador" N. def. (1), 2.a). *Merriam-Webster's Collegiate Dictionary*, 10th Edition, pp. 35–36.

89. W.E Vine, Merrill F. Unger William White, Jr. "Gifts, N. (6)." *Vine's Complete Expository Dictionary of Old Testament and New Testament Words*, Greek section, p. 264.

90. W.E Vine, Merrill F. Unger William White, Jr., "Minister, N. (1)." *Vine's Complete Expository Dictionary of Old Testament and New Testament Words*, Greek section, p. 410.

91. "Energēma, (effects)" (1755), *Zondervan NASB Exhaustive Concordance*, Greek dictionary, p. 1527.

92. ("Mean," N. def. 2.pl., 3.pl.). *Merriam-Webster's Collegiate Dictionary*, 10th Edition, p. 720.

93. W.E Vine, Merrill F. Unger William White, "Know, V. (1)." Jr., *Vine's Complete Expository Dictionary of Old Testament and New Testament Words*, Greek section, p. 346.

94. W.E Vine, Merrill F. Unger William White, Jr., 94 "To know, V." *Vine's Complete Expository Dictionary of Old Testament and New Testament Words*, Hebrew section, p. 130.

End Notes

95   W.E. Vine, Merrill F. Unger William White, Jr., ("Fellowship," N. def. 1.a). *Vine's Complete Expository Dictionary of Old Testament and New Testament Words*, Greek section, p. 233

96   W.E. Vine, Merrill F. Unger William White, Jr., "Fellowship, N. (3)." *Vine's Complete Expository Dictionary of Old Testament and New Testament Words*, Greek section, p. 233.

97   W.E. Vine, Merrill F. Unger William White, Jr., "To worship, V." *Vine's Complete Expository Dictionary of Old Testament and New Testament Words*, Hebrew section, p. 295.

98   Ibid, p. 295.

99   W.E. Vine, Merrill F. Unger William White, Jr., "To worship, V. (1)." *Vine's Complete Expository Dictionary of Old Testament and New Testament Words*, Greek section, p. 686.

100   "Worship, (I)." *The International Standard Bible Encyclopedia*, Volume 4, Q-Z, p. 1117.

101   Ibid, p. 1117.

CPSIA information can be obtained
at www.ICGtesting.com
Printed in the USA
BVHW041623121122
651747BV00018B/54